W9-BZT-089

social work practice

social work Practice

CONCEPTS, PROCESSES, AND INTERVIEWING

Marion Bogo

COLUMBIA UNIVERSITY PRESS

NEW YORK

Columbia University Press
Publishers Since 1893

New York   Chichester, West Sussex
Copyright © 2006 Columbia University Press

Library of Congress
Cataloging-in-Publication Data
Bogo, Marion.
    Social work practice : concepts, processes, and interviewing
/ Marion Bogo
        p. cm.
    Includes bibliographal references and index.
    ISBN 0–231–12546–1 (cloth : alk. paper)
    ISBN 0–231–12547–X (pbk. : alk. paper)
    1. Social service. 2. Interviewing in social service. I. Title.
HV40.B5465   2006
361.3'2—dc22   2005051945

Casebound editions of Columbia University Press
books are printed on permanent and durable acid-free
paper.

Printed in the United States of America

c 10 9 8 7 6 5 4 3 2 1
p 10 9 8 7 6 5 4 3 2 1

Dedicated to LAUREN AVERY

as you grew so did this book

CONTENTS

ACKNOWLEDGMENTS

The impetus for this project came from John Michel, who was senior executive editor at Columbia University Press. We had worked together on my previous book on field education and I knew John to be a supportive and outstandingly helpful publisher, committed to developing social work literature. As in the past, working with him was always a pleasure and I will remember him with gratitude for his encouragement and guidance through this project. I also want to thank Shelley Reinhardt, senior executive editor, Susan Pensak, senior manuscript editor, and Ann Young, editorial assistant, for continuing to direct this project through its final stages. Their advice is deeply appreciated.

The basis for my learning and thinking about social work practice comes from the many clients I have worked with over the years in a range of practice settings, with a wide variety of problems and issues, using a range of intervention models. These raw practice experiences stimulated reflection and analysis and collegial learning from presentation to my supervisors, consultants, and many experienced professional colleagues, especially Marion Soloway and Janet Tanzer. My work at the Faculty of Social Work, University of Toronto provided enriching learning opportunities as we attempted to articulate the elements in social work practice competence and systematically studied social work processes and effective ways of teaching. I wish to thank all those who have participated with me in these activities. They include colleagues at the Faculty of Social Work with whom I have worked in designing and refining curriculum and the field practicum, especially Roxanne Power and Andrea Litvack. I particularly want to thank my colleague Faye Mishna for reading the manuscript and providing information and suggestions that improved the text. Her constant encouragement and belief in the need for this book was extremely important. Also, I have learned from my coinvestigators in research projects where we have used a range of qualitative and quantitative methods to design studies on various aspects of social work practice — A. K. T. Tsang,

Judith Globerman, and Cheryl Regehr. Through teaching and learning with students in a range of foundation, advanced, and specialized practice courses, with doctoral students in a course on teaching and learning in social work, and with field instructors I have worked with in new field instructor seminars, I have had the opportunity to develop and evaluate ideas presented in this text. Finally, my greatest appreciation goes to my husband Norman Bogo for his thoughtful contributions to the manuscript. As a result of his own experience and wisdom as a clinical psychiatrist and psychotherapist, he has provided endless opportunities for discussion and reflection about our respective professional disciplines and practices.

During preparation of parts of the manuscript I was appointed the inaugural Sandra Rotman Chair in Social Work at the Faculty of Social Work, University of Toronto, which provided support for this work.

INTRODUCTION

Social work practice and education have undergone changes in the past half century that have significantly affected the way in which we use knowledge for practice. As I approached the task of writing this book I was struck by how much has changed in our knowledge base since my own graduate-level preparation. In the early sixties there was a very limited set of texts and journals that were used in social work education to prepare students for careers as direct practice social workers or as caseworkers, the term used at that time. The pioneers such as Mary Richmond, Charlotte Towle, Helen Harris Pearlman, and Florence Hollis had developed approaches to practice that built on the central values of the profession and the practice wisdom that had accumulated over time. Theories and practice principles developed in related fields, such as psychiatry and psychology, were integrated into this general body of knowledge. For students learning to practice there was a finite literature that could be studied. Field instructors, having themselves been trained in the same approaches that students were learning, could help students draw the links between their academic learning in university courses and the practice assignments they had in the field agency. One of the strengths of that era was that students learned a circumscribed body of knowledge and approaches in depth. Social work students were taught, either in class, field, or both, how to think about practice and how to enact a practice that flowed from a core of interrelated humanistic values, theories about the human condition, and intervention models. Social workers in direct practice seemed unified in their emphasis on a client-centered approach and a number of practice principles reflected this: start where the client is, go at the pace of the client, value self-determination of the client, support growth and development, provide an accepting, nonjudgmental relationship as the basis for helping, give primacy to client needs rather than organizational administrative requirements, and intervene to change social and economic factors in the client's environment that affect well-being.

The past can be glorified in reminiscences; however it would be false to portray those times as uniformly positive. There were glaring omissions, especially in the tendency to universalize and render diversity and systemic oppression invisible. The insights of feminist theory, antiracism, oppression, and empowerment analyses, and of postmodernist theory had not yet entered the professional discourse. Furthermore, there were few well-designed research studies to investigate social work programs and practices and to examine the outcomes and effectiveness of our work. Practitioners were largely operating on the basis of a collective practice wisdom that had developed over many years, without empirical support for these beliefs. While attention to the environment was always a part of the unique conceptualization of social functioning, the intellectual and practice contributions of Germain and Gitterman (1996) and Meyer (1983), who introduced and articulated the ecological-systemic perspective, were only beginning to influence practitioners. Finally, practice remained "behind closed doors," a private and somewhat mysterious activity. Since one-way mirrors, audio-, and videotape had not yet entered educational technology, students' work was rarely observed, nor did students observe skilled social workers in their practice. Schools of social work were not yet teaching interviewing skills, and students often wondered what good practice really looked like. Obviously, there were many deficits in teaching practice. However, students were taught a core of knowledge as well as a limited number of principles for applying that knowledge, including the following examples: start where the client is, reach for feelings, partialize the problem, determine both presenting problem and underlying problem, and proceed at the client's pace. This set of principles provided guidelines to ground abstract concepts when working with individual clients. These principles were generic insofar as they could be transferred to practice with a wide range of clients, such as late adolescents, adults, and the elderly and across many settings, such as child welfare, family services, and health and mental health. These skills were also useful, with modification, in practice where individual clients and participants were involved in change processes, as with families, therapeutic groups and committees in organizations and communities, in supervision and administration.

In contrast, social work students and practitioners are currently confronted with an ever expanding and constantly changing body of knowledge. Not only is there a knowledge explosion in social work but related fields such as psychology, counseling, psychiatry, and marriage and family therapy offer innumerable new approaches to practice that hold interest for social work practitioners. Many of these new models have been well described, tested, and shown to be effective in use with particular populations in controlled studies. The links between theory, research, and practice are clarified with the advent of treatment manuals developed for these empirical studies. Transferring the findings from studies to the everyday world of practice in agencies, however, has proven to be far more complex than expected.

At the same time that practitioners have been encouraged to use empirically based models, postmodernism and social constructionism have introduced a new epistemology and an appreciation that there are limits to what we "know" and what can be claimed as universal, objective, and true. These doctrines argue that individual meanings are developed through social interaction in specific contexts, cultural groups, and by virtue of social location with respect to characteristics such as race, class, and gender. Furthermore, individual assumptions and meanings are closely tied to language systems. Hence, there are many ways of knowing, understanding, experiencing and defining problems and how they should be addressed. Recognizing the existence of different worldviews may leave practitioners feeling pulled in opposite directions — searching for generalizable proven approaches or working in highly individual ways. Social workers may attempt to stay current with developments by reading the literature, attending continuing education programs, and incorporating new ideas in their work. Or, overwhelmed by the workload pressures of agency practice and the expanding and at times contradictory knowledge explosion, they may rely increasingly on their own experience and a core of practices that have proven useful and meaningful for them over time.

Schools of social work are committed to exposing students to the intellectual debates in the profession, to both traditional and innovative approaches. They try to cover considerable ground from societal to individual perspectives and from philosophical positions to empirical findings. As a result, social work students are likely to find a program of study that is crammed with innumerable bodies of knowledge, perspectives, values, and practice approaches. In individual courses reading lists grow and basic practice texts expand with the publication of each new edition as authors incorporate the latest concepts and debates in the discourse on social work practice. As more specialized models are described and tested students are also presented with an ever expanding range of procedures and specific intervention techniques.

Social work students who are embarking on a lifelong journey of learning to become effective practitioners state clearly that at the beginning they need to learn a core of integrated and interrelated concepts, processes and principles, and skills for practice. Such a core is seen as a place to start, a place that can serve as a foundation throughout one's career; a foundation that provides a sense of being grounded as a professional and engenders confidence that one possesses a core of competencies available for use in practice. An essential component of this core is basic interviewing skills that constitute, in large measure, the way in which any approach is put into practice. However, these interviewing skills do not "stand alone." They must be used in conjunction with knowledge and understanding—of theories about human and social function and dysfunction and of how to provide help and bring about change. Once learned, this body of knowledge and skill can be used in different ways based on the mandate of the agency, the procedures of specific models, specialized information about populations and problems, and the needs of the particular client in the relationship with the worker.

FOCUS OF THIS BOOK

My aim in writing this book was to attempt to provide such an integrated view of theoretical concepts, practice processes and principles, and interviewing skills. Through teaching social work students in both basic and advanced practice courses and providing clinical consultation to experienced social workers in mainstream and ethnospecific agencies, I became aware of the need for a generic text for direct practice or clinical social work courses that would bring together theory, research, and techniques. With the growing findings from studies of practice effectiveness and the increasing number of meta-analytic and systematic reviews of these studies it became a challenge to assist students and practitioners to access and use this new knowledge. Empirical findings are important to guide practitioners and to provide the professional with some confidence that the methods we use will lead to positive outcomes for clients.

The text presents a group of generic theories and skills for use in communicating with adults and adolescents who can take advantage of an approach that is largely based on "talking." Some of the concepts, processes, and skills are applicable to work with children, and examples of such situations are provided as illustrations. However, social workers whose practice brings them into regular contact with children need specialized knowledge to successfully work with this population. For example, a thorough grounding in child development theory is essential for understanding children's growth and behavior as well as some familiarity and competence in using interventions such as play therapy, art therapy, music therapy, and activity groups. There are also a range of interviewing skills designed for work with children that are beyond the scope of this text.

This text is intended especially for students as they begin to learn about social work practice. It can also be used by experienced practitioners who are interested in a systematic reexamination of contemporary social work practice theory, a review of selected empirically based principles, and a summary of interviewing skills. I have tried in the text to provide information at a level that is not so abstract that it is unclear how the concepts may be applied in the real world of practice. Neither is material presented in so concrete a manner that a cookbooklike approach would result. Rather my aim is to provide concepts and practice processes or principles that can be used by practitioners in a flexible and reflective manner so that the social worker and the client can fashion their own unique helping relationship and pathway to positive results.

This text has been influenced by a number of themes that are interwoven throughout the work and bear making explicit. The first theme is that any professional practice in human services reflects a complex integration of a multitude of factors and competencies. Through my work in field education in social work (Bogo and Vayda, 1998) I have taught and learned from social workers and social work professors in Canada, United States, Japan, China, Taiwan, and Sri Lanka and recognized that many general practice principles are understood and used in individualized and culturally relevant ways in local situations. I became interested in understanding how social workers use, adapt, or integrate knowledge in their practice. It is difficult for practitioners to provide full accounts of what they do and why; hence any description of practice can only be understood as "at one step removed" from the actual situation. However, when engaged in extensive reflective dialogues about their work, social workers can articulate understandings and descriptions of their actions that were previously implied but not named or labeled (Bogo et al., in press). What does emerge is a description of practice that is not a linear and direct application of theory. Rather, practice is an intricate, nuanced, interrelated process of action and reflection, with reference to concepts or principles, previous situations and learning from these experiences, and occasionally to findings from practice research. This process occurs in a cyclical, looping, and iterative manner. This view of practice-theory linkage as fluid and implicit is discussed more fully in chapter 1.

A second theme that appears throughout the text provides a somewhat different view. While still recognizing that at one level practice is amorphous and hard to pin down, at another level there are actions and skills used by practitioners that have been demonstrated effective. The text includes descriptions and discussions of these principles and processes and related behavioral skills. This material is derived from the professional literature and from two ongoing research projects. In these projects we aim, with a group of colleagues, to identify and describe some of the processes, competencies, and skills that constitute good social work practice. The first project, funded by the Social Sciences and Humanities Council of Canada, involved an examination of the processes in cross-cultural counseling that result in positive outcomes for clients (Tsang, Bogo, and George, 2003). This study was reviewed and approved by the Research Ethics Board at the University of Toronto and the Research Ethics Boards of the participating hospitals and agencies. In this study we applied process-outcome coding methodologies and textual analysis to transcripts of audiotaped interviews of social workers and their clients. The clients and social workers who agreed to participate in the project were drawn from a range of settings, typical of social work practice: for example, an agency serving adolescents and their families, an outpatient mental health clinic for clients recently discharged from a psychiatric facility, a community health clinic, a family service agency. In all of the situations the social workers were providing the "usual" form of counseling and resources offered by the setting. This study helped to illuminate the processes, activities, and behaviors that workers demonstrated in practice with clients who were different from themselves by virtue of race, culture, ethnicity, religion, gender, age, sexual orientation, and ability. Observations and emerging findings from this study are integrated throughout the text along with theoretical, notional, and experiential observations of practitioners and scholars working in the area of cultural competency.

The second project arose in an attempt to develop more reliable and valid approaches to evaluating the competency of social work students (Bogo et al., 2002). This project is also funded by the Social Sciences and Humanities Research Council of Canada and has been reviewed and approved by the Research Ethics Board of the University of Toronto. In the first phase of the study the aim was to tap the implicit knowledge of experienced social workers and field educators as they described their perception of competent practice (Bogo et al., 2004; in press). Through in-depth qualitative interviews social workers provided rich descriptions of the attitudes, qualities, and behaviors of social work students whom they considered exemplary, average, and not yet ready for practice. Through comparing the findings from the cross-cultural study and this study on competence, a set of helping processes and practice principles emerged, which are presented and discussed throughout the text.

As noted, findings from practice research in helping disciplines, including social work, have been incorporated in this text. Empirically tested models have much to offer to social workers in their practice. One can use a model in its entirety or selectively use processes or techniques that are demonstrated as effective. I have been selective in drawing from this growing literature and have included in this text those principles, processes, or techniques that have been shown to be effective in well-designed research studies and may have a more general usefulness if applied in a wide range of social work situations. Readers interested in the original studies and the specific models can retrieve the primary work through the extensive references provided.

Finally, both the "old" and the "new" are found in the text. Long-standing foundation principles of social work practice, also referred to as "practice wisdom," that have withstood the test of time are incorporated. Many new perspectives offer insightful critiques of traditional approaches; however, the implications for practice are not yet well articulated. Since the aim of this text is to provide frameworks for current practice, material was selected for inclusion when it would further this goal.

LEARNING TO PRACTICE

A final word about learning to practice is warranted. Any text can only *describe* practice; it is only in the actual *doing* of practice that ideas take more shape, are experienced, truly learned, and can become part of the social worker's professional self. Social work education has long recognized this axiom about learning, and all programs prepare competent social workers by providing students with both academic courses and supervised educational experiences in the field. When students are provided with conceptual frameworks to understand what they are doing in the field they report that their learning is strengthened (Fortune, McCarthy, and Abramson, 2001). Some activities that link practice to theoretical concepts and vice versa include making connections between what is observed in specific practice situations and the concepts presented in courses and pointing out and labeling concepts when they are seen in practice. Students value field instructors who provide explanations of client phenomena and related practice interventions in the language of social work theory. Students, course instructors, and field instructors may wish to use some of the concepts presented in this text so that a similar terminology and nomenclature can facilitate teaching and learning across the domains of class, field, and integrative seminars. Similarly, experienced practitioners may wish to review their work on audio- or videotape on their own, with peers or a supervisor, and use the concepts presented in this text as a framework to guide reflection, feedback, self-assessment, and planning subsequent interventions in a particular situation. The process of learning and refining practice and interviewing behaviors is continuous, and I hope that this book can contribute to life-long learning for students and experienced practitioners.

Educational methods for teaching practice, both theories and skills, have been described in numerous articles in social work journals such as the *Journal of Social Work Education, Journal of Teaching in Social Work*, and the *Clinical Supervisor*. It is clear from this body of literature that students appreciate learning environments that model the principles of social work practice (Bogo, 1993; Freeman and Valentine, 1998; Lewis, 1991). Instructors who behave in ways that are consistent with the values and principles they are teaching provide an experience for students that exposes them to the essence of social work (Knight, 2001). Modeling collaboration, respect, relationship building and maintenance are powerful ways of teaching.

The classroom environment is a potent factor that affects students' learning. It provides the milieu in which students may feel respected by their colleagues, connected to each other, and experience a sense of "being in this together." In such environments students report that they feel safe, can risk exposing their struggles and uncertainties in learning, and try out new ideas and behaviors (Bogo, Globerman, and Sussman, 2004a; Shulman, 1987). Experiential learning activities such as role playing with simulated clients and presenting audio- or videotapes to the class for analysis and feedback have been demonstrated to be highly effective methods of learning the content discussed in this text (Collins and Bogo, 1986).

Classroom dynamics however can also compromise learning. In classrooms where bonding has not occurred, where students have expressed strongly held opinions that others experience as insensitive or depreciating, where competition is intense, where problematic histories exist between class members, or where conflict has not been resolved, students report feeling intimidated, unsafe, and guarded (Bogo, Globerman, and Sussman, 2004b; Holley and Steiner, 2005; Mishna and Rasmussen, 2001; Rasmussen and Mishna, 2003). These conditions are not conducive to the self-exposure needed for experiential learning activities or presentation of students' own practice. Classroom instructors need a range of teaching skills, many of which are similar to those used in group work practice and in resolving interpersonal conflict. Drawing on their knowledge of group dynamics and sound teaching skills, instructors can assist students to develop norms for the classroom, learn to be productive members of a learning group, process differences of opinions in a respectful manner, and resolve conflict when it arises. As the teacher responds to a range of classroom situations, students learn about social work processes through observation, modeling, and experiencing them. The instructor's comfort level when dealing with conflict, responses to ruptures that include attempts at repairs, and commitment to a productive environment provide a model to emulate in practice (Mishna and Rasmussen, 2001). Conversely, ignoring classroom dynamics and avoiding intervening when conflict arises also demonstrate stances that students may copy in their practice.

ORGANIZATION OF THE BOOK

The book is organized in three major parts: 1) conceptual frameworks, 2) helping processes and principles, and 3) interviewing skills. Part 1 is entitled "Conceptual Frameworks for Social Work Practice" and examines contexts that affect practice and concepts that inform it. The Integration of Theory and Practice (ITP) Loop (Bogo and Vayda, 1998) is introduced in chapter 1 as a vehicle for examining the multitude of factors that impinge on practice. The ITP Loop has been used in examining social work practice and guiding student teaching and learning in the field practicum. Through the loop metaphor the professional and organizational contexts of practice are examined as they affect the scope of what the practitioner is able to offer and achieve. The professional context is reviewed, including the knowledge and value base that serves as an underpinning for practice. The "personal self" of the student and of the social worker is emphasized and attention is paid to learning to become a practitioner, how the personal self of the practitioner evolves to incorporate a professional self, and ways of thinking about the integration of theory and practice.

Continuing the theme of significant contexts, chapter 2 examines contemporary perspectives that incorporate diversity in all aspects of our work. Social identity characteristics and societal dynamics related to power, privilege, and oppression can be reflected in direct practice. These concepts in the professional literature are introduced as a precursor to further elaboration throughout the text. In addition, key concepts in social work that cross theoretical models are presented.

The third and fourth chapters focus on the relationship as both a context of practice and a crucial dimension for bringing about change. The components of relationship, both with voluntary and involuntary clients, are examined. In chapter 3 fundamental and enduring characteristics of the professional relationship in social work are presented. Theoretical contributions to understanding the relationship are reviewed, especially humanistic and attachment perspectives.

In chapter 4 the extensive empirical literature on the therapeutic alliance is summarized and helping processes, practice principles, and behaviors that derive from this literature are presented. Issues of culture and diversity are examined in the interests of forging this crucial context for practice. Ethical standards relevant to relationship issues are discussed.

The fifth chapter presents frameworks for thinking about change from a variety of points of view. Findings from research on social work practice and from the extensive empirical literature in related disciplines are presented. Change is discussed from the standpoint of the client, from meta-analyses of these studies, and through the lens of a staged process.

Part 2 is entitled "The Process of Helping in Social Work Practice" and includes chapters on the actual stages, tasks, and interventions in practice. Each chapter in this section integrates the concepts presented in part 1 and discusses how these ideas are put into practice through preparatory, beginning, middle, and ending stages.

Chapter 6 considers tasks and issues in the beginning stage. This stage includes the important preparatory work that precedes the first meeting with the client. Activities related to preparing the setting and the worker are considered. The initial stage and its related activities are presented with respect to developing a working relationship and shared understanding between the client and the worker regarding the nature of the issues to be addressed, the goals sought, and the potential methods to reach those goals. An ecosystemic and multiperspective approach is used to examine steps in arriving at an assessment. This approach organizes the questions that the worker needs to consider, the information that must be gathered, the way in which the information will be examined, and finally how goal setting is linked to the conceptual framework chosen. The importance of understanding and assessment as a collaborative activity with the client is a theme throughout this discussion.

Chapter 7 focuses on the middle stage in helping and the processes, principles, and interventions that bring about change. Emphasizing that the social worker is a process expert, this chapter draws on the concepts and empirical findings presented in part 1, "Conceptual Frameworks," to demonstrate how these concepts are enacted in the actual social work session. Throughout the helping process attention continues to be directed to two elements: 1) relationship maintenance and 2) goal achievement. Key themes in the chapter include developing richer and more complex understandings of the presenting problem; working with emotions, cognition, and behaviors; working with themes relating to individual, interpersonal and developmental issues. Identifying strengths, addressing obstacles, developing new perspectives, and taking action are presented. Finally, social workers do not always work to promote change; they also work to support and sustain clients through linkage to and coordination of necessary resources. Helping processes of the case management model are discussed in this regard.

Chapter 8 considers the ending or termination stage in social work practice, from short contacts to those that are longer in time frame. Four key processes are discussed: reviewing progress, consolidating gains, planning for next steps, and processing the emotional bond.

The final section of the text is entitled "Interviewing in Social Work Practice" and consists of one chapter. Chapter 9 provides a detailed discussion of the interviewing skills social workers use in practice. Skills are described and illustrated with examples. Together this set of interviewing behaviors constitutes a skill set that the practitioner uses to ground the concepts and helping processes discussed in the previous two sections of the text. Chapter 9 can be used on its own in social work courses on interviewing or in conjunction with the entire text in social work practice courses at the undergraduate and graduate level, in generalist and clinical programs of study. The chapter ends with recommendations for students about educational processes helpful in learning how to practice social work.

Part I } CONCEPTUAL FRAMEWORKS FOR SOCIAL WORK PRACTICE

THE CONTEXT OF PRACTICE

Mastery of social work practice involves the integration of the knowledge and value base of the profession and a set of core interviewing skills with the "personal self" of the social worker. The behavior of the social worker in the social work interview represents an individual social worker's unique expression of this combination of factors. It is difficult to imagine how effective service could be offered in the absence of social workers' competence in using interviewing skills. It is through our interpersonal actions, the words we use, the attitudes and feelings we convey verbally and nonverbally that we may achieve whatever goals social workers and clients set for their work together. Hence interviewing skills can be seen as the primary tool of practice, and social workers need to know how to use them effectively.

But social work practice is more than technique. It is an integration of knowledge, values, and skill with a personal-professional self. The worker's behavior reflects a set of values and ethical principles, a view of human and social functioning, an ideal about professional relationships, and specific perspectives on helping. Therefore, it is important to remember that the skills discussed in this book are only tools, and their usefulness depends on the rationale or intention underlying their use.

Values reflect the humanistic and altruistic philosophical base of the social work profession. Fundamental beliefs in human dignity, the worth of all people, mutual responsibility, self-determination, empowerment and antioppression, guide assessment and intervention (Reamer, 1999). Ethical codes of conduct and standards of practice specify how these values should be evident in a professional's behavior. As the discipline has developed, some fundamental values and beliefs that have been expressed as practice principles have now received support from new theoretical developments and empirical findings. For example, social work has long valued the notion that a collaborative and strong professional relationship with the client is a crucial factor in bringing about change. Numerous practice models now embrace this concept and considerable empirical evidence also supports this long-held practice principle (Edwards and Richards, 2002; Norcross, 2002; Wampold, 2001). Social workers, guided by this knowledge, use interviewing skills purposefully to forge and maintain alliances between themselves and the people with whom they work.

Conversely, knowledge and understanding of a practice situation remains solely an intellectual exercise unless evidenced in skillful communication with others. Analytic skills enable practitioners to assess situations and plan interventions so that practice is systematic and focused. However, it is through forming a working relationship or alliance with clients that a process occurs where, through dialogue and interaction, workers' insights are offered. The interview is the medium of practice and the site in which intervention is largely delivered. Once again, it is the social worker's skill in interviewing and her communication ability that affects whether professional knowledge will be received and experienced as helpful by the client. Figure 1.1 presents the elements that impinge on social work practice. These components or circumstances are relevant to understanding the process of helping and can also be referred to as the context of practice.

THE KNOWLEDGE BASE OF SOCIAL WORK

This text will present interviewing skills as the application of knowledge in practice and address how knowledge is assimilated for practice. In social work the knowledge base refers to many components; theory, models, wisdom, and specialized knowledge. Social work students are presented with a wide range of theoretical concepts that assist in understanding the human condition, social functioning, and dysfunction. These theories are ever expanding and reflect the explosion of knowledge over the past centuries. What is enduring is the profession's interest in understanding the connections between the person and the situation. Theories therefore will include those that provide explanations of how societal structures may systematically oppress individuals and serve as barriers to social functioning, equitable participation in society, and the realization of their full human potential. Explanatory systems used are drawn from psychological and social theories. These systems provide concepts for understanding behavior with respect to growth, development, and individual and interpersonal functioning in cognitive, affective, and behavioral domains.

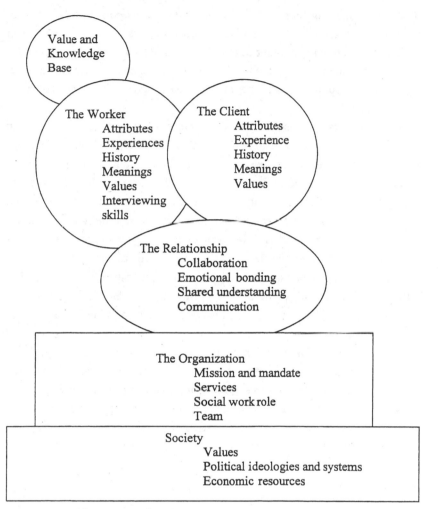

FIGURE 1.1 The Context of Practice

The knowledge base also includes practice models and their related intervention techniques. A model refers to a collection of beliefs about human functioning and what is needed to bring about change with clients who present particular problems and situations. For example, Perlman (1957) developed a problem-solving model for social work to help clients with personal and interpersonal issues. Models generally include techniques or actions that are extensions of the beliefs about the cause and nature of the problem and how to bring about change. Practice models are drawn from a wide range of sources including those developed in related fields concerned with well-being and mental health. Some models are empirically supported, having been studied in a systematic manner by researchers and found to produce positive outcomes for clients. Many models have not been subjected to rigorous testing, yet their proponents claim they are effective based solely on selected anecdotal support.

Social workers have also developed principles of practice through working with clients and conclusions drawn from their experiences. These principles may be referred to as practice wisdom and often reflect both a value stance and a pragmatic way of working. For example, "start where the client is" and "go at the pace of the client" are long-standing guidelines in social work that also reflect the value placed on working in a collaborative manner with the client.

Finally, since social workers often provide help by giving clients relevant information about a range of issues, they use specialized knowledge about conditions, resources, programs, and policies. One unique feature of the profession is that social work bridges the personal and the environmental. As frontline practitioners, social workers are in an excellent position to identify and document unmet environmental needs of groups of people. They are committed to advocate with and on behalf of at-risk populations for the development of necessary programs and services. Social workers therefore need to be highly knowledgeable about the specific conditions that clients present with, from housing, employment, and educational needs to those with special situations, for example, being diagnosed with a particular medical condition, living with violence in intimate relationships, or having experienced abuse in childhood. Box 1.1 provides a brief overview of what can be referred to as the knowledge base for social work practice.

THE SOCIAL WORKER

The personal and professional self of the worker has long been recognized as an important influence on practice and one that can powerfully affect client outcomes. Practitioners bring all their personal attributes and characteristics into their work. Many factors shape our personalities and our personalities in turn affect our work and comfort level in working with various clients. Personal issues related to the past and the present operate as active ingredients in the interpersonal encounter in practice. Social factors, internalized by individual social workers, are also pertinent. Social factors refer to so-

BOX 1.1. KNOWLEDGE FOR PRACTICE

Theories about human behavior in the social environment	Structures, society, physical, economic and political environment
	Power, privilege, and oppression
	Diversity
	Organizational development and functioning
	Individual development and functioning
	Family systems
Practice models, procedures, techniques	Approaches to practice
	Focus on aspects of cognition, affect, and behavior
	Empirical support
Practice wisdom	Values in action
	Practice principles
Specialized knowledge	About populations, conditions, special circumstances, and needs

cial identity characteristics such as age, gender, ethnicity, sexual orientation, economic status, ability, often referred to generically as reflecting culture. Personal factors include unique personal histories in family and community and personality characteristics and styles. Social work students bring their individual personalities, social identity characteristics, experiences, and values to their studies in social work. Through academic courses and field education students develop into professional practitioners, having learned professional knowledge, values, and skills and integrated these components of practice into their personal self. They learn to identify their personal feelings, thoughts, reactions, and the meanings they give to events in their own life experiences. They learn how these factors may operate in their judgments and actions in practice with clients, in both helpful and unhelpful ways. An ongoing commitment of practitioners is to be mindful of the subtle feelings and thoughts that emerge when working with clients. A stance that values self-awareness helps us to learn more about ourselves, to develop more understanding and acceptance of our own internal experiences, and to ultimately be more able to work with a broader range of situations. Through self-awareness practitioners can remain genuine as well as intentional and purposeful in their actions in the interview, rather than reactive to situations they experience as anxiety provoking.

Social workers' behavior in interviews represents a complex combination of experiencing, knowing, thinking, and doing. The ability to use interviewing skills to achieve goals demonstrates successful mastery of these many factors. To reiterate an important point, possessing theoretical and empirical knowledge is not sufficient to help clients; nor is the ability to interview enough. Rather, it is how these components of knowledge and skill come together through the person of the worker that affects whether effective practice may result.

THE ORGANIZATION AND SOCIETY

An important contextual feature of social work arises from the fact that the majority of social work practice takes place in organizational contexts and is defined by the mission and mandate of the employing agency. Organizations in turn reflect the commitment and ability of a society, nation, or local community to care for the social and health needs of the population. Societies vary with respect to their beliefs and values about the appropriate role of the state in meeting universal basic human needs. Political ideologies and systems determine how economic resources will be distributed, the way in which all citizens will be supported, and the way in which disadvantaged groups will be assisted.

The mission of the organization defines what programs and services are offered and the roles for social workers. Social workers may find themselves in organizational contexts that dictate the approaches they will use. Driven by demands for quality and cost-effective services agencies are increasingly more focused on program evaluation. Accountability expectations demand that we review the effectiveness of our work and strive to discover and use the most helpful and efficient methods of helping. Practice research aims to demonstrate which programs, models, and processes lead to desired outcomes. As empirically validated approaches are articulated and adopted organizations are able to serve greater numbers of people. Unfortunately the field has been slow to engage in practice research. Instead new models are often adopted as a result of ideological shifts or attraction to charismatic proponents.

Increasingly, social work practice takes place in multidisciplinary teams. The function, role, and professional activities of the social worker are affected by the way in which the team members organize their work. Where the team is interdisciplinary in composition there may be more or less separation or overlap in roles. For example, social workers in the mental health field have increasingly experienced other professionals' interest in psychosocial aspects of health and illness. In contrast, a social worker in an acute surgical unit is likely to have sole responsibility for these issues.

In primary social work settings teams can provide helpful education and supportive functions for their members. These teams provide consultation on specific clients as well as general continuing professional development for social workers. However in agencies reliant on managed care funding increasingly there is an emphasis on maximizing revenues and as a result there are fewer nonbillable activities such as supervision and consultation (Bocage, Homonoff, and Riley, 1995; Donner, 1996). Similarly, in organizations funded by local or national governments, reduced funding has led to less time devoted to team work. Workers may experience increased isolation and less opportunity for critical reflection on their practice, including the opportunity for developing increased self-awareness.

The social worker's behavior in the interview reflects an amalgamation of many factors—knowledge, values, skills, personal and professional aspects of self—all within the organizational context of service. The way in which these factors find expression in the behaviors of social workers and the helping principles they choose is the result of a complicated cognitive and affective process where theory or concepts are used in some way, filtered through the individual social worker. This chapter will present a range of concepts that can help social workers analyze the links between interviewing skills, helping processes and principles, and the underlying rationale and issues that affect the way in which they are used.

While this text begins with a focus on the worker it is important to recognize that collaboration with the client is a primary feature of social work practice. Practitioners promote an interactive process that enables the client's full participation. The client's issues, circumstances, and reactions influence each step in the process. Practitioners must be flexible, able to provide leadership and a systematic, focused approach and at the same time able to work with the client in an inclusive and responsive manner.

There is a prevailing view of professional competence as the application of rigorous specialized knowledge to problems presented to practitioners. In this perspective knowledge is developed and empirically tested in studies and produces principles, procedures, and techniques that can be applied to real-world problems. Social work practitioners can then search for and efficiently use the current best evidence about what works for a specific question. Referred to as evidence-based practice, this approach recommends that workers learn how to systematically and quickly find empirical literature and critically appraise studies and findings for their validity and usefulness to the situation presented by a current client (Gambrill, 1999, 2001a, 2001b; Gibbs, 2002). Social workers can then use the empirical knowledge to assess clients and design intervention plans. Thyer and colleagues (Thyer and Myers, 1998, 1999; Thyer and Wodarski, 1998) have argued that since researchers have demonstrated the effectiveness of specialized psychosocial treatments, ethical practice warrants the use of those models.

This view reflects the dominant positivist paradigm in contemporary health science professions and is both ethically and intellectually appealing. Certainly our confidence that we can offer helpful services is improved if we have a rigorous base to rely on. However, there are some practical and ideological issues that mediate unconditional adoption of this approach. Evidence-based practice is easily applicable to practice models that can be articulated, defined in treatment manuals, and tested through controlled experiments. In the mental health field this approach has yielded support for behavioral models but is less easily applied to models that are not as readily defined in operational terms. A further criticism is that evidence of effectiveness comes from studies that are conducted on samples that do not fully represent the population of clients served in everyday practice (Raw, 1998). Samples in many research studies use criteria that often exclude clients with multiple presenting problems and symptoms. In a naturalistic study of cross-cultural counseling, we found that many of the clients who approach the participating community agencies for assistance had a wide range of complex problems that included combinations of issues such as family conflict, social isolation and relationship problems, violence, depression, and need for employment (Tsang, Bogo, and George, 2003). Furthermore, outcomes reported in studies are for those clients who participate in the full program being tested and who comply with the approach. Generally, the studies do not investigate the clients who drop out. As a result the samples may represent a more motivated group of clients than those typically seen in social workers' practice. Finally, evidence-based practice assumes the existence of a variety of useful studies upon which social workers can draw. In a recent review and assessment of the extent of research capable of informing practice interventions Rosen, Proctor, and Staudt (1999) found, of the articles published in a sample of leading social work journals, fewer than one in six were reports of research studies. Moreover, only 7 percent of these studies reported on practice interventions, whereas 36 percent of the studies contributed descriptive knowledge, and 49 percent contributed explanatory knowledge. The authors conclude that current social work research falls short of addressing the needs of practitioners for usable information about what works with whom, under what circumstances. While developing an empirically tested knowledge base is of great importance for all professions, it is however premature to conclude that in social work we have such information and that the challenge is only to find better ways of access.

Others have questioned whether sole reliance on empirical validation as a way of deciding how to intervene is appropriate or realistic for social workers (Witkin, 1998). Given the vast number of factors in individuals' lives, in families, groups, and communities, it is impossible to completely predict outcome. An understanding of this complexity and an appreciation of the crucial impact of contextual factors would better serve social workers (Bolland and Atherton, 1999). Others have argued that in a profession that is concerned with humanism and ethical dilemmas artistry is as much a concern as science (Goldstein, 1990, 1999).

The position taken in this text is that practitioners can benefit from a thorough knowledge of evidenced-based approaches, how to access them, and how to think through their applicability when deciding, with a specific client, what approach to use. Gambrill's (1990) seminal work and recent collaboration with Gibbs (Gibbs and Gambrill, 1999) are recommended sources for learning. Empirically supported approaches provide guidelines or specific principles for assessment and intervention. Given the issues discussed earlier, the practitioner needs to recognize both the strengths and limits of sole reliance on any one approach to guide professional work. Rather, it is important to learn how to use practice knowledge derived from research in a flexible way as a lens through which to understand and work with a client. It is the contingencies of the particular situation, that which is unique to the client, that affects the extent to which empirically derived knowledge will be of use. Ultimately, whether a helping system consisting of the client and the worker is formed and maintained and the way that issues are defined will determine what approaches are most useful.

Before the debate in social work about the limits of a positivist perspective, Donald Schon (1983, 1987) questioned whether technical rationality provided a useful intellectual framework for understanding how professional practitioners use knowledge in their practice. He observed that professionals encounter many situations that do not respond to technical, rational, or predictable processes. Instead they face unique and complex problems that do not fit easily into existing explanatory categories. These situations challenge a view of professionals that solely depicts them as having expert knowledge and certainty about procedures and outcomes. As well, professionals are often confronted with situations where there are conflicts in values and technical responses are not sufficient. For example, a school social worker meets with an adolescent boy who is aggressive and getting into difficulty in class with peers and teacher. The social worker knows that the best evidence shows that a cognitive behavioral group approach is effective for aggressive adolescent boys. However, she also knows that the boy's mother died six months ago, the father is having difficulty managing as a single parent of three children, and he has discussed with his son the possibility of the son temporarily moving in with close relatives who live in a nearby town. Furthermore, the pressure of serving many schools with large student populations results in little time for the school social worker to provide long-term and continuous intervention. In this situation there are numerous issues to address at a family and individual level that are beyond a group intervention and may require referral and collaboration with other agencies that provide prolonged service involvement. Moreover, the client is a young adolescent boy who feels that others are making decisions about his life and not seeking his opinion. His involvement in establishing his goals in any service plan will be crucial. With the complexities in this practice example a competent social worker needs more than the ability to apply empirically supported models to practice. The social worker will need to think broadly, to understand the impact of multiple systems on the adolescent's thinking, feelings, and behavior, and be able to work with the boy, his father, and the classroom teacher to focus on what needs to be addressed and how. While the social worker will contribute her knowledge about interventions that work, she will also contribute her expertise in working with people in a process that helps them identify and work on the important issues in their lives that are troubling to them. Social workers practice with contingencies, exceptions, unforeseen events that require them to use general ideas insofar as they can usefully help in understanding unique, individual circumstances. By virtue of recognizing individual diversity, social workers are more often dealing with exceptions to the theory rather than an ideal case that neatly fits the categories.

Schon (1983, 1987) proposed the reflective practice paradigm to capture the way the intuitive know-how of practitioners is brought to bear in their work. When practitioners are confronted with the uniqueness of particular cases, they appear to be able to engage in "a kind of on-the-spot inquiry" (Schon, 1995, p. 40) and consider what is occurring and what actions are and are not successful. This reflection-in-action draws on past experiences with similar situations, formal theories with their general principles, and intuition, to arrive at new insights and hence new action. Unlike the epistemology of technical rationality, reflection-in-action is nonlinear, it happens in the action, and it recognizes that practitioners' experience, wisdom, and insight operate in a way that allows them to improvise. While this capacity is sometimes referred to as intuition, it is far more. Rather, it is a mark of professional expertise, the ability to quickly appraise a situation and decide what course of action to take without going through a deliberate reasoning process.

Hugh England (1986) presented a similar view and stated that the integration of theory and practice is a unique and intuitive process wherein workers do not simply apply formulae. Rather social workers use the theoretical knowledge they possess to construct coherence from the complex situations they see before them. What has been elusive is articulating the process experienced practitioners use to bring these knowledge frameworks into their professional activities.

While working with experienced social workers as they learn to become field educators, I observed that when practitioners are asked directly about the theory or approaches that they use they are taken aback and often respond that their practice is eclectic or intuitive (Bogo and Vayda, 1998). However, through a structured dialogue it is possible for practitioners to stand back from their practice, critically reflect on it, and articulate some of the implicit components that affect their actions in an interview. In a qualitative study addressing how field instructors teach social work students to integrate theory and practice,

Kenyon (2000) found that social workers did not separate theory from practice as university-based educators do. They did not clearly identify the theories they used or describe a systematic application of concepts in practice. Instead, they described a process where, from the very first interaction with clients, they were making meaning of the information they received from the client and the information they gleaned from their participation with and observation of the client. These understandings were described in everyday language and revealed these social workers to be continuously engaged in building a theory about the case. When pressed by the research interviewer, they could describe how they work. In these descriptions formal theories were obvious, although not labeled as such. However, they were integrated into their "talk" about their practice. Through reflecting on their work with the research interviewer they described a process where two activities happened simultaneously; they were actively involved as a participant with the client while at the same time they were reflecting on what was transpiring. Insights gleaned from this reflection would then play a part in directing the next steps taken in the interview. This process was flowing, cumulative, and integrated. Schon (1987) referred to this activity as "reflection-in-action" and noted that "skillful improvisers often become tongue-tied or give obviously inadequate accounts when asked to say what they do. Clearly, it is one thing to be able to reflect-in-action and quite another to be able to reflect on our reflection-in-action so as to produce a good verbal description of it" (p. 31). This opinion is similar to the observations of Bogo and Vayda (1998) and Kenyon (2000) in their attempts to train social workers for the role of field instructor and the task of teaching students how to use theory to guide practice.

From these observations it appears that practitioners accumulate a vast reservoir of knowledge, experiences, and skills over many years. Influences on this knowledge base come from many sources and include significant learning from field experiences and field instructors during social work studies and from practice teachers who exposed students to particular theories and skills and served as role models by virtue of their attitudes and behaviors with students. Many practitioners credit their clinical supervisors as having had the greatest influence on their learning. Observing skilled colleagues and attending workshops are other important sources for new learning. From these experiences each practitioner appears to incorporate her own set of ideas and professional behaviors based on what makes sense to her and feels congruent with her sense of self. This initial core of knowledge and skills constitutes a unique professional foundation for the particular social worker. Over time some parts may be rejected and replaced with new conceptual building blocks. More "pieces" of knowledge are incorporated to create an intricate, complex, multilayered knowledge framework and practice model. Clearly, this is an evolving long-term "project" of constructing, deconstructing, and rebuilding a practice approach. It is an iterative process and one that is stimulated by being in practice. Reflecting on one's practice with a critical eye enables social workers to evaluate their work and examine the effect of specific actions on their clients. Practitioners develop their own way of working as they draw generalizations from these specific instances. As these generalizations are used in subsequent new situations, they may be refined and ultimately integrated into a practitioner's repertoire. Or, if their effect proves to be limited, they may be discarded. The result is similar to a richly colored tapestry in that the practitioner's knowledge base is made up of many different threads. One cannot easily extract particular strands without distorting the whole. However, when practitioners consciously examine and deconstruct their practice they are able to identify those underlying or implicit values, concepts, and beliefs that are seen in action.

This process of knowledge building for practice is presented as if it happens in a structured and systematic manner. In fact it is more likely that it evolves in a less than conscious way, stimulated by those experiences where social workers have the opportunity to discuss their work with others. Social workers have identified the activity of teaching, such as in field instruction, as a motivator to think critically about their practice and identify what they do and why (Bogo and Power, 1992; Globerman and Bogo, 2003).

THE CHALLENGE FOR STUDENTS LEARNING TO PRACTICE

As social work students approach the challenging task of mastering knowledge and skill for effective practice it is useful to keep in mind the view presented above about continuous learning and development. At the end of their first year of social work studies students often reflect on their initial desire for clear, specific, and orderly guidelines and techniques that would help them directly transfer learning from their academic courses to their practice with clients in the field. There is a strong desire to learn skills: what to do and how to do it. Once students begin their field education they report arriving at a new understanding of the links between knowledge and practice, recognizing that connections often are not linear, simple, or direct. Skills and techniques are important, but not enough. Rather, as stated above, practitioners need a variety of theories or models and the opportunity to use them as potential or temporary lens to guide practice. And, they also need to learn how to engage in a reflective process that individualizes the practice situation and helps them work with the uniqueness presented. They need to learn how to simultaneously think about their practice while they are doing it. Students are faced with an additional challenge. They are developing their knowledge and skill concurrently while attempting to offer a competent intervention. While this is true of learners in all professions, it does not lessen the fact that many students experience anxiety and concern that the client is not being well served. This fuels the search for concrete solutions and approaches that might better help clients. As discussed earlier, the field's current focus on empirically supported models reflects a responsible attitude that clients deserve to receive the best approaches the profession has to offer. On the other hand, postmodern perspectives, an increasingly diverse society, and the complexity of the social and structural problems that clients face lead many in the profession to note the limitations of "expert knowledge" and that it is less than universally applicable. As noted, this text aims to take a middle position in this matter. While the knowledge and skill components of the profession will be presented with respect to behavior in the interview, it is expected that students and practitioners will use this information in a critical and reflective manner. That includes recognizing "that one's expertise is a way of looking at something that was once constructed and may be reconstructed, and there is both readiness and competence to explore its meaning in the experience of the client. The reflective practitioner tries to discover the limits of his expertise through reflective conversation" (Schon, 1983, p. 296). This perspective on practice highlights its complexity and that it is an activity influenced by the perceptions, definitions, and values of both the social worker and the client. The Integration of Theory and Practice (ITP) Loop Model (Bogo and Vayda, 1998) is presented in this chapter to assist practitioners, students, classroom and field instructors to reflect on their practice.

At different stages of professional development students and practitioners may chose to focus on different aspects of learning. The elements of professional expertise that have been presented include a range of theories and models, skill sets, and developing a personal practice that integrates these components. While all these elements operate in concert, at various stages of one's professional growth and development a particular focus may make more sense. The goal for students in any professional practice is ultimately to make the knowledge and skills their own.

This text aims to contribute to students' and practitioners' individual "projects" of integrating theory and practice. Where possible the links will be made between professional behavior in practice, such as in the interview, and the underlying derivatives of that behavior—be it theoretically driven, or from empirically derived knowledge, or from professional values, or from personal issues and preferences. Practice guidelines and skills are provided in the service of helping social workers develop a practice that is intentional, rather than unplanned, accidental, or reactive. The purpose guides the action and the actions reflect the worker's personal and professional knowledge base and experience.

LEARNING STYLES

A number of educational theorists have noted that people learn differently and have different learning styles. The concept of learning styles describes a student in terms of those educational conditions under which he is most likely to learn (Hunt, 1987). Many inventories exist to help students who are interested in conducting a self-assessment of their own learning style. A brief review of some of the key concepts can help students get a sense of their preferred style and how that might operate as they approach the challenging task of learning to integrate knowledge, skill, and self in their interviewing behavior. A further issue is that any learning style is not static; it changes depending on such factors as the context and purpose for learning and the nature of the subject. For example, one might learn statistics in a manner different from the way one learns how to interview. Motivation also plays a key role. If we must learn something new to practice our profession effectively and earn our livelihood, we may be more focused and persistent than when learning a hobby or a new sport.

Kolb (1985) described the learning cycle and identified four stages, which also characterize preferred learning styles. In the first stage, called concrete experience, the student learns from his or her feelings about specific experiences and people. Experiences provide a rich resource of information from which one can extrapolate and learn. In the next stage, called reflective observation, the student learns from watching and listening. The learner observes and carefully and thoughtfully examines issues from a number of perspectives. Judgments are arrived at from these observations in a patient manner. In the next stage, referred to as abstract conceptualization, the student learns through logically analyzing ideas. The learner develops an intellectual understanding of a situation, theory is used for planning, and ideas are generated from an analysis of the situation. The last stage of learning, referred to as active experimentation, involves taking a practical approach and learning through doing.

These stages are also defined as preferred learning styles that describe the best possible conditions for various people as they begin to learn something new. For example, with respect to learning how to interview, some social work students will want to begin by recalling their own experiences in interviews and identifying what was and what was not helpful. This experiential and personal reflection provides a meaningful entry for them into learning new material. Other students will want to begin by watching experienced social workers interview through live observation or reviewing videotapes. The chance to reflect on what they have observed will make the concepts and skills come to life. Still other students will want to read extensively and engage in discussion to develop an abstract intellectual understanding of the interview and the skills needed. Finally, there are many students who learn best by doing. Actively experimenting with new skills through role play or actual interviews with clients will provide the stimulus and data for gaining new competencies. Educators acknowledge that it is appropriate to begin learning through using a student's preferred learning style. However, optimal professional learning includes developing the ability to use all domains of Kolb's cycle.

Other dimensions of learning style can be usefully seen not as finite types but as points on a continuum—for example, preferences for more or less structure or preferences for more direction from the teacher as contrasted with more participation from the students. Some learners value an educational environment that is highly structured, led by the teacher, with materials, readings, concepts, and exercises provided in an organized manner. At the other end of the continuum is a nonstructured environment where there is a lot of negotiation about how learning is to take place, how participants will be involved, and what the expectations of the teacher and the learners will be. Adult education approaches, popular in some social work programs, may be experienced as less structured (Memmott and Brennan, 1998). Furthermore, preferences for various styles may vary with the stage of learning of the student. For example, when one is a novice more structure and a teacher-led approach may be more welcomed than in later stages of learning when the student is aiming to develop more autonomy and self-reliance prior to graduation.

Social work students report on the need for safety in educational experiences in order to take risks, to present issues of concern, problems in their practice, or to engage in role plays in front of their peers (Bogo, Globerman, and Sussman, 2004a). Safety can have many meanings, although it generally refers to a sense that the environment is free of danger and others can be trusted. While individual students may experience classroom dynamics differently, generally social work students highlight the importance of feeling connected to, understood, and respected by their peers. Most helpful are classmates who engage with the issues presented, explore topics in depth, and share their own similar practice examples and struggles.

In a study of group supervision trust meant that students had enough confidence to believe that when they risked exposing mistakes, vulnerabilities, and uncertainties the responses from the field instructor and fellow students would be helpful and not deprecating. Comments that were highly critical, shameful, or humiliating led students not only to question their own competence but also to withdraw from group interaction. Energy was directed to self-protection, and students reported becoming guarded about what they chose to share (Bogo, Globerman, and Sussman, 2004a). Similarly, classroom dynamics and interactions between the instructor and students and between students can affect student learning, facilitating or impeding growth (Dore, 1993; Mishna and Rasmussen, 2001; Rasmussen and Mishna, 2003). Contemporary social work classrooms can model valued professional interpersonal processes such as respect and collaboration. An environment that provides room for expressing and listening to diverse perspectives is challenging; both instructors and students need to use group processes to discuss emotionally laden issues of difference, privilege, oppression, and exclusion (Holley and Steiner, 2005; Hyde and Ruth, 2002). Through dialogue greater understanding of others can be achieved as well as insights into self revealed.

THE INTEGRATION OF THEORY AND PRACTICE:
THE ITP LOOP MODEL

Bogo and Vayda (1998) described a process for conceptualizing the thoughts, attitudes, values, and feelings that affect what social workers do in practice. The model is presented in figure 1.2. It can be used as a device for students and practitioners as they consider what influences their behavior in the interview. It has been used extensively in field education to assist students and their instructors to critically reflect on practice and to conceptualize and prepare for subsequent interventions. The material that will be presented in subsequent chapters can be viewed through this loop model as the reader examines the ideas presented. A loop is used to illustrate the cumulative, ongoing, and repeated activities of thinking about, feeling about, and doing or taking some action within a practice situation. Each phase of the loop affects the next in an interactive fashion. While the figure implies a stagelike process, in practice each phase flows into and out of each other.

Retrieval is the first phase in the loop and refers to the recall of the salient facts of a practice situation. An enduring theme in social work is the focus on the person-in-situation, also referred to as person-in-context or person-in-environment. The ecological-systemic perspective is the current metaphor for capturing the profession's central emphasis, the personal-situational-societal nexus that involves viewing the interactions and mutual affects between individuals and their social and physical contexts (Bisno and Cox, 1997). It recognizes that individual capacity, resources, and needs can be enhanced or constrained by familial, community, organizational, societal, and structural conditions. This perspective captures the dual mission of social work, to enhance the well-being of individual clients and ameliorate social conditions that affect all persons. An ecological-systems paradigm focuses the worker to attend to specific phenomena, seek certain types of information for assessment, and address both individual and contextual elements in intervention.

Guided by specific theories of human behavior and models of practice, social workers retrieve information of a biopsychosocial nature. Using individual models, this may include information about the individual's definition of the problem, his behavior, feelings, and/or thoughts. Using findings from neuroscience and health research, this may include information about the individual's health status. Using family systems models, the focus may be on

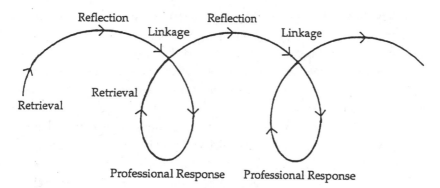

FIGURE 1.2 The ITP Loop Model (Bogo and Vayda, 1998)

key relationships between family members, patterns of interactions, and family roles and structure.

Supported by both empirical findings and practice wisdom, the crucial nature of the relationship between the client and worker, the working alliance, is an area of focus in all direct social work practice. This topic will be discussed at length in chapters 3 and 4. Currently it is noted as an important focus for the worker, and information is gathered about the interaction between client and worker from their first encounter and throughout the process.

Environmental factors in the client's immediate life circumstances and in society provide important information for the social worker, as stated earlier. These include macro issues of an economic, political, and social nature such as entitlements to financial assistance, health and social services, and education. Mezzo issues such as the nature of the neighborhood or community, its resources, supports, and problems are important as well. Contemporary social work theory leads us to consider how diverse characteristics of individuals play a role in their lives, in internal thoughts and feelings, and as they participate in social relations and institutions. An understanding of how structural barriers discriminate against equal access to resources and opportunities remains an enduring theme in the profession. Finally, the nature of the programs and services provided by the worker's organization and the service delivery system must be taken into account.

Reflection refers to standing back from the interview and considering the social worker's personal associations to various aspects of the practice situation.

As already stated, an enduring theme in social work is the recognition that we bring our "self" into our work in many ways. Concepts such as transference and countertransference can assist social workers by elucidating pertinent individual and interpersonal dynamics and will be discussed subsequently. A phase of reflection provides a conscious and systematic method to examine and understand how the personal and professional operate in practice. It makes us alert to the multiple sources of meanings and feelings that are evoked through this type of interpersonal work and it stimulates us to become conscious of the motivations that may lie behind our actions.

The goal of the social worker is to serve the best interests of the client through whatever processes may be useful. The term *process* refers to a sequence of interactions that takes place between the client and worker over a period of time. It is the way the two relate to each other as they discuss the content of the situation that brought the client to the social worker. It also refers to the way they relate to each other as they approach their task of working together. It includes the verbal and nonverbal, the overt and covert meanings of messages as well as the dynamics that are both in and out of awareness. Practitioners reflect on the process from the position of both participant and observer, and they do so simultaneously. This involves moving in and out of the interactional field. It also involves a dynamic tension between the way the worker behaves in her usual way—the personal self—and the way she behaves as a disciplined professional—the professional self (Edwards and Bess, 1998).

Through a type of awareness-in-action, social workers are more likely to provide responses that are intentional and developed to achieve goals rather than unexamined reactions that reflect their spontaneous emotional responses. For example, a social worker preparing a foster child for his second move in nine months is aware that the child's anger at her is eliciting feelings of annoyance. The social worker identifies her annoyance; she has spent hours finding and preparing a new home for this child. She also reflects on how hard it is for the child to experience another rejection and is able to respond to him with compassion rather than act on her irritated reaction. Her reaction is a normal one that warrants recognition and perhaps discussion with a colleague or supervisor. What is important is that this personal reaction is reflected upon, understood, and thereby contained. The worker is then able to provide what the client needs—support and understanding, at this particular point in time.

Social work practitioners can use both long-established and contemporary theoretical frameworks to understand the way in which their personal feelings, thoughts, and behavior operate in an interview. Two perspectives can be integrated: one that focuses on the personality and emanates from psychodynamic theory and one that focuses on social identity and diversity and emanates from social constructivism. The later theory has also influenced current relational-psychodynamic theory, and hence there is overlap. With respect to personality theory, psychoanalytic and psychodynamic theorists drew attention to the ways in which therapists' personalities and personal experiences affect their professional practice. Over time, with the development of relational perspectives, countertransference has been further elaborated and will be discussed in the following section. Social work scholars such as Hollis (1964), Strean (1979), and Schamess (1981) have developed these concepts for social work practice. Recent texts make these concepts accessible for social work practitioners (Brandell, 2004; Goldstein, 1995).

Some social work scholars, not writing in the psychodynamic tradition, have brought contributions of postmodernism and social constructionist theory into social work. Social constructionism views reality and self as co-constructed through interactions with social and physical environments and mediated through language and culture (Gergen and Davis, 1985). Social work writers have drawn from this perspective and focused attention on the ways in which individuals, both clients and workers, are influenced by, process, and internalize cultural and societal messages (Dean, 2001; Dyche and Zayas, 1995; 2001; Laird, 1998). Self-reflexivity is the term used to refer to practitioners' awareness of the cultural influence on the self and the ways in which values, assumptions, and worldview serve as standards and norms by which judgments about human well-being and social justice are made. Previously held opinions characterized as universal are seen as locally constituted narratives.

Although we are not always aware of how issues of the self affect our thoughts, feelings, and behavior in practice, these dynamics often "bubble beneath the surface" and operate at some level in the assessments we make and the interventions we recommend. Furthermore, in a multicultural and highly diverse society particular social identity or cultural characteristics of both the client and the worker are often associated with privilege and power as well as with deprivation and oppression. For example, in a highly racialized society the color of a person's skin may signal a range of stereotypes about background, opportunities, and possibilities. When the worker and client appear to be members of different and distinct groups, each participant may carry societal messages and internalized experiences of advantage or disadvantage into their encounter. Practitioners need to be sensitive to and aware of the way in which these experiences and assumptions operate as expectations for themselves and for their clients. Awareness, however, is not sufficient; social workers also need the ability to work with issues of diversity when they are salient. In the following discussion the dimensions of personality and diversity are presented separately, as they have developed from different theoretical perspectives. In reality they are intertwined, evident in our personal and professional lives, as each influences the development of the other.

Transference and countertransference. The concepts of transference and countertransference, originating in psychodynamic theory, provide useful ways to understand how personal and developmental issues can operate in practice. Traditionally, the term *transference* referred to that part of the client's experience of the relationship that is a manifestation of his intrapsychic dynamics or personality. The term *countertransference* referred to the worker's reactions to aspects of the client and the relationship as indicative of the worker's dynamics and conflicts. The implication was that these reactions would impede the therapeutic process. Within the psychoanalytic tradition this classical view was replaced by writers such as Racker (1968) and Winnicott (1956) who recognized that therapists experience the totality of the client and the therapy, that this experience is not solely a reflection of therapists' unresolved issues but is a normal by-product of intense engagement in interpersonal work. Furthermore it was observed that subjective reactions could be a useful source of data to better understand the client. Hence for social workers both transference and countertransference refers to all the ways in which both the client and the worker experience each other. This current experience is shaped by their personalities, their characteristic ways of feeling, processing information, and creating meaning in relationships. These dynamics are largely unconscious and hence out of direct awareness. Therefore, either participant may behave in ways, both positive and negative, that do not appear to be warranted by the present interactions or purpose of their meeting. Rather, influences from both the past and from current experiences have become internalized and are manifest in the way each individual participates in the helping relationship.

In the past few decades a number of psychoanalytic theorists have emphasized the relational context in which psychological or intrapsychic phenomena exist. In their view therapy is created and shaped by the interaction of both the client and the therapist (Mitchell, 1988; Stolorow, 1994). Beginning with the seminal work of Heinz Kohut (Kohut, 1971, 1977, 1984) self psychology argued that individuals' basic needs centered on empathic connections with others, particularly with caregivers. Empathy is considered central to both development and to the therapeutic process. The term *selfobject* is used to refer to persons or objects that are required to fulfill certain functions that enable individuals to maintain a cohesive sense of self and well-being in childhood, throughout the life cycle, and in therapy. Kohut considered it important for therapists to be self-scrutinizing in order to remain empathically attuned to clients' selfobject needs. Therapists' empathic failures are understood as related to their vulnerabilities stemming from their own current or past selfobject needs that may be intensified when working with a particular client. Social work writers such as Donner (1988), Elson (1986), and Palombo (1985) have brought self-psychology theory into social work and Goldstein's (2001) recent text discusses concepts from both object relations and self psychology for social work.

Intersubjectivity theory in psychoanalysis focuses "on the interplay between the differently organized subjective worlds of the observer and the observed" (Atwood and Stolorow, 1984, p. 41). The emphasis is on the subjective experience of each participant. Both pathological and healthy human development and processes of change arise from and are maintained by the interactions of the subjectivities, be it parent and child, or client and therapist (Orange, Atwood, and Stolorow, 1997). A moderate view of realism is proposed by Orange (1995) who recognizes that inevitably each person's perspective can only be a partial one; through dialogue with others a broader view may be gained. Similar to self psychology, a stance of sustained empathic inquiry is used which provides the therapist's emotional availability, crucial to growth and development (Orange, Atwood, and Stolorow 1997). With respect to the therapist's countertransference, the term *cotransference* is proposed to reflect the importance of the subjective world of practitioners and include their professional theories, personalities, and inputs (Orange, 1995). Rather than viewing their reactions as "counter" or in response to the client, this term captures the notion that there are two persons involved in the helping relationship and each brings forward all of themselves in subtle ways including their way of being, feeling, and making meaning of situations.

Relational theory also contributes to understanding the interactive nature of therapy. The seminal work of John Bowlby (Bowlby, 1969) draws attention to the concept of attachment and that human relatedness is a primary and basic biological need. Relational theorists such as Fairbairn (1952) and Mitchell (1988) emphasize that individuals crave intense attachments and will form, seek, and strive to maintain relatedness in their lives and also in therapy. Early relational experiences are internalized and form a basic relational configuration or internal working model that includes the dimensions of the self, the other, and the transactional patterns (Bowlby, 1969; Mitchell, 1988). While internal working models are formed in the context of earliest relationships they are maintained or reconstructed through experiences and interactions with significant others, such as peer group members, intimate partners, significant extended family members, mentors, employers, and friends throughout adulthood. Internal working models that include beliefs about our needs and the likelihood of others' emotional availability and responsiveness are carried forward into new relationships and affect current behavior. To the extent that they lead to repetitive and predictable behavioral patterns that elicit characteristic responses in others, these expectations or internal working models are reinforced and will persist. These models and patterns are carried into therapy where they can be experienced and examined and new relationship experiences constructed. Hence transference and countertransference can be understood as the enactment of internal working models on the part of both clients and workers. Relational concepts and attachment theory are useful in many aspects of social work practice and have been introduced into social work literature through the writings of Howe (1995) and Sable (1992).

In summary, contemporary views of transference and countertransference (or cotransference) rest on an assumption that early experiences are formed in an interactive social field, occur between people, are internalized and seen in feelings, thoughts, and behavior in subsequent relationships throughout the life cycle and in therapeutic situations. These intrapsychic and interactional patterns then tend to operate in subsequent interpersonal experiences by serving as a lens through which an individual's and others' thoughts, feelings, and behaviors in relationships are experienced and understood. Similarly, in encounters with social workers, where there is an expectation of help, these dynamics are also evident. Using these concepts it is clear that social workers are not objective or neutral participants. Rather, they too bring their history and their subjectivities into the relationship and with the client create a current relationship dynamic.

Many of the feelings and thoughts that practitioners experience are usual and typical of most workers. Some reactions have a more personal meaning. Take a moment to think about some of the practice situations that you have found most challenging. If you have had little experience, what do you imagine would be most challenging for you? What feelings, thoughts, and reactions are stirred up in you?

For example, a student in practicum in a general hospital reflected on how seeing so many ill and dying patients left her feeling sad in interviews and less able to offer helpful professional responses to her clients. It is important to separate out to what extent reactions such as these are "typical," that is, similar to what most social workers in this position would experience, and to what extent these reactions are unique and personal. In discussing this reaction with other students and her field instructor the student became aware that her reaction was a usual one for many health professionals when they begin to work in a hospital. If, on the other hand, reflection helps the student recognize that sad feelings are evoking memories of a recent or current loss of a loved relative or friend, then the meaning of her reactions is an individual one.

While clinical social workers are comfortable with the concepts of transference and countertransference, the generic social work terminology appears to favor the term *use of self*. Nevertheless all agree that the development of increasing self-knowledge may be one of the most crucial aspects of life-long learning for professionals. Edwards and Bess (1998) point out how important it is for social workers to have a systematic inventory of "personal traits and characteristic behaviors which come to them as naturally as breathing. They must be able to identify specifically *how they act* and *what they say* that is unique to themselves as persons in relation with others and that conveys the essence of their inner selves to their clients" (p.97). They recommend that social workers examine their own personal solutions to the challenges they have faced in their lives and how these solutions reflect underlying principles and beliefs about social functioning. Not to be overlooked is to also identify what one enjoys about being a social worker.

Social workers are faced with practice situations that may provoke strong feelings and reactions. Problems encountered can involve loss of loved ones, abuse and violence in intimate relationships, physical and emotional trauma, chronic and deteriorating physical illness, and living in depriving and harsh environments. Individuals are attracted to the profession out of a desire to help others, and it is likely that poignant and upsetting client circumstances will evoke a range of strong feelings such as compassion, responsibility, anger, and anxiety. Self-reflection, consultation, and personal work enable practitioners to become familiar with their own reactions to conditions and people. The reflective exercise on the preceding page can assist in developing self-knowledge.

There are many practice situations that social workers encounter where the client presents issues similar to those the practitioner has experienced. For example many clients value receiving service in ethnospecific settings with social workers who speak the language of the client population. These workers may confront experiences similar to those that they, or members of their extended family, have dealt with, for example, immigration and dislocation, underemployment, racism and prejudice. Sharing comparable life circumstances can assist in building relationships and understanding the client's experience in an authentic and genuine way. It may also cloud the worker's ability to assess and intervene helpfully, especially when the client's reactions to similar situations differ from the worker's, and the practitioner finds herself using her reactions and adaptations as the standard by which to assess the client situation. For example, a worker may value the fact that her extended family, when they first immigrated to North America, had supported each other financially, pooled their earnings from employment, and lived in one home. When faced with a client who resists the help of her extended family, preferring to extract herself from a traditional living arrangement and obligations to her elders, this social worker may find that she is subtly critical and not supportive of the client's decision to live on her own.

Over time practitioners develop effective ways to contain personal reactions in the interview. Generally the process begins by becoming aware of what one is feeling and experiencing in the moment. A worker might ask himself, "What is going on in me right now?" That query can surface a range of feelings and thoughts. This is followed by a conscious cognitive reflection that sorts out the following.

- Is the worker reacting as most practitioners would to what the client is saying or doing, either the content or the process? For example, listening to a client talking about being physically abused by a violent partner would lead most practitioners to feeling upset. Interviewing the violent partner who denies his role in the aggression and angrily states that he was provoked is likely to result in the worker feeling angry and perhaps somewhat frightened.
- Is the worker reacting as she usually does in relationships? For example, some workers do not like hostile people, they try to avoid them in their personal life and find them threatening in their practice.
- Is the worker reacting to issues that are troubling to him currently, or relate to his past, and are evoked by the client's presentation? These issues may be easily linked or the worker may not be fully aware of the concerns and needs to pay attention to his reactions after the interview. For example, a worker who is undergoing a divorce may find working with a couple contemplating separation an anxiety-producing experience. A worker who, in her family of origin, grew up feeling responsible for her parents and younger siblings may find herself feeling overly responsible for and preoccupied by the ongoing suicidal ideation of a depressed client.

Pondering the insights the worker gains from asking these questions will help him sort out to what extent his reactions are by-products of the work, and warrant discussion in supervision or with peers, and to what extent these issues may benefit from personal development and therapy. This intellectual process ideally helps to differentiate the personal and the professional and enables the practitioner to reengage in the interview in a client-focused way. By attending to aspects of the personal self in the work, the practitioner is in a better position to produce a reasoned response, one that is helpful to the client.

Vicarious traumatization. When practitioners work with clients who have been traumatized, they may experience what has been referred to as vicarious traumatization (Johnson, 2002; Pearlman and Saakvitne, 1995). This term refers to the experience some professionals have when working with clients who have been traumatized through events such as physical or sexual abuse, torture, war, rape, or assault. After a considerable time spent listening to difficult narratives and empathizing with clients' pain, practitioners may find themselves feeling unsettled. Connecting with others' extreme vulnerability can challenge the sense of safety and meaning in one's own life and stir up significant issues (Johnson, 2002). Some practitioners report intrusive imagery of the stories their clients have told them. They may have nightmares or experience difficulty sleeping, have headaches or nausea, feel emotionally numb, and feel vulnerable, unsafe, and have difficulty trusting others. This form of secondary trauma, as a result of hearing about clients' trauma, has been identified in a range of helping professionals (Pearlman and Saakvitne, 1995). Therefore, practitioners need to be able to identify what they are experiencing in professional work and access a range of educational, supportive, or therapeutic resources that may enable them to minimize personal occupational stress.

Self-care. To be helpful practitioners need to feel energetic and generally experience a state of well-being. It is important to learn about self-care strategies and discover the methods that work. Experienced social workers describe a range of strategies that help them live with the feelings and thoughts that emerge from their work and with the potential experience of emotional depletion. These strategies can help to contain a type of emotional flooding and preoccupation that can come from active involvement with others who are in pain. Successful strategies help maintain energy, empathic presence, interest, and commitment. Some suggested approaches to self-care follow.

Supportive organizations. The organizational contexts we work in have a profound impact on our well-being. Staff groups and teams, supervisors, and administrators can create nutritive environments where there is mentoring, educational supervision, and encouragement of creativity, development, and learning. Or organizations can demand increasing accountability, unrealistic work productivity standards, and expect risk taking in the absence of structures and personnel that will support frontline staff. Social workers need to use their knowledge and skill to assess both the opportunities and the constraints to bring about organizational change and create positive work environments.

Education, supervision and consultation. That intensive work with persons in difficulty and pain is stressful cannot be denied. Hence it is of vital importance that student learners and practitioners have emotionally supportive professional relationships where they can be open about their struggles, mistakes, and crises of confidence. Such relationships provide important sites for learning, especially with respect to issues of self. When we feel understood by colleagues, meaningful dialogue can occur about what is elicited in ourselves as a result of our work. We can arrive at a more realistic appreciation of our strengths and limits. Sensing that one is a part of a professional and collegial community promotes the vitality and energy that all workers need. As discussed earlier, in a study of conditions that students report as productive for group supervision, we found that having peers who were empathically attuned to each others' concerns, were connected, and offered emotional support was essential. This type of relational base provided the necessary conditions for presenting difficult practice problems and for self-disclosure and exposure of the details of students' practice. Feedback and subsequent learning flourished when these conditions were present. Students reported that competition between students about performance and nonresponsiveness to a student's struggles were corrosive experiences. These conditions seemed to lead to silence in the group, a guarded and self-protective stance, and a retreat from learning (Bogo, Globerman, and Sussman, 2004a, 2004b).

Supervision is no longer the norm for all new social work graduates in their first job. When supervision is provided it is important that it include not only attention to administrative matters but also to the educational aspects of practice in the agency. When agencies do not provide this type of supervision it is especially important for new social workers to find learning opportunities that will provide opportunities for their professional development. In this era, with an ever expanding knowledge base for practice, it can be energizing as well as professionally responsible to see oneself as a lifelong learner. Individual supervision helps apply new learning directly to the case situations with which the worker is engaged. Group consultation, with colleagues that include those more experienced, provides learning from others. There are also workshops, continuing education or online courses, and professional literature that provide new learning, keep one "fresh," and stimulate professional growth.

Primary relationships. Since much of our practice involves us in helping others, social workers need to balance the way they give and the way they receive in their personal, intimate, family, social, and work relationships. Often the role of caretaker or nurturer comes naturally and social workers can find themselves in similar positions with family, friends, and colleagues. It is especially impor-

Take some time to reflect on your current life circumstances as follows. For each category identify both the strengths and the challenges or issues. What would you need to do to improve your sense of well-being? What would others need to do? Is that likely to happen?

ORGANIZATION

Human resources policies and practices about personal and parental/caregiving leaves, conditions of employment, career advancement, and development opportunities

Relationships with coworkers, supervisor, employer

Team atmosphere, degree of collegiality, collaboration, and competition

RELATIONSHIPS

Intimate partner   Children
Family of origin   Extended family members
Friendships and other significant social relationships
Any other significant relationships

PHYSICAL WELL-BEING

What activities do you engage in that are restful, stimulating, or nourishing? Are you doing enough of what you like?

Do you engage in activities that are ultimately deleterious to your health, e.g. smoking, excessive drinking or use of drugs, poor nutrition?

tant to know how to ask for help or support in close relationships. It is equally important to have enjoyable social relationships that are characterized by doing things that are pleasurable. Too often lives get out of balance and an abundance of work, duties, and responsibilities creates stress and demoralization.

Developing physical well-being. Since much of social work practice is sedentary, it is useful to develop a lifestyle that helps maintain health and fitness. Some practitioners embrace traditional physical activities such as regular walking, playing sports, or participating in exercise classes. Others report on the relaxation and fitness they achieve through meditation, yoga, or regular relaxation exercises.

- What specific characteristics of certain clients might make it more difficult for you to form relationships with them? What is it about a client's experience that would be hard for you to relate to or that would create a barrier to empathy?
- What specific characteristics do you have that might make it difficult for clients to form relationships with you?
- What types of clients might you easily form relationships with? What common experiences might exist between yourself and the client that could act to facilitate a connection?
- What risks might occur in forming relationships with those individuals?

IMPLICATIONS FOR PRACTICE

Awareness and understanding of ourselves can assist in better understanding of clients. A steady mindful attitude about our own internal process can help us to monitor our associations to what the client is saying, to better empathize and to gain insight into another's experience. Moreover, attention to countertransference reactions can alert social workers to analyze the source, extent, and nature of the issues presented by self and other in their interaction patterns. Awareness can help restrain practitioners from reacting to clients and encourage instead a search for a facilitative response. The more we know about ourselves, the more likely we are to be able to gain insight into what clients may be reacting to or struggling with. The goal is to use our self-knowledge in the service of the client. For example, a social worker knows that she tends to feel responsible for "fixing problems." When confronted with a client with long-standing difficulties who expresses hopelessness about making any progress, the social worker will spend extra time with the client, often leaving her feeling depleted. With insight the worker can recognize how her own place in her family of origin has been internalized and is being stimulated and enacted in her work with her client. She can also recognize how she is reacting to the client's subtle comment that other workers were more available. These insights can assist the social worker in assessment and also in intervention, leading her to partialize the client problems, choose a finite number of issues to address, and set appropriate limits about the length of the interviews and the time frame for service.

There are many ways to develop self awareness both before, during, and after the interview. The questions in the reflective exercise on the preceding page are based on those developed by Mishna (2003a) and are useful to contemplate prior to engaging in direct social work practice.

In summary, both the client and the social worker come into the helping relationship with their unique personalities and ideas about relationships. These ideas are played out as the two work together to forge an alliance that will help the client. The way in which the two participants interact will stimulate a wide range of conscious and unconscious feelings and thoughts about relationships. Hence, behavior in relationships, including helping relationships, can be understood as shaped by the two participants through the way in which they express and respond to expectations about a wide range of self-in-relationship factors.

AWARENESS OF CULTURAL DIFFERENCE

In this text the term *culture* is defined broadly and refers to the values, beliefs, expectations, and meanings people use to interpret our experiences in the world (Greene, 1994). In this respect culture affects our choices and the actions and behaviors deemed appropriate in a range of situations. Increasingly in North America social work is practiced in contexts of great diversity. Social workers and their clients often come from different ethnic, racial, religious, and class backgrounds. As a result of global migration they may come from different countries of origin, recently or in past generations. There may also be differences by virtue of age, gender, sexual orientation, ability, or a host of other significant characteristics. Perceptions of gender roles and attitudes toward sexual orientation are varied. With legalization of marriage for same-sex couples there is greater recognition of diverse family forms. Disability and health status are also recognized as profoundly affecting individuals and their life experiences.

Culture is neither one dimensional nor static. While frequently the terms *culture* and *ethnicity* are used interchangeably, ethnicity refers to a group of people who share a sense of common ancestry that may be related to language, national origin, traditions, history, or religion (Longres, 1996). Culture includes not only ethnicity but also factors such as gender, class, sexual orientation, ability, and the like and involves the complex interplay between these many dimensions. For example, gender is informed by ethnicity, which can be informed by locality, which can inform how one thinks about and practices religion, which in turn may shape views about sexual orientation (Hardy, 1997). Cultures that affect individuals change over time. For example, as feminism has resulted in more equitable policies in the workforce for women, young females experience their gender and career choices differently than did women in a previous generation. Similarly affirmative action policies and programs increasingly address structural barriers to equitable access to education and employment for African Americans. Legislation that requires institutions to accommodate the needs of individuals with physical, mental health, and educational challenges also provide more accessibility for groups previously marginalized and excluded. These societal changes affect the hopes, dreams, and expectations of individuals who, in some measure, feel part of these groups.

In the past few decades social work and mental health professions in general recognized the need to incorporate an understanding of culture, defined in its broadest sense, into their theories and practices. Building on feminist analysis clinical theorists produced approaches to working with women (Barrett, 1990; Brown 1994; Jordan, 1997; Jordan et al., 1991; Nes and Iadicola, 1989). Similarly, there are increasing numbers of works devoted to practice with gay men, lesbians, bisexual, and transgendered people in social work and related fields (Hunter and Hickerson, 2003; Laird 1998, 1999; Mackelprang et al., 1996). Helping professionals have also developed specialized approaches for practice with persons with disabilities (Mackelprang and Salsgiver, 1999; Solomon, 1993).

Initially, in practice and in the literature culture was equated largely with ethnicity and a number of texts were produced that provide descriptions of the history, dominant themes and characteristics of ethnic groups represented in the American population (Green, 1995; Lum, 1992; McGoldrick, Giordano, and Pearce, 1996). These contributions draw attention to differences among groups along a number of dimensions. For example, norms and expectations about what constitutes a good life, appropriate behaviors at various stages of development and in particular roles, how problems are experienced and defined, and attitudes about help seeking and forms of informal and professional help. Many early texts discussed general concepts and unique aspects of four major ethnic groups: African American, Native American, Asian-Pacific American, and Hispanic Americans. Ethnicity and culture were seen as a client characteristic rather than a dimension of identity and experience shared by both clients and social workers. By framing the literature in this manner the stereotype of the white worker as the professional and members of minority groups as clients was reinforced. Such a depiction distorts the reality that helping professionals all have ethnic and cultural affiliations that affect their work—many social workers are members of visible minority groups and many clients are from the majority and dominant groups in the society.

The contribution of this approach, sometimes referred to as the cultural literacy model, is that it highlights ethnicity as an influential effect on clients, the issues they bring to social workers, and ultimately the processes deemed useful and the outcomes regarded as helpful. However, cultural literacy has been critiqued due to a number of limitations. First, it tends to treat ethnicity as static and stable. Descriptions of particular ethnic groups often appear frozen in time, although they may have been relevant in an earlier period. Descriptions omit recent changes in a particular country that would affect more recent immigrants. The impact of globalization, increased world travel, and the advent of the World Wide Web have also spread popular cultural forms around the world. Universal similarities may be overlooked in the interests of describing unique features of each ethnic group.

A second critique of the cultural literacy approach is that it ignores within group differences and hence is less useful to practitioners in their actual work with individual clients (Dyche and Zayas, 1995). An assumption is made that individuals are simply representations of their cultures when, in fact, families socialize their children to various aspects of their reference groups, and an individual in turn may identify with some dimensions and reject others. Furthermore families in any group are not universally similar, and they mediate interpretations of ethnic forms. While ethnic information may provide some sense of broad themes, it can also produce simplistic overgeneralizations about groups of people that actually perpetuate incorrect stereotypes and support prejudicial attitudes. It is only through understanding the client's internalized culture (Ho, 1995) that a helping professional can begin to understand diversity issues for a particular client. Ho (1995) introduced the notion of internalized culture, referring to what the client believes and identifies with that may be taken from a number of cultural systems, such as ethnicity, age, sexual orientation, class.

Finally a third critique of the cultural literacy approach is a pragmatic one. Since global migration and internationalization have produced communities comprised of people from a vast number of groups and countries, it is nearly impossible for any helping professional to be knowledgeable enough about the history and experiences of a large number of ethnic groups. More general practice principles for working across ethnic and cultural differences are needed. Perhaps more awareness about these differences will facilitate greater creative artistry for developing helping relationships.

An approach has been proposed that recognizes ethnicity as a personal dimension of all people. It also expands the meaning of diversity as ethnicity and includes other salient social identity characteristics such as race, gender, sexual orientation and so on. Hence a professional interview can be seen as a site of cross-cultural encounter between a worker and a client, each with ethnic and cultural identities, with both similarities and differences. Individuals then are seen not as stereotypic representatives of a single culture. Rather, each individual reflects unique differences in their identification with and internalization of aspects of their original ethnic group as well as other cultural systems they reference (Tsang, Bogo, and George, 2003). Social workers practicing in multicultural and multiracial North America need to take into account the variety of characteristics that all persons embody in their cultural and ethnic identities, both clients and workers, and learn how these diverse aspects are relevant in the work with each client.

Dyche and Zayas (1995, 2001) propose an experiential and phenomenological approach where by the worker adopts a position of curiosity and naïveté and tries to listen to and learn from clients about the salient and pertinent features of self, including the cultural self. This perspective is congruent with contemporary social work theory that views culture as individually and socially constructed through interaction with significant others, evolving and changing over time, and dependent on context (Laird, 1998). It requires practitioners to move beyond "the tendency to think in terms of common and fixed characteristics" (Dean, 2001, p. 625). Human behavior is fraught with contradictions. A view of culture or ethnicity as static and fixed renders this complexity invisible. Reductionistic conclusions about the way groups of people think and behave can also unwittingly support prejudicial and stereotypical judgments and result in more limited responses by practitioners.

For centuries, war, natural disasters, and the search for opportunity have led people to North America as immigrants or refugees. When entering a new country people are challenged with adjusting to a new society and to new ways of living and behaving, and often must learn a foreign language. Individuals acculturate in idiosyncratic ways as they deal with the tensions between the former ways of living and the demands and circumstances of the present. Based on both internal and external factors, each individual client will present with his or her adaptation to making a transition and living in two worlds. For example, an immigrant woman from China requests service for her husband whom she reports as depressed in recent months. She describes the couples' experience since arriving in Los Angeles eight months ago. Since she speaks enough English to hold down an office job, living in Los Angeles has provided her with more financial and personal freedom than in Beijing, where she and her husband lived with her in-laws in close quarters. Previously she was expected to care for her husband and his parents as well as to work outside the home. Her husband, formerly a manager in a factory, is unable to find similar employment because of his limited English language skills. He has been compelled to work as an unskilled worker in the food industry. He experiences this job as demeaning and immigration as a disappointment. He mourns the loss of his work position, his social status, and his significant connection to extended family members. In this family immigration and settlement have provided new opportunities for the female member and marginalized and oppressive conditions for the male. The wife's description of her husband's depression can only be fully understood by placing it in the context of profound changes to his sense of self, family, and community in the new country.

Individuals may identify with a variety of groups based on a number of intersecting diversities. Feminist scholars recognize the multiple diversities within the category of woman and that while there are shared common features there are also vast differences. For example, compare the opportunities and challenges of a single mother struggling financially with sole responsibility for supporting her two children, a middle class, professionally educated dual-career lesbian couple who wish to have a child, and an elderly immigrant Iranian widow living with her acculturated Western-educated adult children.

Thinking about diversity requires us to go beyond thinking only about difference. As noted above, the earlier literature presented a view of diversity that implied the worker was a member of the "dominant" society and the client a member of a "minority" group. The reference to minority group was not with regard to demographic numbers but rather to access to power and resources in the society. McMahon (1996) points out those groups with less power are not only defined by ethnicity but also with respect to race and also include women, members of specific social classes, the elderly, and those people with developmental disabilities. Other groups that have struggled for equity are those people with sexual orientations other than heterosexual and people who belong to specific religious groups, for example, anti-Semitism has resulted in barriers and hostile attitudes to those individuals who identify as Jewish or who are defined as Jewish. McMahon (1996) observes that the social context of diversity for these groups is not simply one of difference, but rather of inequality, discrimination, and prejudice. Thus it is crucial to understand the societal context of racism and oppression, which will be further discussed later in this chapter.

Culturally competent service is a function not only of what transpires in the worker and client interaction but is also a product of societal and organizational contexts (Tsang and George, 1998). Clients often present with situations that are, to varying degrees, a result of systemic barriers and a lack of social justice and equity in society. Deprived environments, communities at risk, poverty, and poor health reflect sociopolitical issues that require change. Similarly, agency policies and programs may not be culturally appropriate or may not provide resources useful to clients. Agencies' boards, managers, and frontline workers may be more or less representative of the populations they are meant to serve. Social workers practicing at the direct service level must attend to these contextual factors in the larger systems that affect the nature of the services they can offer to clients. The social change aspect of social work's mission directs practitioners to not limit interventions to the client system, but also to act both solely and with others as advocates for change.

Since an interactive approach to the client and worker relationship is taken in this text, the contribution of both participants to the work that brings them together warrants examination. Germane to a discussion of diversity is the recognition that clients will have perceptions of social workers that may be based on their experiences with people similar to the worker's group. Consequently the worker may be confused by client behavior that does not seem easily understandable in the current context. It may reflect positive or negative experiences with dominant or powerful members of the social workers' cultural group. The behavior may also reflect cultural attitudes about help seeking and expectations about the behavior of professionals. Previous experiences and attitudes may be brought into the practice encounter. Expectations may remain unspoken—expectations that an individual will be treated with disrespect, judged harshly, and not given fair treatment (Proctor and Davis, 1994).

As discussed earlier with respect to countertransference, in any interpersonal relationship both participants, the client and the worker, bring knowledge, understandings, and feelings that operate at conscious and unconscious levels of awareness. Systemic and interactional perspectives draw our attention to the ways in which the two participants work together to create a helping unit, to arrive at shared meaning about why they are meeting, and to bring about change or offer assistance in some way. This approach is enriched with an understanding that diverse cultural experiences (with culture referring to a wide range of diverse characteristics such as race, ethnicity, class, age, gender, sexual orientation, and ability) operate in this interactional field as well as the personality issues generally subsumed under the rubric of countertransference phenomena.

BEGINNING WITH OURSELVES

To achieve competence in interviewing clients who may be culturally different from oneself in a variety of ways it is important to start by developing an understanding of oneself as a cultural being. This involves, as discussed earlier, recognizing that many of our beliefs, attitudes, assumptions, and values reflect a worldview derived from the sociocultural communities with which we identify. Values are further mediated by the way in which one's family of origin interpreted and enacted their ethnic heritage and the way in which each individual comes to view himself. It includes not only seeing oneself as an ethnic being but also identifying other characteristics and significant cultural systems that may be important, such as class, sexual orientation, or religion. It is also noteworthy that social work theory reflects Western values of self-efficacy, autonomy and individualization that may be in conflict with primary values and definitions of self and family held by clients from other parts of the world. Our preferred practice models also reflect these Western perspectives, which come from the culture of the profession (Foster, 1998).

Reflection would then include learning about oneself as a cultural being, getting in touch with surface and obvious ways in which one constructs and evaluates reality. We also need to retrieve and explore cultural constructs that are out of our awareness but operate as potent lenses through which we make judgments. These lenses are, in some way, used to evaluate and guide interaction with clients who are different from us. At another level are the stereotypes, prejudices, and idealizations that social workers have about people from specific groups. For example, many students in social work programs report that growing up in white, middle-class communities has provided little experience of interacting with and having close relationships with people of color, people living in poverty, and people living in dangerous neighborhoods. When receiving practicum assignments that involve practice with clients presenting with these characteristics, these students' energy must be focused on understanding the nature and origins of the attitudes, expectations, and feelings they bring to these encounters. They also need to review the experience of racism and privilege that accrues to skin color. While the beginning social work student, faced with her own fears and uncertainties about her skills as a social worker, might not feel powerful in her relationship with her new client, she needs to attend to the legacy that links color, power and privilege, and oppression and disadvantage in her society. Foster (1998) has identified a range of reactions to the recognition of privilege including denial of difference, excessive focus on cultural issues, guilt and pity, and ambivalence. Practitioners working with clients from a similar background may experience overidentification, distancing, ambivalence, guilt about their own success, and hope and despair.

In a diverse society it is not surprising that individuals experience tension and conflict about their ethnic and cultural identities. Members of a particular group in a society will experience both pride and shame by virtue of how aspects of their culture are defined by other members of these groups as well as by society. Furthermore, through participating in mainstream institutions such as public education, and through employment in large organizations, and through reading newspapers and watching television and movies, individuals are exposed to ways of thinking and behaving that may challenge familial and community values and norms. Exposure to worldviews that are contradictory to original positions can result in responses ranging from increased conviction and identification with original positions, to confusion and ambivalence about one's beliefs, to adopting new perspectives that appear more personally appealing. Indeed, our adult self evolves over time and can be seen as comprising a multilayered internalized culture that is unique to the individual (Ho, 1995).

These comments about internalized culture can be seen as universal and applicable to both clients and social workers. When practitioners attend to the cultural dimensions of clients' experience, their own ambivalences, questions, and struggles about their internalized culture may be evoked. Once again the search for awareness of the underlying beliefs, feelings, and reactions that influence behavior and expectations in our personal and professional life becomes important. Adding a cultural perspective to our understanding of countertransference enlarges and enriches the way in which we perceive human behavior. Learning about this aspect of "self" is not achieved quickly; it involves considerable thought and introspection at deeper levels and is an ongoing process. As social workers the focus is on linking the ways in which societal and familial definitions and values about diversity are incorporated on an individual level.

REFLECTIVE EXERCISE: CULTURE

The following activities are provided as a stimulus for self-reflection. A series of questions focus especially on the cultural aspect of self. Much can be gained by discussing these topics with others in one's reference group(s), such as family, friends, community members, and student or professional colleagues. Using these questions with classmates from different backgrounds can be especially instructive as students can compare similarities and differences in their backgrounds and current positions. Often as we try to explain ourselves to others we are able to crystallize our thinking and gain important insights.

The following questions have been suggested by Nakanishi and Ritter (1992) to guide recall and to begin this exploration of self-in-cultural context.

- On your own consider the messages you were taught as a child about your culture, the world, and acceptable standards of behavior. What were the stories or sayings that were used to convey these messages? Think about categories such as gender roles, parent-child relationships, extended family relationships, expression of emotion, attitudes toward community members and toward "outsiders," sources of help, religion, economic success, the legal system. Add other topics that you feel are important.
- Compare your understanding of your cultural lessons with others from a similar background. This activity will provide the opportunity to sort out those aspects of one's heritage that are cultural and those aspects that are unique traditions of a subgroup or one's own family. There is a mediating affect from other factors, for example, class or caste, country of origin, and religion that renders a universalistic view of culture limited. For example, the cultural experience of a recent immigrant, an upper-class, university educated woman from India, has both similarities and differences from that of a second-generation Indo-American adolescent girl in a working-class family.
- Compare your understanding of your cultural lessons with others from a different background. These discussions will help to highlight similarities between cultural groups as well as differences.

Some thought can be given to how these issues might be experienced in practice. Some examples are the tensions around different expectations about when one can seek help from outsiders, definitions of appropriate gender roles, and preferred child-rearing practices.

- Recognizing that while early family and community teachings have great impact, individuals construct their own self-definitions that may also change throughout the life cycle. Consider your own reference groups at this point in your life. Have they remained stable or changed? What factors affected this? To what extent do you have different self-definitions based on the context you are in? For example, a middle-aged second-generation Italian woman describes herself in different ways when with her elderly immigrant parents, celebrating Christmas with her brothers and sisters and their children, and in her long-term lesbian relationship.
- How comfortable are you currently with people who are different from you along various dimensions? What particular aspects of diversity lead you to feel uncomfortable? For instance, does it have to do with a class, color/race, religious, or sexual orientation difference?
- What feelings and attitudes are elicited when confronted with practice situations that differ from and challenge your values? How do you manage your strong emotions and reactions? How have you learned to engage with clients in a genuine way that is also interested and respectful?

POWER, PRIVILEGE, AND OPPRESSION

Practice that incorporates a diversity perspective is not only about understanding difference. It is also about understanding power dynamics within a social context. By virtue of visible characteristics individuals are perceived as belonging to social groups, groups that have varying degrees of privilege and access to power. For example, depending on the context children and the elderly have less power than early to middle-aged adults; upper-class and middle-class people have more power than individuals in the working class or on welfare. Groups of people are treated differently in society, with some groups experiencing systemic discrimination and oppression by virtue of identifiable characteristics. There are also invisible characteristics that, when known, may present barriers to individuals, for example, sexual orientation, health conditions or disabilities that are not obvious, and affiliation with particular religious groups. Whether or not to disclose the particular characteristic, whether those with power will be accepting and fair or hostile and punitive are matters with which individuals often struggle in many aspects of their daily life. Green (1998) eloquently states that "cultural, racial, and sexual orientation differences are *not* problems in and of themselves. Prejudice, discrimination, and other forms of aggressive intercultural conflict based on these differences *are* problems" (p. 100). Therefore social workers interested in developing competence need to go beyond awareness and sensitivity to cultural difference. An understanding of privilege, power, intergroup relationships, and oppression and their effects on individuals' well-being is also needed to better understand the dynamics of cross-cultural practice.

Power is defined as the capacity to influence for one's own benefit the forces that affect one's life (Pinderhughes, 1989). Social work theorists have explored notions of empowerment and propose that there are multiple aspects of power and oppression: historical, societal, political, interpersonal, and personal (Gutierrez, Parsons, and Cox, 1998). As noted earlier, clients may come from groups who have had negative experiences with respect to oppression and a lack of equal access to societal resources and opportunities to participate in societal institutions. Therefore when clients are ordered by a court to attend treatment programs they may feel yet again that they have little influence over their own lives. Frequently access to legal entitlements for welfare, health, or educational benefits and services are obstructed by complicated bureaucratic procedures. It is understandable that individuals who are constantly struggling to meet basic family needs will experience a pervasive sense of anger and depletion, feeling worn down by oppressive and nonresponsive systems. Feelings of powerlessness and resentment may be transposed into the interaction with the social worker. Personal, familial, and community experiences of oppression can influence individuals in a variety of ways. Despite the best intentions of an individual social worker and her desire to be respectful and understanding, she may be perceived by the client as representative of a particular group simply by virtue of visible characteristics such as the color of her skin. The group may be a more dominant one or one with less power in relevant contexts for the client. Gender will also intersect with other characteristics; for example, a social worker who is white and male will have a different impact on a female black client as compared with a male white client.

Most social workers do not feel they have significant power. The profession is associated with its mission to assist disadvantaged populations, and this value does not hold high status and influence in modern societies, where economic prosperity is a priority value. Nevertheless, in the context of agency practice social workers do have power by virtue of the mandate of their organization, the role they carry, their access to resources, the knowledge they have, and the assistance they can provide. Furthermore, in services that are court mandated, such as child protection, custody and access assessments, and probation, social workers' assessments and recommendations have profound implications for individuals and their families. They can affect, for example, whether children will be taken from their birth mother and father, whether a father will have access to his children, whether a parent must attend a drug treatment program.

Social workers are committed to becoming cognizant of the privileges they enjoy, personally and professionally, both ascribed and achieved. In some regions in the United States privilege and skin color are synonymous. As noted throughout this discussion, they need to be sensitive to the way in which the client perceives them along these dimensions. They also need to be aware of their own feelings about the privileges they have and those they do not have. When workers come from dominant and more powerful groups in society they may experience a range of feelings such as guilt or ambivalence when working with clients from less powerful and esteemed groups. When the worker is from a group with less societal power and working with clients from more esteemed communities there may be a range of reactions from deference to subtle hostility to overt antagonism. Refer to the questions in the reflective exercises on power and priviledge to further develop self-awareness in this regard.

Most organizations have introduced antidiscrimination policies and continuing education in an effort to create organizations and personnel that can provide service to the entire population. Tsang and George (1998) query whether the political atmosphere and demands surrounding cultural appreciation provide an effective learning context. As with any matter relating to personal aspects of the self in the professional role, social workers benefit from clinical supervision, peer consultation, and continuing professional development activities conducted in a supportive environment. In a study of an educational program designed to increase cultural competence of practicing social workers, Williams (2002) found that the creation of a safe learning environment was extremely important to the participants. Since these social workers

REFLECTIVE EXERCISE: POWER AND PRIVILEGE

Equipped with a fuller understanding of oneself as a cultural being, the social work interview can be viewed as a site of cross-cultural engagement. Take some time to consider the following on your own or discuss these issues with colleagues who are similar and different from yourself. McMahon (1996) suggests some of the following useful questions.

- What were your experiences in your neighborhood with groups different from your own? What were your family's attitudes and experiences about these groups? What stories were you told and what advice were you given about socializing, conflict, and power relations?
- What are your early memories of meeting people from groups different from your own? Which aspects were positive and which were negative?
- How aware are you of the dynamics of privilege, or lack of it, in your life course?
- Recall and examine an experience where you realized you had power over another.
- Recall and examine an experience where you realized another person had power over you.
- How might your perception and experience of power and powerlessness demonstrate itself in the work with your clients?

were part of the same organization and worked together during and after the training, they were attuned to the potential affect of the learning experiences on their subsequent relationships. Williams (2002) notes that difference is a topic with the potential for controversy and its discussion can be highly emotional and traumatic for course attendees; they may fear reprisals from fellow learners and experience tensions due to the cultural heterogeneity in the room. Others have noted that when these dynamics in training groups for cultural competence are avoided or not well managed they have the potential to divide learners and inhibit participation (Garcia and Soest, 2000). Practitioners require supportive spaces where they can engage in critical reflection of their work in an open and honest manner. It is crucial to identify and explore strong emotional responses and deeply held opinions that can result from intensive work in situations of diversity. The aim is to promote greater understanding of situations that evoked particular client and worker reactions and develop facilitative client-centered responses.

New conceptualizations of practice aim to highlight the social location of client and worker that take into account culture, power, and identity. Keenan (2004) uses critical theory to deconstruct these concepts and advocates for workers engaging in a continual reflexive process. Creatively using the analogy of a backstitch in sewing, she recommends "a continuous process of questioning one's interpretations of experience (of oneself and others) and one's actions in the service of effective listening to, questioning, and understanding self and others" (Keenan, 2004, p. 545). A similar stance is presented by other clinical theorists who are using postmodern and critical perspectives to understand the relationships between self and sociocultural relations (Kondrat, 1999; Miehls and Moffatt, 2000).

In summary, social work practice takes place in an increasingly diverse society. Social work as a profession is committed to enhance social justice and equity at societal and community levels. Practitioners therefore work to find the most helpful ways to work with clients who are both similar and different from themselves. Culturally competent practitioners are aware that diversity and its challenges arise from societal and familial contexts within their own communities and within the larger society that shape the values, thoughts, and behaviors of individuals. To value diversity is a respectful stance, consistent with social work values, and one that acknowledges many worldviews. An analysis of power, privilege, and oppression recognizes that populations in society do not have equal voice or access to resources. More than a celebration of difference, a diversity perspective is synonymous with social justice. Political, social, and organizational change is often needed to bring about large-scale change. Since social workers in direct practice are part of this broader context, it is crucial to recognize the way in which their social and cultural locations are part of their personal and professional contributions to addressing power dynamics in their work. The goal is to create an empowering experience while offering service to clients.

THE INTEGRATION OF THEORY AND PRACTICE (ITP) LOOP MODEL

The ITP Loop Model was introduced in chapter 1 and has been used as a systematic method for integrating theory and practice. Recall that the first phase of *retrieval* involves identifying the salient factors of a practice situation and is followed by a second phase of *reflection* that guides practitioners to examine the impact of their personally and socially derived perceptions, feelings, and behaviors in their work. In the third phase of the loop *linkage* refers to the way in which social workers use the knowledge base of the profession to guide their practice. Theories and concepts are used to understand and assess individuals and their situations. Social workers will then make decisions wherein, with the client's participation, intervention plans are developed. These plans include who should be involved, what resources can be offered, and what approaches used. When linkage is used in a systematic manner the social worker identifies and labels concepts and principles drawn from a knowledge base. These concepts can potentially explain the practice data and the subjective reactions that have been uncovered through reflection. The explanations and hypotheses that emerge from the assessment will in turn lead to directions for the next phase, referred to as *professional response*. Linkage involves practitioners in an iterative process that moves between the facts and dynamics of the practice situation and the theoretical concepts and practice models that might explain phenomena and suggest interventions. Through connecting theory and practice in this way, social workers gain new practice-related insights and come to understand abstract ideas in a grounded manner.

Drawing on the work of Schon (1983, 1987), the way in which professionals use knowledge in practice was examined earlier. To recapitulate, social workers construct, deconstruct, and reconstruct a cognitive system of understanding until there is a useful fit with the particular situation. This intellectual activity involves an ongoing progression of moving back and forth between abstract, general principles and concrete, specific events and responses.

This iterative and analytical process of linking theory and practice and practice and theory draws from an ever expanding professional knowledge base that includes knowledge of human behavior and the social environment; social welfare policies; values and ethics; models of social work practice; research and evaluation; and diversity, power, and oppression (Reamer, 1994). Practitioners find most useful those theories and models that provide explanations, predictions, principles, and strategies. Models incorporate a unifying theory (or at least a limited, selected set of concepts) that explain why a problem exists and provide a rationale for change strategies. Models also provide a set of principles, procedures, and techniques that guide practice intervention (Ogles, Anderson, and Lunnen, 1999). Social work scholars have produced empirically validated models, such as the task-centered model (Reid, 1992: Reid and Epstein, 1972). They have also developed models that consist of practice principles gleaned from the experiences and writings of veteran practitioners, such as the psychosocial approach to practice (Woods and Hollis, 2000).

Social work practitioners also use models developed in related helping professions such as psychoanalysis and psychology. Some influential models during the twentieth century emanating from psychoanalysis are relational psychodynamic theory (Fairbairn, 1952; Greenberg and Mitchell, 1983; Klein, 1964; Sullivan, 1953; Winnicott, 1965), self psychology theory (Kohut, 1971, 1977, 1984; Wolf, 1988), and intersubjectivity theory (Atwood and Stolorow, 1984; Orange, 1995; Orange, Atwood, and Stolorow, 1997). Psychologists have developed and tested models based on behavioral theory (Bandura, 1986), cognitive theory (Beck et al., 1979; Beck, 1976; Beck, 1995; Seligman, 1990), and some have combined these elements into cognitive-behavioral approaches (Meichenbaum, 1977) to practice. Building on the humanistic tradition in psychology, emotionally focused approaches have recently gained more attention within psychology (Greenberg, 2002a, 2002b; Greenberg and Bolger, 2001). Feminist psychologists have contributed invaluable insights into the psychology of women and have developed models and concepts for psychotherapy (Barrett, 1990; Brown, 1994a, b; Gilligan, 1982; Jordan, 1997; Jordan et al., 1991; Miller, 1987). Postmodern theory and constructivism (Gergen and Davis, 1985) provide a conceptual framework for narrative theory first developed for family therapy and also used with individuals (White, 1991; White and Epston, 1990). The originators of solution-focused therapy, while educated as social workers, developed their approach for family treatment (Berg, 1994; De Shazer, 1985, 1988) although it can be used with individual clients alone.

While some social workers will use specialized models such as those referred to above for particular situations, they also draw from a set of core social work theoretical concepts and practice. Two fundamental themes have been discussed thus far: 1) the self of the worker in relationship to the client, or transference and countertransference, and 2) diversity, power, privilege, and oppression. The following concepts are also presented briefly below as additional themes in contemporary social work practice theory. While they are presented separately, there is overlap between these ideas; taken together they represent a holistic view of social work practice.

Social workers' behavior in the interview may reflect a number of assumptions and beliefs about human behavior and the social environment, the processes that bring about change or that are helpful to support people, and the appropriate role of the social worker. These assumptions inform the way the social worker proceeds, the stance taken, and the frames used that in turn determine which factors are included and which factors excluded in assessment and intervention.

Individual and environment. Individuals have a wide and varied range of characteristics and abilities that potentially enable them to lead satisfying and productive lives. Familial, community, and societal environments can have aspects that are nutritive, supporting, and meet the growing individual's needs at various stages in their life course. Environments can also contain toxic, stressful, and depriving elements. Furthermore, environments may change over time. The goodness of fit between the individual and the environment is the focus of social work (Germain and Bloom, 1999; Germain and Gitterman, 1996). Social work practice models can be placed along a continuum regarding their primary emphasis and focus: from individual change to environmental change or to changing transactions between the two. Clinical or direct social work practice attends primarily to the micro level, assessing what is occurring and what factors can be influenced in the individual's life.

Social workers recognize that change throughout the life course is possible and that helping people experience better environments can significantly affect their well-being. Interventions that aim to change the interaction between the client and their significant partners or family members will make use of specialized couples and family therapy models (see Nichols and Schwartz, 2001 and Hanna and Brown, 1999 for models and concepts). Social workers understand the impact of macro forces such as poverty, unemployment, and systemic oppression on individuals. They recognize the importance of advocacy on a case-by-case level. They also recognize that political and social change must take place if individuals and communities are to truly enjoy equity, social justice, and well-being. To think systemically includes recognizing that social workers practice in the context of environments that can significantly affect the client. While services are designed to meet clients' needs, the agency policies and procedures and the way the team operates with each other and with clients can enable good practice or create barriers to helpful services.

Strengths. A strengths perspective in practice has been advocated as consistent with social work values (Saleeby, 2002b). It focuses on strengths, inner capacities, and external resources of clients rather than pathology, deficits, and problem-saturated accounts. Recognizing that clients are in an active process of coping and surviving, the social worker seeks to understand the factors contributing to that resilience and works consistently to amplify and expand those capacities (Cowger, 1994). Saleeby (2002b) states, "The formula is simple: Mobilize clients' strengths (talents, capacities, resources) in the service of achieving their goals and visions and the clients will have a better quality of life on their terms" (p. 1–2). Cognizant of the power dynamics between those seeking help and those providing it, a strengths focus can potentially reinforce client competence and aid in collaboration. The message conveyed is that the client has the capacity to overcome issues and the worker's role is to assist.

Capacity building. Traditionally the goal of practice has not been limited to helping the client take action and change the presenting problem. It has included helping the client build internal capacities to deal with current and future issues in his life. As a result the practitioner did not "do for the client" but enabled him to "do for himself." To achieve this goal it may be necessary to modify internal factors that impede growth and development. For example, low self-esteem and poor self-confidence can inhibit an individual from actively trying to change his significant environment or relationships. Challenging situations may be avoided whereas, if dealt with successfully, may contribute to self-confidence and a sense of mastery. The habitual use of defensive styles that protect one from experiencing anxiety and vulnerability may also limit assertiveness or behaving in ways that might result in achieving one's full self-potential and having interpersonal needs better met.

Building capacity focuses not only on changing internal states, characteristics and behaviors but also includes helping clients learn how to gain power so they can act on their external environments. Some strategies are raising consciousness about how external structures are oppressive and helping clients gain access to information, resources, and power. Direct practitioners also build capacity through helping clients learn how to be assertive and advocate for oneself in an influential manner.

To achieve significant internal change generally a prolonged period of engagement in a helping process is warranted. Currently both agency-based social work practitioners as well as private practitioners are significantly affected by the policies of managed care organizations. An emphasis on cost containment often limits intervention to short-term contacts (Berkman, 1996; Franklin, 2001). Social workers' assessments must therefore focus on determinants of clients' presenting problems. For example, when lack of information about resources and how to access them is at issue, social workers can provide information, encourage, and guide clients to take action. These processes can be used in short-term work and build self-confidence and internal capacities about affecting ones' environments. However, when more pervasive and long-standing internal factors play a significant role in limiting an individual's functioning, social workers will need to more actively seek services that provide a more sustained helping process.

Feeling, understanding, behavior. Throughout the development of theories of human behavior there has been varying emphasis on the extent to which functioning can best be understood and changed by focusing on behavior, cognition, or feelings or some combination of these elements. Indeed, subspecialties in the helping professions have organized their research, scholarship, and models of practice to reflect a behaviorist, cognitive, or emotional focus. The view presented here is that thoughts, feelings, and behavior operate in a cyclical and interactive fashion with reciprocal effects and influences. Primacy is not given to cognitions (also referred to as thoughts, beliefs, assumptions, perceptions, meanings) or feelings (also referred to as affect or emotion) or behavior or actions. The helping process is more powerful when all aspects of human experience are taken into account (Hill and O'Brien, 1999). In the interests of individualizing practice and using approaches that make sense to clients, the social worker may emphasize one dimension over another, insofar as it appears to match more harmoniously with the particular client's way of experiencing his world. It remains a challenge for practitioners to relate to the unique values, goals, and perceptions that clients bring into the therapeutic encounter.

Persistence and change. Direct social work practitioners appreciate that individuals have developed characteristic ways of coping with internal and external forces throughout their lives. They recognize that individuals have a personality style that has evolved over time (Goldstein, 1995; 2001; Howe, 1995). This unique style is indicative of genetic and temperamental predispositions as well as internalized family, cultural, and community norms and mores. Emanating from the social work value of adopting a nonjudgmental stance, social workers assume that an individual's patterns reflect his best attempts to grow, develop, and meet the challenges presented in his life. However, styles that may have well served a person in earlier stages of his life may be less useful, or even problematic, in later phases. For example, an individual who has experienced a series of foster homes may have developed a strong sense of independence and self-reliance that helped him deal emotionally with multiple moves. This style may interfere however with this individual's desire for closeness and intimacy in an adult relationship.

Social workers believe that individuals have intelligence, insight, and can change habitual patterns. Change is affected by both internal and external factors. Important internal factors are motivation, self-esteem, hope, and belief. External factors that influence change include opportunities and barriers that are presented by others in the individual's significant interpersonal relationships such as intimate partners, nuclear and extended family members, close friends and peers. Work environments can also exert a potent influence on an individual's change efforts. For example, becoming more assertive can be rewarded and encouraged by family members, friends, or employers or can be discouraged or even punished.

Relationship and collaboration. The relationship between the worker and the client is a crucial ingredient in providing a helpful service and social work supports a perspective whereby clients play as full a role as is possible. In specialized approaches the relationship is defined more specifically, but all would agree that an alliance is necessary. It may be useful to think of a continuum with respect to the degree of collaboration and decision making between worker and client. Models can be placed at various points along the continuum. For example, in behavioral and cognitive-behavioral approaches the worker's expertise and professional knowledge is recognized and acknowledged. These approaches are highly structured and include a thorough assessment that results in an individually tailored action plan (Beck, 1995). On the other end of the continuum are postmodern approaches that stress the client as the expert regarding her life. The worker enters into conversations with the client with the aim of searching for joint understanding (McNamee and Gergen, 1992). Some theorists, discussing cross-cultural counseling, note that because the worker and client may come from cultures that are so diverse they must collaborate to develop enough shared understanding of the issues presented that meaningful service can be offered (Dyche and Zayas, 1995; Tsang and Bogo, 1997).

Professional response is the selection of a plan that will inform the next steps in a practice situation. Ideally, from reflection in the current moment or retrospectively, an intentional response is developed and offered. This response represents some selection of the issue of highest priority. As the process of working together with the client proceeds, new information is revealed, additional insights are gained, and the alliance unfolds. The social worker goes through the loop of reflection, evaluation, and linkage again and again, and additional plans and responses may be offered as new understandings and circumstances emerge.

At the beginning of the first chapter a framework for practice was presented in figure 1.1. This framework includes the knowledge and value base of the profession, key concepts and principles of practice, the contributions of the worker and of the client, and the mission and mandate of the organization. The point was made that the social worker's behavior in the interview represents her unique integration and expression of these components. Hence, professional responses, techniques and skills can be understood as the observable expression of these many underpinnings and contributors to practice. As frequently noted thus far, while guided by a broad-based ecological-systems perspective, social workers also use concepts and techniques originally developed in specific models. For example, drawing from client-centered models practitioners focus on developing an empathic relationship and eliciting the client's emotional experience; from psychodynamic models they draw on thoughts and feelings that come out of the client's immediate awareness and explore associations; from cognitive-behavioral models they search for schemas that influence the client's appraisal and understanding of specific events and teach the client to observe, record, and challenge conclusions; and from feminist models they examine how societal or political definitions of women influence the personal way a client thinks about herself and use consciousness-raising and self-disclosure.

As discussed earlier, most practitioners have, through their career, developed a wide array of practices. These practices likely consist of core skills as well as skills and techniques specific to particular models. The "art of practice" refers to the seemingly intuitive and spontaneous way in which professional responses are offered in unique combinations to achieve practice goals. This is more than technical eclecticism. Rather, techniques, skills, or interventions are used in an intentional attempt to find the most helpful approach to work with a particular client. The strength of this type of practice is that it reinforces social work as client-centered rather than driven by preferences of workers or adherence to the most popular model of the day. However, to practice in this manner requires workers to possess extensive knowledge and skills that they have learned and integrated and can use flexibly in practice.

Evaluating progress.   It is crucial for practitioners to include an ongoing reflective stance of evaluation of progress both within and after sessions with clients. When reflection occurs in the interview, as Schon (1983; 1987) has observed, it involves the practitioner in two activities simultaneously: interacting with the client while thinking about the process and outcome. This is the experience of being present and attuned to what is transpiring while at the same time thinking about how the current discussion may be contributing to a future positive outcome.

Reflective evaluation can also take place after the interview is over, through retrieval and analysis of the practice situation. This can be done alone or in supervision and consultation through case presentations or review of segments of audio- or videotaped interviews. The goal is to critically examine whether what is being offered to the client is helpful and what alternative interventions may be more effective. Some degree of hypothesizing may occur and a variety of conceptual lens can be useful for thinking about the situation from diverse perspectives with their related interventions. The activity of connecting speculations to concepts associated with a professional knowledge base has been discussed earlier as a linkage activity.

Evaluation guides practitioners to consider the extent to which their original understandings and assessments were limited or accurate. Reflecting on the process and outcomes of the actions and interventions assists in establishing direction for future work. Increasingly, in social work and related mental health and human services, demands for accountability require that practitioners be able to defend what they do and articulate how it produces change or enhanced well-being for the client. This requires a degree of purposefulness and intentionality on the part of practitioners.

There is a growing body of literature in psychology (Task Force on Promotion and Dissemination of Psychological Procedures, 1995) and social work (Rosen, Proctor, and Staudt, 1999; Thyer and Myers, 1999) argueing practitioners should use those models that have been demonstrated as effective for

particular conditions and situations. However, some researchers in psychology have found little difference between models (Ahn and Wampold, 2001;
Wampold, 2001) and argue that it is common factors across all models that
produce change. Common factors refer to the context of the therapeutic work,
including the client's experience of the relationship and the client's expectation and hope that the help offered will be beneficial (Hubble, Duncan, and
Miller, 1999b; Wampold, 2001). The client's resources and experiences in their
social and physical environment also account for considerable variance in outcome (Hubble, Duncan, and Miller, 1999a).

As noted earlier, the position taken in this text is that social workers can
benefit tremendously from knowledge reported in both bodies of literature.
Regarding empirically based models, social workers can learn to access
practice research literature that provides current information about what approaches have been tested and found helpful under specific circumstances and
with selected populations. When these studies provide practice procedures or
textured descriptions of intervention processes, practitioners find them useful as they provide tools that may be transferred into one's own practice. This
literature is becoming more accessible. Professional journals are available
online and there are an increasing number of systematic reviews of intervention studies that will provide tested practice guidelines (see, for example, the
Campbell Collaboration).

Since there is considerable empirical support for the crucial importance of
common factors across models, it seems that, at a minimum, practitioners

should attend to these components in their efforts to reflect on the effectiveness of their work. Too often, even when an approach is not working, we continue to do more of the same. Through a conscious and purposeful reflection on these core factors workers can make immediate changes that might increase the possibility of more successful results. Each of the salient common ingredients will be elaborated on in-depth in subsequent chapters. The questions in the reflective exercise on the preceding page may help practitioners focus their reflections and evaluate their work with specific clients.

LEARNING TO INTEGRATE THEORY AND PRACTICE

There are many ways to learn to think about how theory and practice come together. Bogo and Vayda (1998) have used the exercises on the following page successfully with students and field instructors both in the classroom and in the field setting.

An example of applying the stages in the loop model to examine and plan practice is also provided by Bogo and Vayda (1998). First, using the stage of *retrieval*, they describe pertinent facts in a family situation from the perspective of the practitioner, a white female social worker, in her mid-forties, who is working in a women's shelter. The client is described as a thirty-four-year-old woman with three children, two girls of six and eight and a ten-year-old boy. Her parents and many members of her large extended family emigrated from Italy as children and live in the same city. This woman has experienced physical abuse by her husband numerous times and has sought refuge in the shelter twice in the past year and a half. She then returned to her husband, in part through the influence of her parents and brothers who believed that was the right thing to do. She has a grade 10 education and has never worked outside of the home.

After a few interviews the social worker uses *reflection* to examine her thoughts, feelings, and reactions to this woman. The client's situation is in some way reminiscent of her own. She too had been in a heterosexual common-law relationship that had become abusive when her partner increased his consumption of alcohol. Counseling helped her to leave that relationship, support herself with a daytime job, and complete her social work studies on a part-time basis. Through reflecting on the differences between herself and her client, she recognizes that her middle-class background, educational opportunities, and knowledge of how to get the help she needed allowed her to leave the abusive situation. She is aware of her impatience with the client for

having returned to her husband and of her subtle negative judgments of the
client. In separating her own experiences and opportunities from those of the
client, she feels more ready to listen to the client and try to understand and
empathize with her situation.

The practitioner uses linkage to draw upon social work's diverse knowledge base including information about cycles of abuse, the impact of police

practices in charging the abusers, and attitudes toward marital stability in the client's community. She can also access the practice and empirical literature on approaches to working with women living in violent situations and can, together with the client, develop support and safety planning strategies, utilizing both informal and formal sources. Successful approaches that involve extended family members identified as supportive can be used, as can resources for financial support, subsidized housing, vocational training, and day care for children.

The next *professional response* involves formulating an intervention plan that takes all of the above factors into account and begins with a discussion with the client about what choices she feels are immediately necessary and possible. Since the client is strongly considering returning to her husband, a safety plan for herself and her children must be developed that could include neighbors, extended family, and police. The client has commented frequently that her parents, brothers, and cousins are close.

Chapters 1 and 2 have examined the context of the interview and focused on the social worker's contribution to practice. Social workers are both members of a profession and workers in an organization. Therefore their work represents knowledge and values drawn from their profession as well as procedures and practices reflecting the mandate of their employing agency. In many instances these two influences are complementary; however in some cases they present contradictory expectations. The way in which social workers carry out their roles depends on their ability to navigate the demands presented by these two "masters." Also of crucial importance is the worker's use of self. This refers to the way in which personality, social identity characteristics, reference groups, family and community experiences have been internalized and are evident in the values held and the judgments made. We are part of our society and in some way reflect the privileges and disadvantages we have experienced. A major theme in the first two chapters is that individuals who are committed to human service practice continuously strive to understand how their own thoughts, feelings, and motivations are brought forward into their work.

Another important theme of the first two chapters of this volume is that the integration of theory, research, and practice is a challenging and complex activity. Currently it is a subject of some controversy in the professional social work literature. Empirically tested approaches hold the promise of providing social work with a scientific base. As well, the exceptions presented by the unique circumstances of clients require flexible workers who, while knowledgeable about approaches that work in controlled research studies, are at the same time attuned to the client's definitions, preferences, and needs.

Thus far this book has focused on the social worker and the way the organizational, professional, and psychosocial factors affect practice. However, it is crucial to remember that the client is primary in influencing outcomes. What can be achieved is highly dependent on the client, her aspirations, resources, opportunities, and environments. Therefore, the important issue is how the social worker can participate with the client to achieve the best possible outcome. Social work has historically been client-centered in its value base and in its practice models. Further support for this time-honored tradition is provided by contemporary research in social work and related helping professions. In the next two chapters we will examine concepts, processes, and interview behavior that promote a collaborative approach through a specific type of professional relationship.

THE HELPING RELATIONSHIP

CHARACTERISTICS AND CONCEPTS

{3

CHARACTERISTICS OF THE
SOCIAL WORK RELATIONSHIP

THE CRUCIAL CONTEXT

The organizing principle in this text is that the social work interview is the medium through which much of social work practice takes place. It provides the context within which services are delivered. Regardless of philosophical, theoretical, and practice preferences all social workers use the interview to work with the client. What is unique about professional social work helping that affects the social worker's behavior in an interview? Many beginners wish to provide immediate "help" to clients and conceive of social work practice as consisting of listening, getting the facts, and then offering advice or assistance through a problem-solving approach. Rather, social work practice is a particular form of helping that emanates from a mission to enhance social functioning by alleviating external conditions and addressing individual factors that affect well-being. A systematic helping process unfolds within a unique type of professional relationship.

The perspective taken in this book places the relationship at the core of practice; a process unfolds based on a client-centered interpersonal relationship whereby the social worker provides the necessary conditions that a particular client needs at a specific moment in time. As the practitioner interacts with the client, information is shared, joint perspectives or assessments are developed, and interventions are planned and implemented. Research evidence supports the conclusion that the relationship is the most crucial determinant of outcome (Horvath and Bedi, 2002; Norcross, 2002; Wampold, 2001). Helping relationships don't just happen; they develop over time and may experience ruptures and repairs as the participants work together in the interests of the client. Information, behaviors, feelings, thoughts, and meanings are described, explored, and reexamined. A continuous cycle of helping involves the client and the social worker in a collaborative effort at producing change. Promoting well-being is not exclusively reliant on the interpersonal aspects of the helping process. The social environment, resources, and supports in the client's life are crucial. Programs, services, and opportunities can address and fill important gaps. However, the difference social workers in direct practice can make in large measure takes place in the interview, and it is the relationship between the client and worker that provides the crucial foundation upon which social work intervention is built. In chapter 1 figure 1.1 highlights the many contextual influences in professional helping, and this chapter and the following chapter focus on the relationship.

THE IMPORTANCE OF PROCESS

Social workers know a great deal about the process of change, a process that comes about through providing a relationship context in which individuals and families can examine their needs, strengths, abilities, and supports. They can also be helped to identify the challenges, obstacles, and problems that interfere with or block achieving their goals, improving their relationships, and realizing more adaptive social functioning. There are many constraints and challenges that clients face; environmental, interpersonal, and individual. For example, regarding the environment, clients may lack resources or knowledge about how to obtain necessary assets or they may experience harassment and exclusion based on social location and personal characteristics. Challenges of an interpersonal nature occur when social networks and relationships engender conflict. Relationships may be nonsupportive, place unrealistic demands on individuals, or are abusive and provoke negative and harmful behaviors. Constraints may also be of an individual nature when issues of self-esteem, self-defeating thoughts, or fears of disrupting an uncomfortable, but known, status quo may keep an individual trapped in a situation that does not meet her needs. Of special interest to social workers is the "goodness of fit" (Germain and Gitterman, 1996) between clients' needs, rights, capacities, and aspirations and their social, economic, and physical environments.

The hallmark of social work practice is the expertise of the professional to engage in a helping conversation, or interview, that encourages the client to get in touch with their inner strengths and abilities so as to "figure out" the issues with which they are struggling and alternative ways of thinking, feeling, or acting in relation to these issues. Social workers provide "a space and a place" where, working together, practitioners and clients can examine the nature of the problems, the persons involved, and the relevant external forces and circumstances. The emphasis is on maximizing the client's participation as the two individuals work together and collaborate.

A helping "space and place" appears to assist clients to explore and experience their own feelings and thoughts at deeper levels. In an ethnographic study of therapy for family problems, clients were interviewed about the factors they believed helped them to change (Gehart-Brooks and Lyle, 1998). Clients reported that they developed a more complete understanding of their situation through the process of talking it out with an attentive and supportive professional. The professional was seen as objective, since they were not personally affected by the content under discussion. Participants experienced relief expressing themselves to another person. They reported being helped through having the professional listen and validate their experiences. Change came from the dialogue and the helpfulness of the practitioners' questions; both simple questions that clarified the details and dynamics of the problem as well as questions that challenged clients' assumptions and positions. Of interest is that clients' viewed suggestions made by the therapists as helpful but almost never followed up on them. Rather, clients described how, through dialogue, they were able to arrive at their own new perspectives. The give and take in the conversations stimulated clients' thinking. This in turn led to new perspectives and behavioral, emotional, and cognitive changes. The researchers concluded that within the context of an accepting, supportive relationship clients experience enough safety and trust to be open to consider alternative ways of looking at the presenting troubling situation and related issues. This collaborative stance appears to help clients generate their own interpretations and new perspectives that make sense to them.

A SITE OF CROSS-CULTURAL ENGAGEMENT

Collaboration is even more crucial in North American communities that are characterized by great differences in their population. Migration from around the globe has created diversity in communities. It is not unusual for both social workers and their clients to have emigrated from different countries and to not share life experiences and worldviews. However, as discussed in earlier chapters, members of a particular country or ethnic group do not uniformly internalize all aspects of the dominant culture. Individual preferences (Ho, 1995), patterns of nuclear and extended families, local conditions, and immigration histories can have a profound impact (Falicov, 1995). Social identity characteristics, such as, for example, gender, social class, educational and employment level, and religion, intersect with ethnicity and produce complex, layered, and multifaceted individual identity. Hence, one cannot realistically draw overall conclusions about an individual based on his original country or ethnicity.

Diversity does not only refer to values, beliefs, and behaviors connected to ethnic and national origins. Social workers recognize a vast array of factors that contribute to salient aspects of individuals' identity and belief systems. Especially in societies with a history of slavery or where dominant majority groups have oppressed members of minority groups, historical and political aspects of power and privilege are salient factors in interpersonal relationships. Social workers are particularly aware of factors related to race, gender, sexual orientation, and ability.

A humanistic perspective leads us to recognize that there are many commonalities among all individuals. However, by combining diversity perspectives with the principle of individualizing the client, the challenge of forming relationships now takes on more complex meaning. Professional practice must expand to provide time and space to understand, explore, and incorporate these differences when they are relevant to the issues under discussion.

KEY COMPONENTS *client centered practice*

How does this view of a professional relationship, and its accompanying behavior in an interview, differ from the way we conduct ourselves as an interested friend or helpful family member? In fact, many beginners in social work have been identified as "natural helpers" and are accustomed to family members and friends seeking their advice and input when faced with problems. Three features distinguish the professional social work relationship: 1) that it is client centered, 2) that the social worker remains aware of the many ways in which one contributes personally and professionally to the outcome, and 3) that the social worker's behavior is therefore intentional and purposeful.

First of all, the exclusive purpose of the relationship is to provide service to the client. In other words, the work is client centered and focused on helping the client to tell his story, to identify his needs, and to consider what can be done to alleviate current concerns. This is different from reciprocal relationships where there is give and take and it is expected that the interests and needs of both parties will be met. While social workers learn from and are often inspired by their clients, their strengths and resilience, this learning is a by-product, not a goal, of the work. Rather, the role of the social worker is to use her knowledge and expertise solely in the client's interest. The aim is to provide the context for growth and change to occur for the client.

The professional relationship, across all helping professions, is conceived of as different from a social, sexual, or business relationship. By virtue of the influence the worker may have over the client, if the worker engages in dual or multiple relationships with the client, a conflict of interest occurs. Each professional body develops a Code of Ethics and Standards of Practice to protect clients from dual or multiple relationships with the practitioner. Practitioners have the responsibility to behave ethically and not violate the boundary between a professional relationship and other types of relationship. Whenever professional helpers are uncertain about their feelings or actions with respect to upholding this standard, they are advised to seek assistance from supervisors or consultants.

In addition to maintaining an exclusive focus on the needs of the client, a second component is needed for a professional relationship, which is that the social worker is aware of what she is contributing to the practice situation, both personally and professionally. Recall the discussion in chapter 1 and the contemporary view of transference and countertransference as all the ways in which the client and the worker experience each other that are shaped by their personalities, their cultures, and their characteristic ways of feeling, processing information, and creating meaning in relationships. Some of these dynamics are unconscious, and hence out of direct awareness, while others are familiar and known to us from our past history. A range of characteristics and reactions are carried forward into our professional work. The nature of the relationship that can be developed in any dyad of client and social worker is affected by these issues. Through self-awareness practitioners can tease out the extent to which their internal states and personal reactions reflect their own personality or are responses to interactions with clients. When self-awareness is not sufficient, social workers turn to supervision and consultation.

Within the interview practitioners need to adopt a stance where they are both a participant and an observer of self and of other. This is a complex requirement—far different from the spontaneous, undisciplined, and natural way we participate in friendships and family relationships. This position includes being genuinely involved with the client in an honest, present, and active way while at the same time being aware of the impact of the client and his circumstances on one's own feelings, thoughts, and immediate spontaneous judgments. Keeping in mind the earlier discussion of transference and countertransference in chapter 1, consider the ways in which practitioners' personal aspects affect the work with the client. Personal reactions can provide helpful data about the practice situation or they may represent values and issues in the social worker's life that could interfere with client progress if reacted to or shared before they are examined and understood. A continuous process of development of self-knowledge helps practitioners stay client centered and energized by their work rather than reactive, anxious, or emotionally depleted.

In addition to a focus on the client, and self-awareness of the practitioner, a third component of a professional relationship is that the practitioner aims to behave in an intentional way. That is, the practitioner's comments originate from thinking about the current process and how it can achieve the desired outcome. The relationship context has been shown to affect significantly whether clients gain from professional intervention (Bachelor and Horvath, 1999; Norcross, 2002). Therefore it is important that practitioners stay attuned to whether the client is experiencing the relationship as helpful and focused on his goals. The worker then uses this information to guide her remarks and interventions. This intentional activity integrates thinking and action and is evidenced in our behavior in the interview. As such, it is different from the unplanned reactions and natural responses that characterize our usual interactions with friends and family.

Although social work practitioners and scholars accord importance to relationship, there is a paucity of new theorizing in social work since the early conceptualizations. In those formulations the characteristics of the relationship were defined as comprising warmth, acceptance, empathy, caring concern, and genuineness. A nonjudgmental stance and positive regard were also seen as necessary to produce the trust and mutual respect that can lead to collaboration on agreed upon goals (Biestek, 1957; Northen, 1995; Perlman, 1957, 1979; Woods and Hollis, 2000). Early theorists defined the social work relationship as one in which the practitioner was highly present and created a real relationship (Edwards and Bess, 1998). Coady (1993; 1999) reviewed social work literature and empirical studies in related fields and concluded that the ability to develop and maintain this type of relationship still remains the cornerstone of helping. He recommends that social workers find ways of expressing this "heart/mind-set" (Coady, 1999, p. 70) in their own unique and natural ways.

Historically, and in contemporary practice theory, there is support for the importance of a human and caring presence in professional practice. Goldstein (1990) argued that the profession should not overlook the humanistic and artistic aspects of our work as we strive for more theoretical, empirical, and technical complexity. In an editorial in the influential journal *Families in Society* at the beginning of the new millennium, Goldstein invited social work scholars to share their thoughts about the profession. Experienced educators and researchers noted the challenges and opportunities provided by the growing use of technology, the need to establish the effectiveness of social work interventions through research, and the growing bureaucratization of social work. Emilia E. Martinez-Brawley reflected on the best of social work in the past and stated that "professional social work attempted a fusion of the most enlightened principles of the helping arts with the most concrete applications in aiding those who were less fortunate. Humane, open and highly ethical actions kept the client, the person in need, at the center" (Goldstein, 2000, p. 5). She encouraged the profession to remain concerned with human existence, to strive to understand and care. In a similar vein Weick (1999) has argued for a return to the roots of social work as a caring, relational profession.

The important characteristics of social work relationships are presented in virtually all current texts on social work practice (see for example Compton and Galaway, 1999; Hepworth, Rooney, and Larsen, 2002; Kadushin and Kadushin, 1997; Murphy and Dillon, 2003). While definitions of particular aspects of the relationship vary, they all reflect a set of qualities similar to those presented in Coady's (1999) literature review, and these qualities will be reviewed in the next section. As noted in chapter 1 theoretical concepts in social work are formulations about phenomena related to the human condition and to processes of change. When empirical findings support these formulations, practitioners can have confidence in their potential usefulness for practice. This is the case with the concept of relationship. There are now abundant empirical findings to support the importance of relationship in bringing about change (Bachelor and Horvath, 1999; Norcross, 2002). It is not surprising that this is the case, as when an individual is in a relationship in which one feels understood and safe opportunities exist for positive growth. There is a greater likelihood that an individual will be more open, share salient features of the situation, even when those features are painful. With additional relevant information the practitioner can arrive at a more informed assessment and focus on the important factors. Moreover, in a positive relationship a client will feel enough support to explore issues heretofore avoided, take risks, and attempt new behaviors.

Theoretical concepts, such as the helping relationship, are often presented at an abstract level that requires practitioners to individualize the concept and tailor its use to the unique needs of each client. Furthermore, the way in which a concept or principle takes shape in practice is through the social worker's verbal and nonverbal behaviors, interviewing skills, personal style, and stance. In the remainder of this chapter and in the following chapter concepts pertaining to the professional relationship will be discussed and empirical support presented. General principles and process guidelines for using these concepts will also be offered. Interviewing behaviors and skills that social workers actually use to carry out these principles will be introduced in part 3.

WARMTH AND CARING CONCERN

Warmth refers to a friendly attitude on the part of the social worker that, when accompanied by concern, conveys an interest in the client's well-being. The worker is sincerely interested in the client and the difficulties he is experiencing. She conveys her commitment to finding possible ways of helping him arrive at a better situation. The personal, emotional, and painful individual issues are considered, as well as the client's social, economic, cultural, and physical circumstances. When needed programs or services are difficult to obtain, concerned workers are those who persistently search for resources and advocate for their clients. Some clients will have difficulty engaging with a worker, may remain silent and minimally responsive in initial meetings, or struggle to convey what issues are pressing. Concerned workers are persistent and patiently stay involved, understanding that this behavior may reflect an aspect of the distress or difficulty that has brought the client to the service.

Warmth and caring concern are, to some extent, elusive qualities to demonstrate since they reflect the internal feelings of the social worker and her idiosyncratic ways of self-expression. Students often wonder how they can be warm, concerned, and interested while maintaining professional boundaries and distance. Too often professionalism is incorrectly equated with a cool, aloof, distant, and impersonal demeanor. The challenge is to be able to be professional, which means being appropriately objective and using specialized knowledge and skills, while at the same time demonstrating genuine human concern, interest, and warmth.

Social work values, as well as practice theory, support the importance of the next cluster of characteristics variously referred to as acceptance, positive regard, respect, or a nonjudgmental attitude (Hepworth, Rooney, and Larsen, 2002). The profession's values are rooted in concern about individual well-being and social justice. Among the core values are individual worth, dignity, and respect of persons (Reamer, 1994). Respect refers to showing concern for and esteem toward another person. Proctor and Davis (1994) highlight that in professional relationships where the worker is white and the client is black social workers need to be cognizant of their clients' experiences in everyday life. They note that disrespect and lack of goodwill is a feature of many clients' lives and strongly recommend that social workers use respectful behaviors such as addressing clients by their full names, giving clients full and undivided attention, listening attentively, and not disrupting the session by answering the telephone. Respect and consideration are shown through such basic activities as starting and ending sessions on time. Privacy is important in order for clients to feel their confidentiality is respected. Therefore a meeting space should be arranged with this in mind and also must provide a comfortable setting, one that is free from barriers to communication. In hospitals and other institutions workers can show respect by knocking on a patient's door rather than entering the room without permission. Respect is shown when workers provide a rationale for the questions they will ask and the information they will require. As well, clients can be encouraged to ask any questions they have about the helping process and agency programs and services. While respectful behaviors are universally important, Proctor and Davis (1994) point out that they can begin to build bridges across racial differences.

Traditional and contemporary writers in social work agree on the fundamental issues in acceptance and positive regard, that of accepting and valuing the client while at the same time not approving of particular behavior. Acceptance rests on the belief that all people have the right to be heard, understood, and helped (Heinonen and Spearman, 2001) and therefore social workers value people as they are (Perlman, 1979), appreciate and affirm clients as people (Murphy and Dillon, 2003), and offer warm goodwill (Woods and Hollis, 2000). To achieve this stance two issues need clarification. One is the difference between valuing the person while not valuing the behavior. The other is the place of self-awareness. With respect to the first issue of client's behavior, social work theorists are clear and in agreement that acceptance does not mean that social workers also approve of, condone, like, or agree with negative behaviors on the part of the client. Thus the dictum to adopt a nonjudgmental stance is made with regard to the essential human nature of individuals. It still preserves the social worker's commitment to social justice and equity and to taking a stand with regard to behaviors that are violent, oppressive or degrade others, are illegal, or are a danger to the client.

When social workers practice with clients who do not voluntarily seek their services, acceptance becomes a crucial feature of the work. Two studies are informative, given that they investigated clients' opinions about what helped them in their interactions with child welfare workers (Drake, 1994) and with municipal social service workers (Ribner and Knei-Paz, 2002). These clients all had lengthy experiences with service bureaucracies and had encountered many workers over the years. They had experienced workers who were hostile, judgmental, and rude. They recalled with great fondness those worker-client relationships where there was "a feeling of being accepted for who they were, of not being criticized for failures in life or as clients" (Ribner and Knei-Paz, 2002).

Psychologists within the experiential tradition in psychotherapy have also described the importance of a therapeutic attitude of unconditional valuing (Greenberg, Rice, and Elliott, 1993). At a basic level positive regard provided by the clinician has the potential to counteract the client's own negative feelings and thoughts about himself. In this approach change is produced through the client experiencing and processing important feelings and thoughts. The client can more fully turn his attention to these therapeutic activities when not distracted by concerns about the clinician's judgments about the client's thoughts and feelings. Where the client experiences unconditional valuing from the clinician, he feels heard, understood, and accepted and has confidence that any interpersonal misunderstandings can be resolved between them. This perspective appears congruent with social work values and is useful for those aspects of practice that focus on the internal and interpersonal life of clients.

The second issue that affects social workers' ability to maintain a nonjudgmental stance is the way they can work with their personal and social attributes that affect building a relationship. A universal truism is that we all constantly make judgments in human interaction. As discussed in chapter 1, as we develop our professional self we aim to identify and understand the values, attitudes, and standards that are present at a more or less conscious level, what personal meaning they have for us, and how they are present in our professional judgments and preferred actions. As the profession of social work has become increasingly aware of diversity, self-awareness is also understood within the context of intergroup dynamics and historical and current relations of oppression, power, and empowerment. The issue for the individual worker is to be aware of his social location and the privileges and barriers that accrue to him. How do factors such as gender, race, ethnicity, sexual orientation, religion, class, ability, frame the way in which the worker views his clients and the way in which clients view the worker who is different from them in some way? For example, while the individual social worker may believe that he approaches all clients in an open and equal manner, by virtue of his social location and a host of characteristics that he embodies and may display, he will be perceived as having more or less privilege. In some instances clients will generalize from their experiences with others of the workers' group and may be wary, wondering whether the relationship will repeat previous oppressive and disempowering encounters. In other instances these differences may be evaluated as positive, again based on generalizing from previous encounters. Or, differences may not be seen as significant. The question is, does the difference make a difference in this encounter, and, if so, in what way? Practitioners then need to consider how they can engage the client to work with them to address and resolve these issues.

An understanding of social location, privilege, power, oppression, and exclusion can assist practitioners in understanding the importance and limits of the relationship qualities of offering positive regard, acceptance, respect, and a nonjudgmental stance. As noted earlier, social workers need to be self-reflective about the way the color of one's skin is interpreted within their society. How is color related to their own experiences of privilege and power or disadvantage and oppression? How have these dynamics operated in their lives in a range of social contexts, such as with family and friends, and in educational and employment environments? Have there been situations where they were benefited and situations where they were marginalized? Social workers need to also understand how they have made sense of these experiences, how they have been incorporated or rejected, and how they are present in their own feelings, thinking, and behavior. While social work as a profession prizes social justice and equity, at an individual level self-reflection may reveal situations where factors such as color, class, social and economic status, and the like provided and continue to provide benefit. To what extent have societal attitudes and belief about personal and social entitlement been absorbed and play out as implicit and unexamined attitudes in our practice? When workers from backgrounds of privilege hear and appreciate the oppression of others, Pinderhughes (1989) cautions that they need to learn to manage their own feelings of guilt or shame, which can also affect their perceptions and judgment. A range of concepts and approaches to assist practitioners in taking culture and diversity issues into account have been proposed (Gutierrez, 1990; Lum, 1999; 2000; McIntosh, 1989; Sue, Ivey, and Pedersen, 1996).

Reflecting on the foregoing description of the characteristics of professional relationships, it is apparent that the literature in social work, as well as in related helping professions, describes an ideal that we can only continually strive toward. In chapter 1 concepts and methods for developing self-awareness that assist practitioners move toward these ideals were presented. It may be helpful to those new to social work to recognize that learning is an ongoing and lifelong process that has the potential to lead to increased self-knowledge and practice effectiveness. The process is iterative and includes formulation, action, reflection, reformulation. It involves thinking about and planning for practice, interacting with clients, reflecting on practice, resurfacing salient personal and social issues that affect practice, and then reworking issues. In this way social workers develop the "personal self" through professional activities. This is both the challenge and joy of being a social worker.

When clients feel that the worker has positive regard for them, emotional bonding has a chance to occur. If clients feel connected, they may be more able to consider the practitioner's contributions to their work on key issues. Contributions include offering support and information as well as exploring and challenging thoughts, feelings, and behaviors (Goldstein, 1995; Hepworth, Rooney, and Larsen, 2002; Woods and Hollis, 2000). In the absence of a relationship with enough of a bond, clients are more likely to experience challenge as criticism, blame, or confrontation leading to self-protective reactions or withdrawal. Rather than achieving open discussion and examination, the opposite occurs.

This description of a relationship draws from the concept of a holding environment, a place where there is enough affirmation of the individual and her worth that anxiety producing feelings, thoughts, and situations can be explored and better understood. The concept of the holding environment derives from the work of Winnicott (1958, 1965) who used terms such as the *good enough mother* and *holding environment* to refer to the ways in which the mother is able to offer emotional security to the developing infant and child. Winnicott drew analogies between these concepts and psychoanalysis; similarities to social work clinical processes are discussed by Applegate and Bonovitz (1995) and Brandell (2004). When the client feels enough acceptance and security in the social work relationship, she can disclose uncomfortable aspects of her life. Discussion of painful issues may stimulate potent feelings of anxiety, rage, or sadness which the client experiences as overwhelming. Within a connected and calming holding environment practitioners can offer sustaining and supporting responses so that feelings do not overpower the client but rather are contained. Therapeutic responses emanate from the characteristics of genuineness and concern, empathic listening, and a nonjudgmental stance. When such attitudes and behaviors engender a feeling of safety in the client she may be able to become more reflective of her situation and related feelings and engage in a mutual search for understanding and ultimately reprocessing experiences and examining choices.

For example, a psychiatrist and marital counselor referred a female in her mid-forties to the social worker for individual counseling to help her deal with the discovery of her husband's affair of one-year duration. Members of this family are originally from the Middle East but have immigrated or sought refugee status in the United States over the past twenty-five years. As a teenager the client sought refugee status on a visit to her older brother and his family. Subsequently her widowed mother and younger brothers and sister joined the family. Following cultural convention, the client was introduced to a number of young men whom the family deemed appropriate and after a few such meetings chose to marry her present husband, expecting that they would both come to love each other. She and her family believed that he would be a good husband and one who would take good care of her. The couple has been married for twenty years and report that they are westernized in many respects.

After an initial period of turmoil following the discovery of the affair the couple decided to remain together, in part because their Middle Eastern culture frowns on divorce. They have begun to attend couples therapy, and the husband has decided to end his affair and states that he hopes to become a faithful husband. However he complains of his wife's bitterness toward him and avoidance. The family consists of four children who range in age from five to sixteen. In couples therapy he states that she is too involved with the children and does not concern herself enough with his needs. Upon learning of the affair the wife was extremely distraught, could not sleep, and on her family doctor's recommendation saw a psychiatrist and is taking antidepressant medication.

In the first individual session the client shares her perception that she is experiencing pressure on many fronts to "get over" the husband's affair—from her own extended family members, from psychiatric interventions, and in couples therapy where the focus is on moving forward. In individual counseling the social worker adopts a stance of listening, encouraging the client to explore her feelings, and reflects to the client the hurt and pain she expresses. In many meetings the client is extremely distraught and tearful and rages about the way her life has developed. The worker responds with respect and validation; she is supportive and involved in her presence, availability, and the reflective and empathic comments she makes. Over a few sessions the client states that she feels the individual counseling is "for her" and the only place where she is able to talk about how she feels and not be told to do something with those feelings—"get over them, put them aside, or carry on." The helping context allows her ultimately to explore and express her rage at her husband's betrayal and her anger at the cultural dictates and extended family values that have left her so dependent on her husband. As she progresses she also examines her anger and sadness about the ways in which she has accommodated to others' needs and ignored her own. As she and the social worker proceed to examine possible future choices and reflect on their work, the client comments that what has helped her is that she could count on the practitioner to "be there and understand me, not tell me what I should be feeling or doing."

Thus far we have discussed two groups of relationship characteristics: warmth and caring concern, and acceptance, positive regard, respect, nonjudgmental attitude. Why are these characteristics so important for the helping process? When people are confronted with a problem and recognize that they must seek help, they usually feel distressed and vulnerable. When individuals are ordered by a court or required by their employers to seek help they experience a loss of autonomy and ability to control their own lives. They also may experience positive anticipation and hope that they will receive something of value, and some sense of relief simply by taking the first step of trying to do something about a situation or problem that is troubling to them. Hence, in the initial meeting with the professional potential clients may feel a range of emotions from anxiety, skepticism, and helplessness to optimism, hope, and positive expectation. Through providing the qualities of relationship discussed thus far, the worker can begin to build an emotionally supportive connection. The client's experience of these facilitative qualities appears to operate as a necessary step toward producing an atmosphere where clients feel safe enough to risk discussing and exploring their anxiety-provoking or painful issues. The development of such a relationship involves sensitivity to timing. As in any interpersonal relationship, safety and trust do not develop instantly. Rather it is through ongoing experiences that we learn about the others' trustworthiness. We learn what we can expect from the other, whether the worker will be constant and reliable in her emotional availability, attitudes, and behaviors. In short-term interventions, where the work is limited by time constraints, social workers need to be even more skilled at demonstrating these qualities in a way that helps clients to develop trust more quickly than in situations that are open-ended.

The link between relationship building and intervention in actual practice is less linear than the description offered thus far. Practice is a process, a series of interactions over time that progresses through stages where worker and client gain greater familiarity with each other. As in any dyad, the behaviors of each person affect the other and produce subtle, mutual adaptations as the participants cocreate a working relationship. For example, if the worker is able to convey respect and challenge at the same time, she may be able to demonstrate to clients that she is committed to them and cares about those things they do that are, for example, self-defeating. If the client then reacts with anger, the worker who can listen to the client, understand the anger but not react defensively to it, and continue to work with him demonstrates "staying power" in the face of uncomfortable interactions. It is through the worker's ability to work with these two dimensions, support and challenge, and remain involved that trust is built. Again, note the similarity to the concept of the holding environment (Winnicott, 1965.)

The following activities and behaviors are some basic ways in which social workers convey warmth and caring concern, acceptance, positive regard, respect, and a nonjudgmental attitude. These interview behaviors emanate from a strong commitment to social work's humanistic and liberal values. They reflect a belief in the intrinsic worth and dignity of all individuals and that the uniqueness and individuality of each person is of value (Hepworth, Rooney, and Larsen, 2002). Without this value stance these interviewing skills can seem mechanistic and hollow.

BOX 3.1. RELATIONSHIP-BUILDING ACTIVITIES AND BEHAVIORS

- Attend to the client's need to feel comfortable by being on time, holding interviews where it is convenient for the client, such as in a home visit, and, if holding an office interview, arrange the meeting place in a way that will be comfortable for the client.*
- Convey concern through constancy and availability. This includes returning clients' telephone calls promptly, following through on tasks such as providing information, making a referral, and obtaining promised resources.
- Offer nonverbal behaviors such as a warm smile, a welcoming and attentive gaze; an expression that matches the client's feelings can convey interest.
- Offer verbal behaviors such as frequent encouragements and speaking with a friendly and interested tone as you ask questions and provide information or offer comments.**
- Active and attentive listening and communicating in verbal and nonverbal ways show that the worker is intent on understanding the situation as the client experiences and understands it. This stance is in contrast to an overly structured or constricted one where the worker presents herself as an expert, seeks to obtain only certain information, and offers premature judgments, interpretations, and solutions.
- Convey acceptance through paraphrasing and restating what the client said in a way that demonstrates the worker's concern that he has understood what the client has expressed. The tone is open and accepting, inviting clarification from the client.
- Allow time and space for clients to tell their stories free from judgment by the worker.
- Adopt a mindful, reflective stance in the interview where participation and self-observation come together through self-awareness and avoidance of habitual and unprocessed reactions. Self-observation is not solely limited to personality, but also to understanding how social factors connected to diversity and power are linked to personal and present relationship building for the client and the worker.

*Compton and Galaway, 1999.
** Kadushin and Kadushin, 1997.

GENUINENESS

Rogers (1951) is credited with introducing a humanistic approach to psychology and his work has been influential in related helping professions, including social work. He proposed three core conditions for helping: empathy, warmth, and genuineness or congruence. Earlier, the attitude of warmth, as described in the social work literature, was presented. Empathy will be discussed later in this chapter.

Genuineness refers to being open, real, and sincere in the helping relationship. The worker however, while behaving in an authentic manner, is still functioning within a professional context. This involves the challenge of "being real," but in a way that ensures it is client focused and facilitates the work. Professionalism should not mean being phony and hiding one's self behind an aloof, distant, expert mask. Nor does it mean impulsively sharing feelings and impressions. Rather it is a "disciplined spontaneity based on the therapist's accurate self-awareness of his or her deeper levels of experience and shared in a facilitative manner at a therapeutically appropriate moment" (Greenberg, Rice, and Elliott, 1993, p.20).

Another aspect of genuineness has to do with being honest in a responsible and nondefensive manner. Especially when social workers are delivering bureaucratic or court-ordered decisions and know this information may be disappointing to the client, an honest recognition and communication of their own feelings can reflect their sensitivity. Clients of child welfare services reported how much they valued workers' honesty and genuine interest in them (Drake, 1994). For example, the worker who states that she will try hard to work together with the family, even though she knows they would prefer that she not be there; she further notes that she would feel the same way. Genuineness also includes knowing one's own limits; if a worker cannot answer a question it is important to convey that and seek out the information rather than provide vague or inaccurate responses.

Similar to findings about clients required to work with child welfare authorities, Ribner and Knei-Paz (2002) found clients of social welfare institutions valued workers who softened the experience of being "needy." Such workers did not deny the reality of the client's situation or the requirements and limits of welfare provision. However, the respondents experienced as helpful those workers who were genuinely involved with them as people and who did not see them simply as problems. For example, genuine workers would inquire about the clients' life in general, not only financial and employment related issues, and show interest in clients' pleasures and hopes.

Finally, it is not unusual to have "second thoughts" after an interview is over. Through reflection practitioners reevaluate a session and can gain new perspectives on the client and their work together. Workers can return to the next meeting with the client and reveal that they wonder if they misunderstood the client's comments and reopen a discussion. Workers who admit they drew inaccurate conclusions or made unhelpful comments can apologize and in this way demonstrate genuineness.

Two stages of genuineness were suggested by Carkhuff (1993). The first stage occurs at the beginning of any human interaction and includes conventional and natural ways of responding to persons in relationships. This can be thought of as a quasi-social stage with general comments and inquiries offered in a natural way. In the second stage, as a result of working together over some period of time, greater understanding of each other likely has developed. Practitioners can then more freely be themselves, modeling an openness that can help clients also achieve openness and share information important to the work.

Congruence refers to the consistency between the worker's behaviors, feelings, and attitudes. For example, if the worker feels warmly toward the client and is concerned about her, these attitudes will be demonstrated through the kind of questions and remarks made, such as asking about the client's well-being in a friendly and interested way at the beginning of the session. The client is likely to experience an authentic and real connection. Conversely if the worker verbalizes his concern but does not demonstrate it in his behavior, the client will understandably question how committed the worker truly is to helping. For example, a worker is providing counseling to a couple for their relationship difficulties and mentions that there appears to be considerable stress as a result of both parents working outside the home to support the family and their need for child care for their young school-aged children. When the couple complain that they have not been able to find affordable after-school care for their children, the worker states she will look into this. This promise is not followed up, and the couple wonder whether this worker is really interested in them or whether they are simply "another case."

In order to achieve this stance of genuineness and congruence we need to understand those internal processes that interfere with our ability to be fully present and available. When we are preoccupied by our thoughts, feelings, and judgments it is more difficult to be authentic and genuine. For example, when workers feel overwhelmed by the complexity of a client's circumstances, out of a desire to be helpful, they may offer reassurance that is false or at best conveys only a superficial understanding of the multiple factors operating in a client's life. As discussed in chapter 1, an ongoing process of self-awareness and understanding helps practitioners attend to their own internal feelings and reactions to the client, develop ways to deal productively with issues, and achieve greater comfort in practice. Supervision, consultation, and personal work are all potential resources in this process. These activities enable practitioners to integrate the personal and professional self and achieve a level of authenticity that is comfortable for them and helpful to clients.

Constraints to offering facilitative relationship conditions may not only be about our reactions to the client, but may involve other issues such as concerns for oneself that are spilling over into the work. Students, for instance, report that they become preoccupied with the level of their knowledge and competence in the interview. While trying to understand what the client is saying they become self-conscious about their skills and uncertain about where to focus and in what direction to take the interview. Finally, the work environment of organizations exerts a powerful impact on all human service professionals. Increasing expectations about worker productivity and workload may create realistic pressures that interfere with our ability to be centered and present in interviews. For example, social workers in hospitals report that the team's expectation for quick discharge of patients contradicts social work principles to fully involve their clients in developing the best plans for themselves (Globerman and Bogo, 2002). All these situations get in the way of being genuine in the interview.

Despite all good intentions and professional tools it is inevitable that practitioners have negative feelings or judgments about some clients that interfere with their ability to be truly present and available to the client. Social workers struggle with the boundary between genuineness and professional restraint. While being authentic implies sharing perceptions with clients, these may be destructive to the client if not made in a purposeful and considered manner. Murphy and Dillon (2003) capture the complexity involved in drawing a distinction between genuineness and total honesty. They state, "We need to be selective, always considering the impact that our remarks and behaviors have on our clients" (p. 83).

In summary, as with other relationship characteristics presented, genuineness is an ideal stance to which we strive. It can best be understood by reminding oneself that it is in the service of the professional role. Self-awareness helps to differentiate between our internal reactions, the client's contribution, and the processes that result from the interaction. Ultimately, genuineness is controlled, as it is offered to advance the client's progress toward meeting his goals.

EMPATHY

Social work practice theorists embraced the contributions of Carl Rogers (1951; 1957) in his assertions that empathy, warmth, and genuineness were not only necessary conditions but also sufficient for activating the healing and growth potential of clients. The important role played by these core factors has been demonstrated in a number of research studies conducted on the outcomes of psychological counseling and psychotherapy. However, the contention that these conditions are sufficient has not been supported (Bachelor and Horvath, 1999). While these studies have been critiqued for measurement limitations, researchers do agree that these core conditions are associated with positive outcome (Horvath, 2000) and facilitate the change process across all counseling and psychotherapy models. They can be considered as "common" treatment factors (Beutler, Machado, and Neufelt, 1994).

Social workers recognize the importance of contextual factors on well-being and change and hence have not totally adopted Rogers' theoretical formulation. However, they have seen the congruence between Rogers' emphasis on the relationship as crucial and social work's perspective that the relationship is both the foundation and the context for change. Furthermore, his delineation of the characteristics of the helping relationship parallels social work's century-old client-centered and humanistic focus. It is understandable that social workers have been interested in the theoretical contributions and research studies conducted in humanistic and experiential psychology. This well-articulated body of knowledge is a good fit with social work's client-centered values and can usefully be integrated into social work practice.

The Rogerian relationship stance emanates from his belief in the importance of helping clients become aware of their inner experiences and the feelings and meanings that are connected to their behavior (Hill and O'Brien, 1999). He believed that a client's subjective experience guides his behavior. Hence the only effective way for the helper to be of assistance is to gain an understanding of the internal life of the client. This entails reaching for an emotional and intellectual appreciation of the internal frame of reference from which the client interprets and experiences himself and his situation. It includes being both participant and observer. As participant, empathy involves aiming to experience the client's subjective perspective, to feel as she feels. As observer, empathy involves remaining separate enough from the client's feelings that the practitioner can better understand the client's situation. As Murphy and Dillon (2003) observe, empathy is "the ability to immerse oneself in another's experience without losing one's own sense of self" (p. 88). It is proposed that empathy serves two purposes; through an attentive focus on the client and his experience a bond is forged and in-depth information is obtained about the client.

Within the humanistic and experiential tradition of psychology, a contemporary elaboration of the concept is presented by Greenberg, Rice, and Elliott (1993). In their description of empathic attunement they state, "Clients build a stronger sense of their own experience by having their experience recognized, responded to, and thereby validated by their therapists. Having one's own feelings understood and accurately reflected back to oneself in both a verbal and nonverbal manner helps one to experience the feeling more fully and with increased confidence that 'this is really what I am feeling.' Feelings are often inchoate, emerging from a highly subjective, idiosyncratic, inner world for which there is no formal descriptive language. When the experience is symbolized and shared, it is confirmed as being what it is by the other's understanding of it" (p. 20). On the part of the practitioner, achieving empathy requires a consistent focus on the client and some degree of artistry. From the client's perspective, having one's experience understood is essential to creating an alliance.

Within the psychoanalytic tradition of self psychology the concept of empathy was developed by Kohut (1957) and self psychologists. He began with the principle that individuals need empathic connections with others, particularly empathic responsiveness from caregivers to normative developmental needs. He further theorized that the need for others to fulfill a range of psychological functions endures beyond childhood and throughout life. Similarly, in the helping process empathy is central (Kohut, 1984). Empathy is defined as the therapist's ability to engage in "vicarious introspection," immersing oneself in clients' experiences, and to understand how they perceive and feel about their lives. While striving for a focused empathic attunement, the inevitable empathic failures that occur provide opportunities to further examine and understand the subjective perspective of the client (Wolf, 1988). Empathic breaks where, for instance, clients feel disappointed, misunderstood, or fearful the therapist wants to abandon them offer emotional data that can lead to understanding and change.

In common across theoretical perspectives about empathy are two components of empathy that facilitate the helping process: understanding and communication. The clinician strives through the dialogue to recognize the client's feelings and thoughts and then to communicate that understanding to the client. Hunches, reflections, and comments are offered in a tentative way in the service of building joint understanding. An empathic comment offered in such a way demonstrates the worker's desire to understand the inner frame of reference of the client through active listening, following or tracking the client, and trying to hear themes and patterns throughout the client's narrative. To truly listen, without evaluating, or attempting to interpret the issues from any particular theoretical framework the clinician needs to be nonjudgmental, focused on the client, not distracted or preoccupied with her own inner issues or beliefs about the preferred directions for the other.

As the practitioner develops an appreciation of the affective and cognitive experience of the client he also tries to find the words to share his understanding. The worker aims to express the essence of what the client is struggling with and to share that in a respectful way that invites dialogue. Clark (2003), in an analysis of the strengths and limitations of empathy, notes that often the conceptualization of empathy as a tool of sustained mutual inquiry is overlooked. Rather than the worker searching for an "accurate" reflection of the client's feeling and thinking, empathic comments can be viewed as an important aspect of interpersonal communication between client and worker. Comments serve the goal of collaboration, as the worker aims to arrive at a joint understanding with the client of what the problem or issues are that are troubling and, ultimately, what may be areas for work. Again, with a warm, accepting, and respectful stance on the part of the clinician, the client can agree or disagree with the clinician's empathic comments. When the communication appears meaningful, the client will feel validated and supported by feeling understood. When the client disagrees, where there is a growing bond and trust, the client is more able to directly verbalize, or indicate in some way, disagreement. Together client and clinician can continue their dialogue, moving onward until they find enough meaningful shared understanding.

This type of empathic communication is more than simply reflecting what is expressed and what is seen. It especially involves exploring what is implied.

Topics and issues may be bubbling beneath the surface and are troubling to the client even though he is not able to easily articulate them. By attending to nonverbal expressions of joy or pain, to evidence of discomfort, such as rapid breathing, flushing, clenching fists, and the beginning of tears, a sensitive social worker can empathetically focus the conversation. Underlying thoughts, issues about which there is guilt, shame, conflict, or mixed feelings can be explored.

Timing also plays a part in arriving at understanding another person. As the client and worker have many interchanges the worker will learn more about the client's experiences, issues, and interpretations of life circumstances and the present situation. Increasing information assists the worker to better understand the client's internal life and hence to respond in ways that are more attuned to the client. Moreover, clients may appreciate the worker's sustained attempts to understand them as helpful in and of itself. These processes do not happen immediately. It is reasonable that in any relationship individuals need to feel relatively confident that when they disclose painful or difficult thoughts and feelings the other will respond supportively and empathically. This would especially be so in a professional relationship, where the practitioner is unknown to the client. Over a period of time and with multiple experiences with the worker the client will learn and trust that he will not be shamed, judged negatively, or humiliated. An expectation of safety, however, does not develop until a number of such experiences have occurred.

EMPATHY AND DIVERSITY

The concept of empathy has been critiqued by social work scholars as failing to account for the impact of the cultural and sociopolitical context on experience (Keefe, 1980; Pinderhughes, 1989). They query how one can experience and understand the feelings and cultural meanings of those who are vastly different from oneself simply by trying to feel as the client is feeling (Devore and Schlesinger, 1996; Green, 1995). They caution that without knowing about the cultural context of behaviors, thoughts, and feelings social workers will inadvertently use their own personal, cultural, and social frames of reference to understand the client's experiences. To act "as if" all human experience is universal prevents us from learning about the diverse and unique worldview or cultural frame of reference of the client (Green, 1995). Furthermore, each of us possesses many diverse characteristics that produce our uniqueness. When these characteristics are viewed within a political context it is apparent that they affect our access to resources and opportunities and challenge the notion of universal equality.

How has professional social work addressed issues of culture and diversity? Social work has long recognized both universal and particular aspects of human behavior. On the one hand the profession identifies common principles that can be applied in a general way. On the other hand we are aware that there may be diversity between worker and client by virtue of a host of attributes such as race, ethnicity, gender, age, socioeconomic class, sexual orientation, ability, educational background, religion, country of origin, and geographic locale, referred to under the general rubric of "culture."

To briefly review the discussion in chapter 2, the cultural literacy approach advises practitioners to gain knowledge about the cultures of their clients and study their history, backgrounds, and characteristics (Devore and Schlesinger, 1996; Green, 1995; Lum, 1999; 2000; McGoldrick, Giordano, and Pearce, 1996; McGoldrick, Pearce, and Giordano, 1982). Originally, this approach drew the attention of helping professionals to the important cultural context that was missing from assessment and intervention. More recently, with the recognition that there is substantial within-group variation in all populations and cultures, many writers have proposed an alternative view. Rather than professionals presenting themselves as knowledgeable about a client's culture, the worker adopts a stance of learner and conveys interest in learning about the cultures that are significant for the client, from the client's perspective (Dean, 2001; Dyche and Zayas, 1995, 2001; Tsang and Bogo, 1997; Tsang, Bogo, and George, 2003). The goal is to understand the client in her context, her current relationships and life experiences, and her internalized cultural schemas and understandings. To take this position requires practitioners to be aware of their own values, attitudes, and judgments and to be sensitive to how these assumptions are a part of their personal and cultural belief system and operate in more or less overt or subtle ways in their practice. As Schon (1987) so elegantly described, this is the nature of all professional practice; practitioners operate in a zone of complexity and uncertainty where uniqueness and diversity pose a challenge to so-called universal theories and practices. The hallmark of this type of professional work is the ability to tolerate ambiguity and remain committed to understanding the particularities of the client. A stance of openness is well captured by Dyche and Zayas (2001) who state, "Receptive listeners prefer to experience and describe another's world rather than to define or assess it. They look for narrative coherence instead of truth" (p. 247).

The cultural learner model proposes that practitioners aim to listen attentively and openly to clients' stories so that they may better understand their experiences and the feelings and meanings associated with them. Writing from a
postmodern perspective, others have proposed a similar stance. For example,
Anderson and Goolishian (1992) recommend operating from a "not-knowing"
position and Laird (1998) refers to a "learner stance." In some respects these
perspectives are similar to adopting a nonjudgmental stance, as discussed earlier. The difference is that the new approaches specifically draw attention to
understanding the client not only through individual and interpersonal lenses
but also through cultural group membership within a society.

Academic writing may present these two approaches, cultural literacy and
cultural learner, as polar opposites, although they both have insights to offer to social workers forging relationships with people who are different from
themselves. Practice can be conceived of as a site of cross-cultural engagement
where both client and worker have expertise that needs to be used in a collaborative enterprise aimed at addressing the client's needs (Tsang and Bogo,
1997). The worker's expertise is about human behavior in general and the process of change. Some knowledge about the characteristics of specific groups
can provide some general themes and may be useful as a background reference point. However, a collaborative, process-oriented approach that recognizes that clients are experts about themselves appears more useful. Such an
approach uses a dialogue with clients to learn the ways in which the values, attitudes, and behaviors of their significant reference groups play a role in their
lives. Green (1995) proposes that empathy in cross-cultural practice consists
of a serious and interested stance. Through active listening and inquiry the
worker tries to convey that it is important for the worker to understand the
client's views. Rather than assume commonality by tuning into one's own feelings, the worker adopts a learner stance and seeks to discover the underlying
personal and cultural meanings behind the client's concerns. He recommends
paying attention to key worlds, metaphors, and other linguistic elements as entry points into exploration of implicit meanings. This type of empathy is used
as a communication device as the worker conveys what he thinks he has heard
and invites feedback. Through a joint dialogue, enough shared understanding
of the client's situation develops so that some helpful activities can be undertaken. This stance not only serves the goal of assessment, it also builds the
relationship as the worker demonstrates his keen interest in learning about
the unique personal, cultural, and societal frame of reference of the client.

Many examples of this type of learning approach emerged in our research on cross-cultural counseling (Tsang, Bogo, and George, 2004). In an agency dealing with adolescents, a social worker saw a mother and daughter together to help them deal with the adolescent's failing performance in school and the conflict between them due to such issues as setting a curfew upon which they could both agree. As the worker began the discussion of curfew with them, she inquired about the mother's experiences as a teenager. The mother was an immigrant from an urban center in Africa and had been raised with standards that prohibited a teenage girl from going out without being accompanied by a relative. She had always therefore been accompanied by a brother, and they would return early in the evening. The social worker invited mother and daughter to contrast their experiences. The teenager was born and raised in North America and believed, with great conviction, that she was an independent person, well able to go out alone in the evening. The interviewer asked the mother how growing up with those standards had affected her. The mother went on to explain how she had been able to accommodate since "that was the way it was for everyone," however, she had convinced her parents to allow her to attend school in Europe after completing high school and, even though she lived with close family friends, she had enjoyed considerable autonomy then. As the worker drew the parallel between the mother's and the daughter's similarity in seeing themselves as able to take care of themselves, mother and daughter softened their oppositional positions and began to talk and listen to each other more openly. During this discussion the worker took the opportunity to ask the clients to let her know if, during their time together, she said something that did not make sense because it was not true of their culture. She elaborated, asking them to tell her should they feel there were things she needed to know to understand them and their situation.

EMPATHY AS AN INTERACTIVE CONCEPT

Empathy and the other components of relationship discussed thus far are described primarily as qualities offered by the social worker through a particular stance and associated behaviors. What is less obvious is an interactive view of the relationship. That is, how are the qualities and behaviors of the worker affected by the client and how do the client's responses to the worker in turn affect their ability to develop a productive working relationship?

Horvath (Horvath, 2000; Horvath and Bedi, 2002) observes that studies on the effectiveness of counseling and psychotherapy reveal that it is not the worker's actual behavior as measured by objective observers that accounts for positive gains. It is the client's subjective evaluation of the relationship with the worker that is associated with success. Hence, it is important to attend to how the client experiences both the relationship and the worker's understanding of the client's situation. Efforts are needed to obtain feedback from the client about how he evaluates the helpfulness of the worker. Furthermore, not all clients experience and evaluate the dimensions of empathy in a similar manner. In a study of clients' perceptions of the therapist's empathy Bachelor (1988) found that the empathy offered by practitioners was experienced and valued differently amongst a sample of clients who were drawn from a community clinic population. She identified four distinct styles. A large number of clients (44 percent) valued empathic responses that conveyed an intellectual or *cognitive* understanding of their innermost experience or subjective state. Thirty percent of clients valued communications that were *affectively* oriented, that conveyed that the helper was emotionally involved with the client and feeling as she was. The third style was labeled *sharing* and reported by 18 percent of clients as the worker sharing personal opinions or experiences that are related to the issues confronted by the client. Finally, 7 percent referred to *nurturant* empathy and valued the supportive, attentive, and caring presence of the practitioner.

In a related study Bachelor (1995) again found that clients varied regarding the value they attributed to empathy in professional relationships. The qualities of facilitative relationships, such as respect, a nonjudgmental attitude, empathic understanding, and attentive listening were valued by close to half of the sample. Another 40 percent of respondents described a positive relationship as one that resulted in greater self-understanding. They attributed gains in their self-awareness to clarifications made by their therapists to issues they discussed. Only 10 percent of clients viewed a positive relationship as a collaborative effort where both the therapist and the client have joint responsibility for bringing about change.

These studies suggest that it is unwise for practitioners to assume that all clients will experience the empathy they offer in the same way. Clearly, there are individual appraisals and preferences. The general facilitative relationship characteristics of warmth, caring concern, acceptance, positive regard, respect, and a nonjudgmental attitude are likely to provide a useful starting point for work with all clients. As social workers strive to use the principle of individualizing the client, it is useful to remember that clients do not value equally the various aspects of empathy. Some will prefer a focus on cognitive understanding, others on emotional attunement, and others on support and nurturance. And, some clients are less concerned with an empathic stance and instead prefer a worker who provides considerable self-disclosure. Differences in clients' preferences may also include the degree of formality versus informality, the degree of warmth and friendliness as contrasted with a more neutral style, the degree of direction, structure, and activity on the worker's part, and the balance between support and challenge (Norcross, 1993). Moreover, clients may change their preferences through the course of the helping process, especially as more familiarity and trust develops.

This group of research studies suggests that it may be helpful for practitioners to be attuned to the way each individual client responds to their stance, behaviors, and comments in the interview. The nature of the relationship may need to be negotiated initially and over time as comfort and familiarity are established. Practitioners will therefore need to develop a flexible repertoire of relationship stances that suit different clients' needs and expectations so that they can bend and adapt aspects of their interpersonal style to achieve a more optimal fit with each client. This principle is similar to the social work notion of "differential use of self" and captures a characteristic of experienced, competent practitioners entailing the ability to use different aspects of their personal and professional style in a variety of ways to join with clients. Some examples are being more active with less verbal clients and more nondirective with clients who are able to more easily express issues of concern and what they need; in an emergency being able to move quickly and act in a range of roles, and, in longer term involvement, being able to go slowly and be patient; knowing when to be challenging and confront client issues and when to sit back, listen, and say little; being able to work with adolescents and adults and vary the use of language, degree of formality, and stance to match the age-appropriate style of the client; and knowing when to use humor and when to remain serious.

The following activities and behaviors are some of the ways in which social workers facilitate empathic communication in the service of building working relationships and developing enough shared understanding of the client's situation to enable effective helping to proceed. The related interviewing skills are elaborated on in part 3 of this volume.

ATTACHMENT THEORY AND THE HELPING RELATIONSHIP

A discussion of concepts that assist practitioners' understanding of the relationship can be enriched by the contribution of attachment theory and research. Originating with the work of John Bowlby in the 1950s, this body of work has demonstrated that continuity exists in personality and social development (Bowlby, 1988). Attachment theory is introduced here as it adds depth, complexity, and richness to assisting us to individualize clients. Furthermore, there is a substantial body of supporting empirical work. Two concepts arise from this work that are useful for practice: 1) the client's way of relating reflects her underlying beliefs and ideas about relationships and 2) the client's characteristic ways of relating will also be seen in the manner in which the client relates to the practitioner. Hence the relationship has the potential to help the client change his beliefs about relationships by offering a different relationship experience.

There is a vast literature on attachment theory and the accompanying empirical studies it has spawned that is beyond the scope of this chapter. Rather, selected ideas that can be useful in practice are presented here, and readers are encouraged to pursue the work of attachment theorists and researchers. Attachment concepts are congruent with the notions about empathy and the therapeutic alliance reviewed thus far.

Individuals have basic beliefs about relationships. Bowlby (1988) proposed that humans have basic needs for care, nurturance, and emotional connection and an infant's attachment to his mother or substitute caregiver arises from numerous responses to the infant's needs. Accessible and responsive caregivers provide a sense of attachment and this in turn leads to the development of secure bonds. Attachment and caregiving are affected by such factors as parental characteristics, children's characteristics such as temperament, the fit between children's needs and caregivers' capacities, and stresses and supports in the external environment. Ainsworth (Ainsworth et al., 1978) studied the relationship between children and their caregivers based on babies' responses to brief separations from and reunions with their parent in a lab situation, referred to as the Strange Situation. Initially three attachment styles were identified: secure, insecure-avoidant, and insecure-ambivalent. A fourth style was identified by Main and Solomon (1986) and described as disorganized/disoriented.

From early experiences with caretakers individuals develop notions about self, other, and relationships, referred to as internal working models of attachment, relationship schemas, or scripts (Baldwin, 1992; Bretherton, 1993). These internal working models are internal representations that have thoughts and feelings associated with them. They constitute our self-image, especially about our worth, lovability, dependency, effectiveness, and sense of self as good or bad. These models about others include expectations about their availability and accessibility, dependability, lovingness, caring, responsiveness, cooperativeness, and trustworthiness. Relationship models include what we expect as patterns in relationships, for example, that relationships are easy and rewarding, need work, or are essentially dangerous and exploitative. These relationship models predispose us to habitual forms of relating to others or of demonstrating our attachment styles in significant and intimate relationships.

Attachment styles can change throughout the life course based on life experiences in the family. For example, when stable care giving patterns are disrupted because of illness, unemployment, war, forced relocation, or other traumatic and disruptive events, attachment styles can be affected. When unstable caregivers' life experiences change and enable them to be more present and available, or when more giving and available individuals become part of the caregiving system, more secure attachment styles may develop. Important mediating factors that affect the development and persistence of particular attachment styles are the individual's temperament and resilience and the characteristics of caregivers and others in the social environment (Landy, 2002).

Individuals' way of relating to others reflects internal working model. Internalized ideas about self, other, and what one can expect in a relationship are brought forward in relating to significant others in current situations. Especially when adults seek emotional connection in intimate interpersonal relationships attachment styles can be seen to be operating. Individuals engage in habitual patterns; the expectations we have of others, our appraisal and interpretation of their actions, and the emotions that are stirred up reveal our internal working models (Hazan and Shaver, 1987; Johnson, Makinen, and Millikin, 2001; Johnson and Whiffen, 1999).

As noted, Ainsworth and colleagues (Ainsworthet et al., 1978) and then Main (Main and Solomon, 1986) identified attachment styles in children. Researchers have studied attachment in adults and have found that adult attachment styles are in general associated with specific relationship behaviors and concerns (Kirkpatrick and Hazan, 1994; Simpson, 1990). For example, securely attached individuals were more trusting, committed, and satisfied in their relationships. Those with avoidant attachment styles tended to avoid commitment and intimacy and were less trusting of partners. Those with preoccupied attachment styles were concerned with their partners' predictability, trustworthiness and dependability. More recently researchers and clinicians have applied the concept of attachment to the study of couple relationships (Johnson and Whiffen, 2003).

Attachment styles describe some predominant trends that can assist in understanding consistent thoughts, feelings, and behaviors on the part of an individual in relationships. They are, however, not absolutes and individuals may demonstrate a range of styles, especially under stress or when threatened with loss in a meaningful relationship. It is useful to think systemically and regard our internal life as developing and changing in relation to our external experiences; affecting and being affected by others. As we participate in interactions with significant others and take in new information and experiences we can change our internal working models. Repetitive positive or negative themes that emerge in relationships with partners, peers, mentors, and employers can confirm or disconfirm an individual's internal working model of self and relationships.

Individuals relate to the helper in ways that reflect internal working models about relationships. As with all significant relationships individual ways of making sense of and behaving in important interpersonal relationships can be displayed in the way the client relates to the helper. The client expects the practitioner to respond in ways that confirm his internal working models and expectations of self and of other. This is especially so if the client approaches the worker with the expectation that assistance of some form will be provided. The professional relationship can be seen as analogous to a caregiving relationship. The parallels are especially obvious when an individual needs more assistance from another, for example when in a time of distress. When the practitioner can offer availability and responsiveness some degree of comfort is experienced by the client. Such responsiveness would be offered in a selective manner depending on the attachment style of the client.

Practitioners can help clients develop alternative internal working models about relationships. Clinical practitioners who use attachment theory to inform their work focus on understanding the impact of early and current attachment and loss with the aim of changing thinking, feeling, and behaving (Bowlby, 1988). The following practice principles are associated with this type of in-depth work. They can also be used in more general ways in all forms of direct social work practice, regardless of the particular theoretical model applied.

First, the worker aims to understand the client's view of self, of other, and his expectations of relationships from the client's description and from reflecting on the current interactions with the client and associated feelings. Attachment researchers posit that models are kept stable when others behave in a way that confirms them (Hazan and Shaver, 1994). Therefore, the worker's self-awareness is crucial so that practitioners can distinguish between their own idiosyncratic or countertransference response to the client and what might be the typical response of others to the client's behavior in relationships. With an understanding of the client's expectations the worker is better able to avoid reacting in a way that will confirm the client's most negative expectations. By refraining from behaving in a way that reinforces the typical relationship experiences of the client the worker provides an opportunity for a new type of interaction experience to occur. Learning from this therapeutic relationship will hopefully generalize to expectations and behavior in the significant relationships in the client's life.

Second, to the extent the helping relationship is emotionally engaging and continues over some prolonged period of time it has the potential to change internal working models through providing a secure base. The practitioner can provide the empathic qualities that demonstrate accessibility, interest, and responsiveness by simply being there for the client in a way that is different from others in his life (Howe, 1995). The offer of support and assistance through the worker's steady, consistent availability leads to trust. This may build slowly over time, through numerous contacts and interactions, or may arise from offering support and instrumental help in a time of great need. This new and important relationship encounter becomes emotionally important to the client, is internalized, and provides the client with new beliefs or alternative internal working models about self and other that are now available for use in future social interactions.

Third, when client and practitioner can work together over some period of time, within the context of this secure and trusting relationship base, the client can explore past relationships in some depth and the associated feelings, thoughts, and behaviors. The client can examine how past and current experiences are linked, including whether salient themes from the past are active in the here and now between the worker and client. Since discussions of past relationships may stir up painful emotions, the client's experience and growing expectation that the worker will provide an empathic and nonjudgmental response provides comfort (Sable, 1992). The opportunity to experience open communication in an atmosphere of acceptance and interest demonstrates what a close relationship can be like. The practitioner's behavior is an example of how professionals, using attachment concepts as a theoretical base, are able to engage in a differentiated and selective manner to meet the specific needs of each client. Furthermore, through the practitioner drawing explicit connections between the past and the present the client develops an expanded understanding or new narrative about his history, development, and recent learning about self and ways of relating to others. These new learnings can in turn be used in relationships in the client's life.

Many ingredients interact to form the helping relationship between the worker and the client. This chapter has presented the fundamental and enduring characteristics of the professional relationship as defined in social work and further developed in related helping disciplines. Theoretical contributions from attachment theory can also provide specific concepts and an overarching perspective to understand the importance of the relationship. Practitioners have a wide range of concepts to use in building and maintaining this crucial context for growth, development, and change.

THE HELPING RELATIONSHIP

FURTHER DIMENSIONS

THERAPEUTIC ALLIANCE: EMPIRICAL SUPPORT
FOR THE IMPORTANCE OF THE RELATIONSHIP

Despite the centrality of the relationship concept in social work, there has been little empirical investigation. Research in social work practice has largely focused on the effectiveness of various interventions and emphasized measuring outcomes (Poulin and Young, 1997; Reid, 1994; Reid and Fortune, 2003). The study of the role of the relationship in helping has largely been undertaken by disciplines such as psychology, counseling, and psychiatry through studies of a range of variables that effect outcome in psychotherapy. These variables include client expectations and presenting symptoms, interventions of specialized models, and the alliance between practitioners and their clients. Studies have been conducted in a variety of settings and with a range of practitioners, including social workers. While there may be differences in ideology, theory, and nomenclature between professional disciplines, there are sufficient similarities between the study populations, their presenting problems, and the actual practice models and people and problems that social workers encounter and approaches they use that attention to this work is warranted. Findings from these studies have produced knowledge that is useful to social workers and can be easily adapted.

Originally outcome studies were conducted to demonstrate the effectiveness of a specific intervention model (Bachelor and Horvath, 1999; Lambert and Bergin, 1994; Orlinsky, Grawe, and Parks, 1994). In a number of meta-analytic studies researchers have concluded that psychotherapeutic or counseling interventions are effective and that no particular treatment model is more effective than another for a range of individual problems (Bergin and Garfield, 1994; Norcross, 2002; Wampold, 2001; Wampold et al., 1997); all models produce "approximately equal benefits generally" (Ahn and Wampold, 2001, p. 254). This conclusion spawned an extensive discussion in the literature in psychology and psychotherapy on the common factors that exist across specialized models such as psychodynamic, cognitive-behavioral, and humanistic. The reasoning was that, if one model is not superior to another and all models produce change, there are features common to all approaches that account for improvement.

Considerable theorizing and meta-analyses have identified these common factors. Grencavage and Norcross (1990) summarized five main areas: 1) client characteristics, such as expectation, help-seeking activity, and distress level, 2) therapist qualities, such as cultivating hope, and offering warmth and positive regard, 3) change processes, such as the opportunity for expression of feelings, and acquisition of new behaviors, 4) treatment structures, such as the use of techniques and the exploration of emotional issues and the inner world of the client, and 5) relationship elements, such as the development of the alliance between practitioner and client. Lambert (1992) proposed a similar scheme of four therapeutic factors as the ingredients that explain positive improvements across models. These factors are extratherapeutic, common factors (which include the relationship), expectancy or placebo, and techniques. Furthermore, Lambert (1992) found that 30 percent of the successful outcome across models was accounted for by the relationship factor.

These studies provide a compelling argument for training social workers and other helping professionals to be proficient in activating these common factors. Ahn and Wampold (2001) note "the importance of interviewing skills, establishment of a therapeutic relationship, and the core facilitative conditions…is supported by the empirical evidence" (p. 255). Hubble, Duncan, and Miller (1999) observe that since relationship factors are so influential professionals need to develop their own style as they work with these therapeutic factors in their practice and partner with clients to assess the fit between what is offered and what the client finds helpful.

The characteristics of helpful relationships emerging from these empirical studies and meta-analyses mirror those characteristics of the relationship presented in the social work literature (Coady, 1999; Perlman, 1979), in humanistic and client-centered psychology (Greenberg, Rice, and Elliott, 1993; Rogers, 1957) and in psychoanalytic self-psychology (Kohut, 1957; 1984; Wolf, 1988). To summarize, they include the caring aspects of empathy, warmth, acceptance, and validation that create safety. Within such a relationship practitioners can encourage risk taking and mastery, which leads to change (Hubble, Duncan, and Miller, 1999).

In this era, which prizes empirically based intervention models for social work (Thyer, 2000), it is important to note the finding that the relationship affects outcome supports long-standing beliefs, theories, and practices according the relationship centrality in social work practice. Psychotherapy researchers have reconceptualized the concept of relationship as "a therapeutic alliance" and pinpoint its salient dimensions. Bordin (1979, 1994) provided a definition of the therapeutic alliance that goes beyond the traditional social work notion of relationship and has been used in designing measures for research purposes. Rather than viewing the relationship as composed of characteristics and qualities that are offered by the social worker, as discussed earlier, he defines the alliance concept as consisting of agreement between client and therapist on goals and tasks and the emotional bond that develops between them. The concept encompasses the interactive dynamics and collaborative processes between the worker and the client, again a concept congruent with social work practice theory and values.

THERAPEUTIC ALLIANCE DEFINED

Bordin (1979) proposed three factors that constitute the therapeutic alliance: 1) an emotional bond or connection, 2) agreement on the tasks of the work, and 3) agreement on the goals of the work. The first factor is the bond and refers to the emotional quality of the relationship between the client and the worker. It includes the degree to which the client feels that the worker understands, respects, and values him (Safran and Muran, 2000). The client feels connected to the worker in a way that is meaningful and important. The bond encompasses some aspects of the helping relationship discussed earlier such as the worker's empathic attunement and understanding of a client's thoughts and feelings, acceptance, and a nonjudgmental stance. It provides the emotional base that holds the relationship together as the client and worker experience the progress and setbacks of intervention. For example, an adolescent client new to the country had been encouraged by her social worker to initiate conversations with classmates to show her interest in making friends. The client tells the worker, angrily and tearfully, that no one responded to her efforts and that she felt like a fool and more of an outsider. This client feels that she can tell her worker that her advice was useless and that the worker does not understand what it is like to be different. Because an emotional bond has been established, the client believes that the worker will listen and keep trying to help her. In the absence of such a bond the client may blame the worker for giving bad advice or simply not return.

The second factor in the therapeutic alliance is the goal of intervention and refers to the general objectives of the work and the degree of agreement about the purpose of meeting together. In social work the principle of "starting where the client is" refers to giving primacy to the client's definition of the issues to work on. Individual social workers also have their own view of optimal social functioning, and this plays a role in contracting. For example, a client in an acute hospital might expect the social worker to help him exclusively with discharge planning and admission into a rehabilitation setting close to his home. The social worker might view this objective as only one part of the goals of working together. Other goals might be helping the client adjust to the psychological and social implications of a serious accident that resulted in paralysis and permanent loss of function. Meeting a client's expressed immediate needs is viewed as important and valid. Providing concrete resources may constitute sufficient service for the client at this stage of his adjustment. Or it may solidify his perception of the social worker as a valued helper with whom he can work to deal with other aspects of his physical condition. However, most social work practice takes place within an organizational context or service program. The acute hospital may limit the amount and span of time that the social worker can devote to the client and in this way set limits on what goals can be addressed. In practice these three perspectives, the client's needs and wishes, the social worker's knowledge and assessment, and the organization's policy, must be negotiated in setting goals.

Over time goals of intervention may change and new tasks or activities will be introduced. For example, while working with a young couple referred by Child Protective Services to help them learn parenting skills, a social worker in a community agency may discover that the father's employability is limited by his lack of literacy. The worker may also initiate an assessment to determine whether the client may have a learning disability or refer him to an adult literacy program.

The third factor in the therapeutic alliance is the task of intervention and refers to the activities, methods, or procedures of the particular intervention plan. It may include the roles and responsibilities of both the client and the social worker in bringing about change and the degree of agreement between them. For example, the parents of a child who is having difficulty controlling his anger might expect that the social worker will see the child individually or in a play therapy group. The social worker may agree and also recommend regular family sessions as an important part of bringing about change. While the parents may be reluctant to participate, if enough of a bond has developed they may be able to discuss their mixed feelings and then accept the worker's recommendation.

This three-part formulation of the therapeutic alliance provides a multi-dimensional view of working effectively with clients. At the beginning of the relationship, when there is little emotional bonding, it is likely that agreement on goals and tasks is of great importance as the worker has not yet established the credibility to reframe or enlarge the work together. However, as the bond increases the client may become more hopeful about achieving additional goals. This can lead the worker and client to develop new plans, which include engaging in activities about which the client may have initially felt skeptical. Similarly, when there is progress as a result of successful interventions the relational bond is strengthened. In this respect the three components of the therapeutic alliance are mediated by each other and together produce the facilitative conditions for growth and change. For example, the young father was initially too embarrassed to discuss his inability to read with the worker. As he and his wife learned parenting skills from the worker and experienced her as helpful, caring, and non-judgmental, he was able to discuss his frustration about his employment prospects. With encouragement from the worker he was able to attend classes and learn how to read. His wife was supportive of his time away from the family as she had been actively involved in developing this plan.

It is not unusual despite the best efforts of all participants for progress to be slow or not evident at all. When a bond exists between the practitioner and client they can discuss this without the client feeling blamed or judged. Together they can explore factors that may have been overlooked, information withheld, or deep-seated attitudes and feelings that are not easily modified. Discussions about a lack of progress can strengthen the relational bond when the worker demonstrates her commitment to facilitating the client's progress.

COLLABORATION AND PARTNERSHIP

Earlier we discussed empathy as an interactive concept. Even if the worker believes she is offering the best qualities for a therapeutic alliance to develop, ultimately the client will determine whether that is so. With a notion of alliance expanded beyond an emotional connection to include agreement on goals and tasks, the interactional viewpoint is established. Therefore, social workers need to actively learn about clients' initial and ongoing experience of their work together. By focusing attention on clients' overt and subtle reactions to workers' interventions, much can be learned. Some clients prefer a more formal rather than informal relationship; some find a focus on internal aspects of their life more helpful than a focus on the external. Some clients favor an approach that is oriented toward behavior, others to thoughts and explanations, and others to feelings. For example, the social worker observed that her young adult male client avoided eye contact and offered little elaboration of his responses whenever she asked about his past relationships in his family of origin. Despite the fact that his presenting concern was how he could tell his parents that he was living in a gay relationship, talking about past family relationships brought about discomfort. Recognizing this, the worker could make this explicit or maintain a focus exclusively on the present. By introducing her observation the client could further explore his discomfort (that he felt he had disappointed his parents in his educational and career choices and that coming out to them would be another disappointment). Or the client could provide information about his view of change (that he believed that long excursions into his past would take a lot of time and not help him with the immediate concerns he was facing).

Workers can make the collaborative process more explicit. In the first session they can state that the work will involve active participation by the client in setting goals and tasks. They can discuss the usefulness of regular feedback about the process, especially whether the client experiences the worker as understanding, affirming, and helpful. Practitioners can also build in regular and periodic discussion of these aspects. Instruments developed for research purposes specify the factors associated with alliance and can serve as a trigger for such discussions and can easily be used to evaluate the process aspects of the work (Horvath and Greenberg, 1986). These self-report instruments can be administered at the end of each session.

Poulin and Young (1997) developed the Helping Relationship Inventory (HRI) for social workers and their clients. While this instrument reflects the alliance components of task, goals, and bond as defined by Bordin (1979), it also incorporates the language and activities of social workers when accessing services, such as advocacy, linkage, and coordination. In an initial test of the client version of the instrument they identified two groupings of items: a structural component and an interpersonal component. The structural component consists of questions about the extent to which the worker and client discussed specific issues and how much input the client felt he had. The specific issues were goals, problems or concerns, how client and worker would work together, actions the client would take, actions the social worker would take, and how progress would be assessed. The interpersonal component consisted of questions about the client's perception that the worker helped the client think more clearly about himself and his difficulties, instilled belief in the client, was similar to the client in some ways and had similar views, and inspired hope. The researchers referred to the interpersonal component as an inspiring or motivating factor.

This inventory can be used in both research and practice to evaluate the strength of the relationship and to facilitate discussion about it. Students and their clients independently and simultaneously completed versions of the HRI and discussed the results at the next session. The researchers report that students and their clients discussed items where there were marked differences or where ratings were lower than most items. Using the inventory served as a structured way to evaluate and redirect practice. It helped identify additional areas of concern and it made discussion of the working alliance explicit.

Workers who seek and use feedback from clients have the opportunity to truly individualize their practice. This involves adapting the worker's stance, intervention activities, and expectations. Workers need knowledge of and comfort with a range of therapeutic behaviors and a versatile and flexible stance. This perspective seems congruent with the contemporary practice realities that take diversity into account, as discussed earlier.

This view of practice grounds ideas of collaboration, mutuality, and partnership. Social workers do not do things to clients; rather they come together to engage in activities that help the client meet his goals. Therefore a reasonable starting point is to learn what the client wants to achieve and hopes will be different because of meeting with the worker (Hubble, Duncan, and Miller, 1999). Since goals are often expressed in vague and general terms it is useful to break them down into manageable parts or partialize the problem. Goals may expand or become more specific through new learning and the accompanying insights that emerge. Hence it is important to see this type of work as a dynamic and evolving process.

SELF-DISCLOSURE

Self-disclosure is a somewhat controversial topic in the helping literature with different views about its helpfulness, depending on the theoretical model and the practitioner's belief in its effectiveness and her level of comfort with sharing personal information. Unfortunately there is a dearth of useful empirical studies to help clarify the issues and provide data to sort out the different claims made by particular models (Hill and Knox, 2002). Ethical principles also guide practitioners' decisions about self-disclosure.

Obviously social workers reveal information about themselves by the way in which they dress, whether they wear a wedding ring, the pictures and decorations they place in their offices, and so on. That self-disclosures arising out of spontaneous and unconscious processes are likely to happen is also acknowledged and the earlier extensive discussion about self-awareness can assist workers in this regard. Again ethical principles about appropriate professional standards and behavior apply. For example, it is not appropriate for social workers to share their personal fantasies and social, sexual, or financial circumstances (Reamer, 2001).

What is worthy of consideration is whether and under what conditions self-disclosure may be helpful when used in an intentional manner. The guiding principle reflected in much of the literature in social work and related helping professions gives primacy to the potential usefulness to the client. The desire to share a private incident or personal feelings with a particular client should be examined in relation to the worker's motivation and associations. Does the worker believe that it will convey empathy, increase the bond, or motivate the client to take a course of action? Does it arise from an attempt to highlight similarities between the worker and client or to lessen a power differential and is it likely to achieve that goal? Reflecting on these dynamics may illuminate motivations that are more personal and related to emotional or relational needs of the worker and incidental to the client. For example, a young female social worker confronted with an older depressed male in an outpatient psychiatric day program reacted with irritation to the client's boastfulness about the high status of his family. She disclosed to the client that her parents also lived in the same neighborhood and belonged to the same religious and social organizations. While this disclosure may have been cloaked in the guise of promoting similarity, further reflection revealed that it stemmed from her perception that the client was elevating himself above the largely lower-middle-class staff. It was not helpful to the client, however, who responded to her disclosure with concerns about the confidentiality of their sessions. Reflection on the part of the worker revealed her understanding that the client felt shamed about his depression and experienced a palpable blow to his self-esteem. His statements about his background were attempts to bolster his shaky sense of self and convey to the staff that he was "more than a psych patient."

Traditional psychoanalytic and psychodynamic approaches viewed self-disclosure as reflecting worker countertransference. Rather than share personal information about themselves or respond to clients' requests for information about their personal lives, practitioners would explore the client's motivation for asking a particular question. For example, if the practitioner stated that the next regular session would be canceled as he would be away and the client asked where the worker was going, rather than immediately respond the worker would explore the client's thoughts and feelings about the worker's absence. The focus would remain on the client's reactions, which might reveal his concern about a growing dependency on the worker or a fear that the worker was interviewing for a job in another city and would abandon him. The rationale for avoiding a factual response to the question was that it might close the topic or divert attention from the important issue, the client's experience of the worker's absence, to a superficial discussion of vacation plans. In contrast, in client-centered and humanistic approaches self-disclosure was considered an aspect of authenticity and essential to demonstrating genuineness and positive regard (Wells, 1994). Similarly feminist theorists use self-disclosure to equalize the power differential between client and worker (Brown, 1994a, b) and to transmit feminist values and foster a sense of solidarity (Mahalik, VanOrmer, and Simi, 2000).

Clinical social work theorists drawing on self psychology have proposed that self-disclosure can promote empathic attunement and responsiveness when used in a thoughtful and intentional way to strengthen the relationship bond (Goldstein, 1997; Palombo, 1987). From this framework self-disclosure is categorized in at least three ways. Practitioners share information with clients that they believe is in the service of creating participation and collaboration. Hence, social workers might spontaneously, or in response to a client's query, share factual information such as the school they graduated from, how long they have been with the agency, their marital status, whether they have children, and where they were born and grew up as children. A second type of self-disclosure is about the worker's feelings, thoughts, or reactions when in a situation similar to that of the client. For example, a client is undergoing medical investigation for cancer and the worker has had such an experience in the past. In discussions of the client's situation the worker discloses aspects of her own feelings, thoughts and reactions as she dealt with the medical system, with friends, relatives, and coworkers, and with her own anxieties and fears. A final type of self-disclosure relates to the worker's more personal response to a client's story. For example, a client who has been assaulted in a deserted subway tells the worker that she is now afraid to go on the subway alone. The worker responds that she would have the same reaction as the client—that the client's fears are emotionally understandable to the worker.

Recall the earlier discussion of diversity and the importance of striving to understand the client's experiences when they are very different from those of the worker. In an attempt to work across differences, social workers may use self-disclosure to demonstrate similarity with the hope of creating an emotional bond and connection or provide role modeling. Sharing experiences of difficulty may enhance confidence on the client's part that even though both are different there may be enough common experiences and understanding. For example, an African American male social worker in his late thirties has been working with a Native American woman in her mid-twenties through her employee assistance program. She has received a promotion as a section head and presents with feelings of general anxiety. The client was raised on a reserve not far from the medium-sized urban center where she attended university, excelled in her management and business courses, and later found employment in a large financial institution. As the worker came to know the client's family and community history, he observed that, similar to himself, this client was now operating in an environment where she was a minority and where she felt extremely burdened to demonstrate her capabilities, especially since being recognized for her achievements and promoted. The worker had experienced similar feelings through his graduate education as he was aware of the high expectations he placed on himself and that his family reinforced. Through success at his work and developing greater understanding of the interplay between historical factors related to race and his own personal and family history he was able to feel comfortable with himself and his accomplishments. In his work with this client, his personal narrative was introduced over time. It was brought into sessions in relation to the issues and feelings the client raised. The client later reflected that hearing about the worker's similar struggles was inspirational and gave her much hope.

Self-disclosures that are not well-thought out, however, can have the opposite effect. In the interests of leveling a power differential with a thirty-five-year-old immigrant male from Sri Lanka, the twenty-five-year-old white female student, in a government-sponsored vocational retraining program, discussed difficulties adjusting to life in a new country and the downward employment mobility the client was experiencing. The student shared her experience moving from the West to a large Eastern city for university education and how disorienting it had been for her. The client was deeply offended by this disclosure, feeling that it trivialized his experience. He forcefully told the student that she had no idea what it was like to be a visible minority in a country where white people made decisions about who gets jobs and who gets into government programs. He elaborated that even though he spoke English well locally born people reacted to "his accent" and often stated that they could not understand him. This client was reacting to what he experienced as too simplistic an attempt on the part of the student to draw similarities between them. The privileges she had by virtue of her upbringing and color limited adequate empathy from her perspective of his struggle with the disadvantages and barriers he faced daily.

When considering using self-disclosure, practitioners can also consider the expectations of the client. For example, if the client, by virtue of age, culture, or class expects the worker to adopt a formal posture, then self-disclosure may be ineffective in forging a relationship and may undermine the credibility the worker needs to establish. On the other hand, when clients are unfamiliar with social and health services, disclosing information that the client is requesting or might benefit from demonstrates respect and provides useful data about the educational background of the social worker, what the role consists of, and how they might be of help. As noted above, comments about similarities between worker and client can in some instances interfere with bonding. However, if the worker has had some meaningful interactions with the client's culture, through personal associations or living in the client's country of origin, this may assist in building a relationship. As practitioners come to learn and know their clients over time, they can better anticipate the potential effect of self-disclosing comments. Timing remains a central factor in achieving an optimal equilibrium in the practitioner-client dyad.

Practitioners can assess, to some degree, the impact of an intervention by observing how clients respond to it, and this is also true with self-disclosure (Hill and Knox, 2002). Responses may be immediate or may have an impact on the work over a longer period of time. The client may think about the content of the worker's disclosure after the interview, which in turn may influence the way the client is processing the issue under attention. The client may prize the fact that the worker shared information with her, adding to the bonding in the relationship.

Some useful reflective guidelines are provided by Murphy and Dillon (2003) to evaluate the impact of the social worker's self-disclosure on the client. They recommend examining how the client made sense of the information, any feelings they had about it, and whether it affected the working relationship. In addition, the worker can consider whether it achieved the desired effect, whether they should discuss directly with the client her reaction to the disclosure, and in retrospect consider whether it was useful.

SELF-DISCLOSURE AND ETHICS

Reamer (1999, 2001, 2003) has written extensively on ethics in social work practice and his contributions are extremely illuminating when applied to self-disclosure. Too much self-disclosure, he proposes, can inadvertently stimulate boundary crossing. Reamer (2001, 2003) notes that while not all boundary issues are problematic or unethical, many are. The distinction is made between boundary violations and boundary crossing. In boundary violations clients may be exploited, manipulated, or coerced, and harmed if practitioners pursue intimate relationships with them. For example, sexual or business relationships with a client are clearly unethical. Similarly, Brown (1994), writing from a feminist perspective, points out that boundary violations include situations where "the client becomes an object for the satisfaction of certain needs and desires on the part of the therapist" (p. 33), needs for sexual gratification, for entertainment, for information, or for a source of intimacy. When the practitioners' needs take precedence over the client's and the worker behaves in an impulsive and self-centered manner, there is greater risk of distorting what can be considered helpful to the client.

In contrast to boundary violations, boundary crossing refers to interactions with clients that arise from the workers' emotional needs and manifest in many ways such as forming friendships with clients, engaging in personal self-disclosure with clients, affectionate communication with clients, and seeking out clients through community groups and activities. Engaging in personal relationships after therapy has ended is problematic, since both parties do not enter as equals. The previous hierarchical nature of the relationship casts a shadow over the present and former clients can more easily be exploited. Furthermore, while the client may gain a friend he looses a counselor as he can no longer return for service should the need arise.

Self-disclosures that arise out of practitioners' unmet emotional and relational needs may convey their wish for a personal relationship with the client and "sharing personal details may be a way to set this process in motion" (Reamer, 2001, p. 110). Personal sharing in such circumstances is clearly inappropriate. There are however circumstances similar to the example of the counselor in the employee assistance program presented earlier where "practitioners may self-disclose for more altruistic purposes, deliberately and judiciously choosing to share personal details—usually modest in scope—in an effort to empathize with clients, offer clients support, align with clients, and provide a constructive role model that clients may use in their efforts to address their own issues" (Reamer, 2001, p. 166). Reamer concludes that when it is unclear whose interests are being served the ethical principle that guides self-disclosure is "that it is done for the client's benefit within the context of the therapeutic process" (Reamer, 2001, p. 112).

In conclusion, it appears that self-disclosures may be useful in some situations. They may serve to enhance the relationship bond, normalize or validate client reactions, and provide alternative ways of thinking or behaving in difficult situations. The guiding principle for their use is that the practitioner thinks that the information will assist the client. Therefore, workers need to attend to their own motivation for sharing personal data and examine whether it arises from their need or from a legitimate assessment of the potential usefulness to the client. Consideration should also be given to whether the information will burden the client and lead him to avoid sharing certain types of material with the worker in the future. And whether it will confuse the client about the boundaries in the relationship and the focus of the meetings must be anticipated.

THE ALLIANCE OVER TIME

As reviewed earlier, there is considerable empirical support for the strong connection between the working alliance and outcomes. Furthermore, the strength of the alliance in the early sessions is highly predictive of the outcome. Horvath and Symonds (1991) conducted a meta-analysis of fifteen years of psychotherapy studies and concluded that there may be a limited period, between the third to fifth session, to establish a working relationship that provides enough of a foundation to prevent premature termination thereafter. Hence it is important for practitioners to be keenly attuned to the nature of the developing relationship from the outset. Especially in the early sessions practitioners need to pay attention to whether the client feels respected, heard, and understood. Discussions about the nature of the work and the client's perceptions about the relationship can reveal those elements that are important to amplify and expand. For example, a female client who had been sexually abused as an adolescent by a cousin who was a frequent visitor to her family related the circumstances of this abuse in each meeting with the social worker. After eight sessions the worker and client reviewed their work together and the client stated that she was beginning to feel better, some degree of relief, and a diminishing of the anguish that had for so long accompanied her recollections of the ongoing abuse. She commented that the most helpful aspect of their meetings was that the worker listened to what she had to say and validated her feelings by confirming her subjective experience. In contrast to earlier therapeutic services she had received, she observed that the worker did not attempt to "make her feel better" through pointing out her strengths, nor did she attempt to have her problem solve and find strategies to block or control her thoughts. Rather, she simply listened and commented on how understandable it was that she was angry that her family did not protect her, that she was saddened by her own timidity and fear of retaliation if she disclosed the abuse to anyone, and that she continued to experience anxiety when faced with family gatherings.

As the work proceeds, practitioners need to pay attention to subtle, as well as overt, indicators about whether the client perceives the meetings as helpful. For example, mixed or negative feelings about the interviews can be expressed through missed appointments, reluctance to book subsequent meetings, the client's lack of initiative in introducing topics for discussion, a general appearance of boredom, distraction, and lack of involvement. Or clients may wonder out loud whether they are really making any progress, whether they need to continue coming to see the worker, or question how long they will need to attend. Practitioners need to sort out to what extent these types of behaviors are expected reactions to the uncertainty of any helping process, indicative of the particular client's style and reactions to the legitimate struggles he is experiencing, and/or responses to some aspects of the worker and the approach being used. If a worker is maintaining a nondirective stance when the client repeatedly asks for more concrete suggestions and more structure, then it is understandable if the client questions whether he will gain anything of value by continuing. Or the client's behavior may indicate his perception that the worker is not empathically attuned; a comment or line of discussion may have been experienced by the client as a break in empathic connection. Or, the client's questioning may reveal aspects of his usual reactions, in this instance to think about leaving a relationship when he feels frustrated and that he is not getting his needs met.

When reviewing the helping process the client may comment on aspects of the worker's behavior or stance that the client is not experiencing as helpful. The client's observations might not match the way the worker sees himself, and it is very difficult to suspend our natural tendency to defend ourselves and to explain what we really meant or intended. It is essential, however, to listen carefully to the client's perception and aim to understand her view and to communicate that understanding. When clients learn that difficulties in interpersonal relationships can be discussed and both parties can gain clarification and more knowledge about each other and their interactions, new learning occurs through experiencing a different type of relating (Safran and Muran, 2000).

As in all relationships, there is likely to be fluctuation over time. When the work progresses and improvement occurs, the client may develop a stronger bond with the worker and feel more hopeful about achieving some desired goals. There may be periods when the client feels that progress is not being made or that the worker is not interested enough, or available enough, or does not truly understand. These strains, breaks, or experiences of being "stuck" are referred to in the literature as ruptures (Safran and Muran, 2000). Relational work can be seen as needing ongoing attention between the two participants. The practitioner has the responsibility to address problems that are overt and to be sensitive to behaviors that are less obvious and may indicate disjunctions in the alliance. Alliance researchers all agree on the importance of discussing with clients, when feasible, the relational dynamics, focus, activities, and outcomes of the work. The activity of trying to repair ruptures improves the sense of collaboration and partnership (Bachelor and Horvath, 1999; Hubble, Duncan, and Miller, 1999; Young and Poulin, 1998).

The activities and interviewing behaviors in box 4.1 are some of the ways that practitioners use to facilitate the alliance (Bachelor and Horvath, 1999; Hubble, Duncan, and Miller, 1999; Young and Poulin, 1998).

RELATIONSHIP BUILDING WITH INVOLUNTARY CLIENTS

Relationship building has been discussed thus far with regard to clients who initiate contact with a social worker or who accept a referral and have some interest in seeking help from a professional. Social workers also practice with clients who present as a result of being ordered by a court or pressured

BOX 4.1. ALLIANCE BUILDING: INTERVIEWING ACTIVITIES AND BEHAVIORS

- Elicit the client's expectations and hopes about receiving help, preferred goals to work on, problems to be addressed, and how worker and client will work together.
- Regularly inquire about the client's perceptions and experiences of how the work is progressing: what is helpful, what is not helpful, what is missing, what does the client believe would help? Does the client feel understood? Are the worker and client talking about topics that are important to the client? Does the worker's way of proceeding make sense to the client? The use of structured self-report questionnaires at the end of sessions can facilitate discussion of components of the alliance.
- Be attentive to the client's reactions to what the worker provides in the session, for example, how comments, questions, and suggestions are received.
- Follow up on between-session plans and inquire whether they were carried out and with what effect. If plans were not carried out, explore whether this was a result of alliance factors, such as lack of agreement on tasks.
- When clients request elements in the relationship or in interventions that are possible and appropriate, workers should attempt to meet them. For example, a client who requests that in addition to discussing job seeking the worker also tell him what he should actually say and do can be engaged in role-playing.
- When clients request elements in the relationship or in interventions that are not appropriate workers should discuss this and invite clients to work with them to find alternative possible solutions. For example, when an isolated client asks the worker to go to a movie, rather than only explain that this is not possible the focus can be redirected to how the client can connect with others in their life so that isolation and loneliness are alleviated. It can also be helpful when the worker talks about the "unusual nature" of therapeutic relationships and acknowledges the client's frustration or disappointment with its limits.

by another person to seek help. Social workers in the criminal justice system, child protection, and mental health services frequently work with clients who were ordered to attend a specific intervention program or seek counseling in order to avoid a jail sentence, to gain access to their children, or to leave a mental hospital and live in the community. Interventions can include, for example, anger management groups for abusive men, group and individual programs for alcoholism and drug addiction, regular individual counseling about work adjustment, social relationships, or parenting for young mothers of children in foster care, and rehabilitation programs for persons living in sheltered housing. While not mandated for service by the courts, many clients seek social work services at the behest of others. Some examples are children and adolescents who are referred by a teacher as a result of aggressive behavior in a class or when the teacher has observed some signs of internal distress, employees who are referred about their absenteeism, depression, or suspected alcoholism, partners who believe that counseling will help with the other's mood or behavior in a close relationship, and friends and family who are concerned about an individual's behavior, which they appraise as self-destructive.

The experience of being told by an institution or by an employer, friend, or family member that one is deficient in some way and needs professional help is generally experienced as an attack on self-esteem and self-control. Individuals will have a range of emotional reactions, such as anger, depression, and confusion, and often feel victimized, demoralized, and demeaned. It is a challenge for practitioners to offer the qualities of the relationship discussed in the previous chapter in the face of anger, hostility, or defensiveness. In such circumstances social workers need to simultaneously understand and balance two dimensions: first, how the client experiences and understands his situation and the reasons he is seeing the worker and, second, the nature of the behavior and the way it is a threat to others (Rooney, 2002). A nonjudgmental stance can be achieved by striving to understand the person in his context. In the face of the client's anger and rejection of the worker and the service she is trying to offer, professionals can become defensive and define clients in negative and pejorative ways as "unmotivated" or "resistant." Practitioners' assumptions, judgments, and worldviews may be revealed in these immediate emotional and behavioral reactions to clients who are not cooperative. Ivanoff, Blythe, and Tripodi (1994) recommend that workers reflect on and examine these personal views and how they are manifest in their work with these clients. When court-ordered clients differ from social workers, with respect to poverty, race, and ethnicity, interpersonal differences in privilege and power are exacerbated by the power of larger systems such as the criminal justice system. Structural and systemic discrimination can severely interfere with the worker's ability to be client-centered and humanistic in practice.

Recall the key components of the therapeutic alliance discussed earlier— the emotional bond, agreement on goals, and agreement on tasks. Examining these factors when clients are involuntary reveals the necessity for adapting practice principles to enhance the potency of these components. With respect to creating an emotional bond, some social work scholars have argued that because of the social control aspect of mandated services it is unrealistic to expect clients to engage in a characteristic collaborative and generally positive helping relationship. Rather than aiming for a relationship of trust or openness, they recommend establishing a practical working relationship (Cingolani, 1984; Slonim-Nevo, 1996). Experienced practitioners however, are less pessimistic. For example, Borash (2002), reflecting on twenty-five years of working with court-ordered clients, recommends offering empathy regarding the client's initial reluctance and hostility, as a way to engage and develop a bond. Instead of attempting to deal with denial and other defenses head on he offers comments such as "It must be hard being forced into a program that you don't think you need" (p. 21) and "It sure makes sense to me that you wouldn't take kindly to being forced into a group and that, if you really thought that others were trying to change you, you would resist" (p. 22). Such comments begin to mirror and validate the client's experience and feelings. They slowly build some degree of safety that allows involuntary clients to risk letting down their guard enough to share some of the vulnerability and pain underlying the presenting problems and behaviors.

With respect to achieving agreement about goals to promote the alliance, workers need to address the fact that initially it is not likely that agreement about goals will be present or easily achievable. The client is attending because someone else has ordered or coerced him to attend and has defined the presenting problem. The client's goal may be to find a way to avoid continuing. Or the client may agree that there is a problem, but may not agree that it is the one for which they were referred. For example, an employee referred to the company employee assistance program for absenteeism and counseling about alcohol consumption agrees that absenteeism is a problem but attributes it to stress from an increased workload and a demanding supervisor. There needs to be some period of discussion between the social worker and client where the client has the chance to reflect on the question of goals, weigh the pros and cons of change, and consider whether it is in his own interest to participate in the counseling. Such a discussion may result in a hesitant realization that there is some overlap between the client's desires and the service goals. For example, a male client was ordered by the court, because of domestic violence, to attend an anger management group. Eventually he was able to identify that he wanted less acrimony in his marriage, and if he could learn something in the program that would help him and his wife, then perhaps the group could be useful. The research on working with involuntary clients identifies that when clients acknowledge that changes are in their own best interest the gains made are consolidated more so than when they are made in order to comply with the demands of external agencies or to attain rewards (Rooney, 1992).

The third factor in alliance directs practitioners to work toward achieving agreement on tasks. However, with court-ordered clients there are likely to be many tasks that are not negotiable. The literature recommends that the social worker clarify from the outset her dual role within the system that has mandated the intervention and within the therapeutic activity (Behroozi, 1992; Ivanoff, Blythe, and Tripodi, 1994; Regehr and Antle, 1997; Rooney, 1992). The following should be described: the expectations of the program or service, the role of the worker including her authority and under what circumstances that authority will be exercised, what is expected of the client, time lines and potential consequences, the worker's reporting responsibilities, and limits to confidentiality. Drawing on extensive practice experience, Waldman (1999) introduces the work on tasks by reframing counseling as "providing a podium for clients to tell their stories, to be heard, as well as a space for conversations that may reveal new behaviors" (p. 507) that can be used in future stressful situations to prevent repeated involvement with police and child protection authorities. For female clients she describes therapy as a gift to help them reflect on their lives.

Consistent with the alliance concept with voluntary clients, where aspects of the intervention are negotiable, the worker should strive to involve the involuntary client as fully as possible and inquire about how the client views attending, what he thinks he can gain, what activities make sense to him, and what issues are important to discuss.

ETHICS AND THE SOCIAL WORK RELATIONSHIP

In the discussion of self-disclosure and ethics earlier in this chapter mention was made of the overriding characteristic of ethical professional practice; that the relationship with the client is exclusively for the purpose of addressing the client's needs, not the worker's needs. The following practices assist in maintaining this focus; a structure is set for interviews including their frequency, the meeting takes place in a formal setting, a focus is agreed on, and a set of procedures is used that other professionals would agree reflect contemporary ethical practice principles. Contacts that take place outside the formal setting are consistent with practice in some agencies. For example, social workers in outpatient mental health settings, child protection, intake and community care for the elderly regularly meet clients in their homes. Many agencies expect practitioners to file a schedule of their visits with the office. These visits are consistent with patterns of service delivery in the setting and do not cross a boundary into a friendship relationship. In some situations the client will offer a cup of tea or a cold drink as a sociable and welcoming gesture, and it is appropriate to accept this. Social workers may also meet with clients in informal settings. For example, a social worker has accompanied an upset adolescent to a meeting with the principal at her high school to discuss an alternative plan to expelling the student for poor attendance. After the meeting the social worker might meet with the adolescent to debrief its outcome in a nearby coffee shop. Social workers in medical settings may take a family member to the cafeteria to meet following an upsetting experience with a terminally ill relative. Although these interviews are held in informal settings, their purpose is to assist clients with their immediate emotional needs in a setting that is convenient and also affords enough confidentiality. Regardless of setting, it is useful to bear in mind Murphy and Dillon's (2003) statement that "the clinical relationship, while friendly in tone, is to be maintained as a working one, not as a friendship and not as a prelude to a friendship. Sexual contact between clients and clinicians is strictly prohibited" (p. 248).

BOUNDARY ISSUES

Boundary issues can occur when practitioners face potential conflicts of interest stemming from dual or multiple relationships. Social workers' relationships with clients are based in their roles as helping professionals. Practitioners have a fiduciary relationship to their clients. Fiduciary relationships emanate from the trust that clients must place in professionals because of professional specialized knowledge and the unequal power in the relationship. Dual relationships arise when social workers also assume a second role with clients, such as friend, employer, teacher, business associate, family member, or sex partner (Kagle and Giebelhausen, 1994). While some situations of boundary issues may be unclear, others are not. Reamer (2001) defines boundary violations as follows. "A boundary violation occurs when a practitioner engages in a dual relationship with a client or colleague that is exploitative, manipulative, deceptive, or coercive" (p. 5). Examples of such violations are sexual involvement with current clients, gaining client acceptance for fraudulent billing for reimbursement of services, or influencing clients to provide expensive gifts or include the social worker in their will. These situations put the social worker in a conflict of interest between two roles; the worker's duty to serve the best interests of the client is compromised by serving his own interest in a sexual or business relationship. The code of ethics of professional associations such as the National Association of Social Workers, the Canadian Association of Social Workers, the American Association of Marital and Family Therapists specifically prohibit dual relationships and situations where practitioners are in a conflict of interest that compromises their ability to serve the best interests of their clients. In a study of NASW code violations over ten years Strom-Gott-fried (2000) found that boundary violations account for as much as 56 percent of all ethical complaints.

Less clear are those situations Reamer (2001) calls boundary crossing that are not inherently unethical since they are not exploitative, manipulative, deceptive, or coercive. However, as in the case of self-disclosure, there can be boundary crossings that, while they are expected to be helpful to clients, create unanticipated negative outcomes. These situations are complex, not easily written as regulations, and require thought and consultation. In addition, some behaviors that are helpful to some clients will have a negative affect on others. For example, a female social worker shared personal information about having been sexually harassed at her workplace, a situation similar to the one faced by the client. She revealed that she struggled with the situation on her own and was very fearful to take action. Finally, she filed a formal complaint at her work setting that produced a positive outcome for her. The client became confused with this revelation. Was the worker suggesting that the client do the same? Would she think less of the client if she did not follow through? Why was the worker telling the client such personal information? Did she want to become her friend? However, for another client such a revelation is extremely helpful. She sees that she is not alone and others including the social worker, whom she respects, have dealt with similar situations successfully. The client feels supported through this self-disclosure and empowered to act.

Ethical issues are analyzed in a thoughtful paper by Ringel and Mishna (2005), who argue that students need opportunities in practice classes to openly think through ethical dilemmas they encounter in field practicum cases. Since ethical guidelines are frequently presented in prescriptive terms, they observe that it is difficult for students to raise examples where they were troubled, confused, or

BOX 4.2. PRACTICE PRINCIPLES FOR BUILDING HELPING RELATIONSHIPS

- Develop a climate of trust by offering the qualities of warmth and caring concern, acceptance, positive regard, respect, and a nonjudgmental attitude, genuineness, empathy, and a commitment to understanding and working with diversity. These qualities are associated with providing a secure base.
- Attend to both verbal communication and nonverbal cues to understand the client's experience of the helping relationship. Ultimately it is the client's perceptions that determine whether a facilitative relationship has been created.
- Recognize that client preferences for processes that are helpful vary based on a host of individual personal and cultural factors. Individualize understandings of clients in their personal, cultural, community, and societal contexts. While general knowledge about populations may be useful, it is only through dialogue with individual clients that an understanding of the meaning of general themes in the lives of individuals can be gained.
- Use the helping relationship, when appropriate, as a base to create new internal working models of self, other, and relationships. The professional relationship can provide potent new emotional and cognitive learning experiences.
- Build and maintain a positive alliance through an interactive and collaborative process. The success of the alliance depends upon the degree of congruence between the client's expectations, perceptions, and experience of the process and what client and worker are actually doing together. The partnership is successful when clients feel that they are working toward meeting their goals, in ways that make sense to them, and that they are connected to a helper who is interested and understanding.
- Pay attention to the quality of the alliance between the worker and the client, especially in the initial sessions, and also throughout the work. Workers who individualize their approaches are more likely to achieve positive outcomes.
- Adapt generic principles for practice with involuntary clients. Workers need to be especially clear about all aspects of their dual roles when functioning in both a therapeutic manner and as an authority within a criminal justice system.
- Take into account ethical principles in forming and maintaining professional relationships.

in fact bent the rules. Drawing from student case examples, they discuss ethics related to three situations; gift giving and receiving (when to accept, what types of gifts to accept), flexibility or formality in the treatment frame (whether to meet clients outside the office), and continuing to see clients after termination (especially when termination occurs because the student's practicum ends rather than client's needs having been met). Useful practice guidelines are recommended to assist in thinking through appropriate responses to these ethical dilemmas about boundary issues. With respect to the first issue, gift giving and receiving, students and practitioners are advised to consider the following: what role is played by countertransference factors; the stage of treatment and symbolic meaning of the gift, for example, a modest gift at termination has a different meaning than a lavish gift during a difficult middle stage; the client's cultural background and values whereby a small token at particular times is conventional and would be considered impolite if rejected; gender considerations such that a gift from a male client to a female worker may be a seductive gesture; and the personal meaning of the gift for the client.

With regard to the second issue, flexibility and formality in the treatment frame, Ringel and Mishna (2005) advocate opportunities for discussion and reflection in academic classes, with field instructors, and ultimately in consultation with seasoned professionals to explore the particular challenges and potential gains or difficulties if one agrees to or declines a client's request for extra treatment meetings such as going for lunch, taking a walk together, attending a graduation, wedding, or family celebration. Ethical issues related to termination will be discussed subsequently in chapter 8.

PRACTICE PRINCIPLES FOR BUILDING RELATIONSHIPS

In summary, this review of the concept of relationship in classical and current social work perspectives and from empirical studies in social work, psychotherapy, and psychology all support the enduring notion that the interpersonal connection between the client and the practitioner is a crucial component of practice. New knowledge developed in related fields can be used and adapted when appropriate for social work practice. Students and practitioners value conceptual frameworks that can inform practice and provide an intellectual foundation for guiding the use of interviewing skills. Box 4.2 presents a summary of principles that can assist social workers in forging and maintaining the crucial foundation of practice, the helping alliance or relationship.

TOWARD UNDERSTANDING CHANGE $\Big\}$ 5

GENERIC PRINCIPLES

Key concepts that inform contemporary social work practice were introduced in earlier chapters of this volume and can be briefly summarized as follows. Individuals' lives are intricately linked to their social context, including their social and physical environments. Individuals are diverse along many personal and social identity characteristics including age, gender, sexual orientation, ethnicity, and ability. Either privilege or disadvantage is related to social dimensions such as race, class, and gender and influence individuals' access to power or experiences of oppression. The professional relationship provides the crucial context for change, and it is through a collaborative partnership with clients that help is offered and used. A strengths perspective empowers clients through the use of interventions to address not only presenting issues but also to build clients' capacities to deal with future issues. Principles that address change processes were also introduced; feelings, cognitions, and behavior are intricately intertwined and affect each other. Change efforts need to take into account both persistence of patterns and desire for change.

Before moving to an examination of the processes and principles of helping, specifically the structure, tasks, interventions, and related interviewing skills, it is worthwhile to consider further the dynamics of change in greater depth. What are social workers interested in when we refer to change? How does change come about, both naturally and when individuals are working with a professional? What is it that leads clients to feel that professionals have assisted them in changing their situations, their attitudes, feelings, and behaviors? Even when change is not possible, what transpires in the helping encounter that leads clients to feel supported through times of great stress or loss? A fuller understanding of the subtle and illusive ingredients and processes of change can help us craft more effective professional approaches.

Social work has embraced the ecological-systemic perspective to provide a broad framework for understanding the situations individuals, families, and communities confront (Germain and Bloom, 1999; Hartman, 1994). An understanding or assessment of what constitutes and contributes to a problem should logically lead to identifying what needs to change. Hence the eco-systemic perspective defines the professional territory of social work and assists workers in identifying which systems and relationships should be included in intervention plans.

The focus of change in direct social work practice may be directed to one or the combination of three areas: individual, relational, and environmental. Individual change refers to changes in an individual's thoughts, feelings, behaviors, and includes, for example, changes in aspirations, attitudes, the meanings given to experiences, gaining more knowledge, developing more positive feelings about self, accepting aspects of one's past, and increasing one's capacity to bring about change in one's own life. Such changes may lead to individuals developing different adaptive styles that leave them more resilient to cope with further challenges.

Relational change refers to changes in significant relationships such as those with intimate partners, family members, close personal friends, and colleagues and employers. It can include, for example, changes in the way individuals within the relationship communicate, handle conflicts, and gain satisfaction. A change in relationships generally requires involvement of all key participants in counseling. In some instances only one individual is willing to attend counseling. A focus on the interaction patterns the client is caught up with or contributing to can still be productive.

Environmental change refers to changes in circumstances or resources in an individual's environment that have a significant effect on well-being and social functioning. It can include, for example, gaining better housing, moving to a neighborhood with a greater sense of community cohesion and resources to support child development, or changing employment to work with a productive and affirming team. Environmental changes may result from planned and direct intervention or occur by chance. For example, a new neighbor may suggest that she and the client take turns babysitting for each other's children. This in turn may provide a young couple with the needed, but previously unaffordable, break from constant child care and the opportunity to spend some time together as a couple. Social workers also practice with highly vulnerable client populations where the goal is to help clients live in the community rather than in institutions. Stability, rather than change, in individual functioning and surrounding supports is the aim. For example, when working with an individual who has a chronic and severe mental illness goals may include regular visits with the health care practitioner, compliance with a medication regime, stable relationships with the staff in a group home, healthy nutrition, and attendance at a social club. A clinical case management approach that includes environmental intervention and counseling for the client is recommended (Walsh, 2000). This approach is discussed in greater detail in chapter 7.

When examining the dynamics of change processes the eco-systemic perspective does not provide a well-articulated understanding of how change is actually brought about. Instead, since the earliest days of the social work profession, practitioners have developed a number of general practice principles to guide change efforts. These principles reflect ideas about change derived from humanistic values, beliefs about the human condition, and insights emanating from practice experience. These principles are described in widely used texts such as Compton and Galaway (1999), Hepworth, Rooney, and Larsen (2002), Murphy and Dillon (2003), and Sheafor, Horejsi, and Horejsi (1997). Representative of practice wisdom are principles such as start where the client is, go at the pace of the client, value self-determination of the client, support growth and development, provide an accepting, nonjudgmental relationship as the basis for helping, and intervene to change social and economic factors in the client's environment that affect well-being.

SPECIALIZED MODELS

A range of specialized theories and models provides particular explanations of human and social function and dysfunction which in turn serve as the underlying rationale for a series of change processes. Some of these models are exclusive to social work and others were developed in related human service professions such as psychology and psychiatry. Clinical social workers have found some of these models helpful and have incorporated them in professional literature and practice. While there are hundreds of specialized models, both Brandell (1997) and Turner (1996) present a selection of approaches that social workers have embraced.

Key theoretical concepts that have had the greatest impact on practice were referred to in chapter 2. For example, practice with individuals has been influenced by concepts from psychodynamic theory and its contemporary developments in object relations theory (Fairbairn, 1952; Greenberg and Mitchell, 1983; Klein, 1964; Winnicott, 1965), self psychology theory (Kohut, 1971, 1977, 1984; Wolf, 1988) and intersubjectivity theory (Atwood and Stolorow, 1984; Orange, 1995; Orange, Atwood, and Stolorow, 1997). From psychology social workers have been influenced by humanistic and experiential therapy (Carkhuff, 1993; Rogers, 1951), behavior theory and therapy (Bandura, 1986) and cognitive theory and therapy (Beck, 1995). Feminist theory and therapy (Jordan, 1997; Jordan et al., 1991) has strongly influenced many social work practitioners. Similarly family systems theory and therapy (see Nichols and Schwartz, 2001 for a review of family therapy models) has had great appeal for social workers engaged with family problems focused on children and adolescents as well as adult difficulties. More recently solution-focused therapy (De-Jong and Berg, 1998; De Shezar, 1985) and narrative and postmodern theory and therapy (White and Epston, 1990) have been of interest to social workers. Social work theorists have also developed unique models such as the problem-solving approach (Perlman, 1957), psychosocial therapy (Hollis, 1964), task-centered casework (Reid and Epstein, 1972), crisis intervention (Parad, 1965; Roberts, 2000), the life model of practice (Germain and Gitterman, 1996), a strengths approach (Saleeby, 2002a, b), and an empowerment approach (Gutierrez, Parsons, and Cox, 1998).

Specialized approaches or models provide a particular way of understanding human and social functioning and of defining problems or difficulties. Each model rests on a set of concepts about two dimensions: 1) a view of function and dysfunction and 2) a view of change. Models vary in the degree to which concepts of function and dysfunction are explicated and the degree of empirical support available to support these concepts. Models also vary in the degree to which the understanding about how to bring about change is translated into principles and techniques. Some models provide abstract discussion about principles with the expectation that practitioners will find their own ways to enact these principles and meet clients' unique needs. Other models provide specific guidelines and techniques, which may be found in treatment manuals.

Proponents of each model make claims about its effectiveness, and in some cases an impressive body of empirical findings is available to support those conclusions. Social workers are advised to investigate the specific body of literature to determine the extent to which the context, sample, and methodology of a study warrants confidence in its conclusions and whether the findings can be generalized to social work situations. It is now well recognized that there are many ways of achieving the same objective and a range of approaches may be useful to bring about desired outcomes.

While most texts present models as if they are separate and discrete, as discussed in chapter 1, in actual practice concepts, principles, and techniques from a variety of approaches are generally integrated into a professional style over time. Few practitioners are purists adhering to only one model. Practitioners' styles reflect their preferences, the clients they serve, the results they have obtained from using various models, and the agency mandate. The ITP Loop Model, introduced in chapter 1, provides a systematic approach to review, reflect, and recall the links between the conceptual frameworks and personal attitudes that students and practitioners bring to their work. When engaged in tracing the origins of interventions used, practitioners often comment on the eclectic nature of their work. For example, while a practitioner may espouse a strengths approach, an analysis of her interviewing techniques may reveal her affinity for emotionally focused work, associated with humanistic client-centered theory and psychodynamic approaches. In addition, techniques of different models often appear similar when used in practice.

The fact that many practitioners have an eclectic approach is supported by the findings of a study about social workers' use of theory. In a national study of a random sample of experienced clinical social workers respondents reported that they use an average of eight theoretical formulations in their practice (Timberlake, Sabatino, and Martin, 1997). The choice of approach was accounted for by the interplay of the nature of the client's problem, the targets of intervention, and the time frame available for work.

STUDIES OF SOCIAL WORK PRACTICE

The debate about the superiority of models was introduced in chapter 1. Recall that there is considerable empirical evidence from studies of counseling and psychotherapy to support the conclusion that common factors appear to account for change across models studied, such as psychodynamic, cognitive-behavioral, and humanistic (Bergin and Garfield, 1994; Hubble, Duncan, and Miller, 1999b; Norcross, 2002; Wampold, 2001). Unfortunately, there have not been extensive studies of practice models developed in social work to determine their effectiveness, nor have there been the meta-analytic work and systematic reviews of studies that yield general principles and practice guidelines that are useful for practitioners (Gambrill, 1999; Rosen, Proctor, and Staudt, 2003; Thyer, 2000). Social work scholars have distinguished themselves in developing value-based theories and interventions that honor and empower individual clients. Only recently, especially in the past decade, are social work researchers increasingly testing intervention programs and conducting reviews of these studies with the aim of arriving at a data base that can produce guidelines for practice. For example, Reid and Fortune (2003) conducted a systematic review and analysis of empirically tested social work intervention programs in direct practice with client systems. Programs reviewed were those that aimed at change or alleviation of problems in clients' circumstances and met research methodological criteria. Of the 107 studies reviewed, group programs accounted for the majority (59 percent), with individual intervention used in 20 percent, family used in 9 percent, and mixed methods in the remainder. The authors also examined problem areas and interventions used and concluded that two distinct types of effective programs could be identified. The more prevalent type was the group modality and consisted of structured cognitive-behavioral interventions that used skills training, education, and group processes. The second type was mainly individual in focus and resembled a case management approach with concrete services and use of relationship. Reid and Fortune (2003) conclude that there now exists a number of studies that could be helpful in building practice guidelines. They note, however, that these studies do not reflect "the world of everyday practice [where] one finds considerable attention to any number of approaches that one finds little of in these tested programs—for example, generalist, ecological, solution-focused, and psychodynamic" (p. 70). Furthermore, they observe that while the majority of studies were about group interventions, the great majority of social work practice is conducted in an individual format. In the absence of an extensive body of knowledge about change generated in social work, practitioners must turn to information derived from studies in related fields.

UNDERSTANDING CHANGE FROM THE CLIENT'S PERSPECTIVE

The social work literature on client motivation often presents clients as either motivated or unmotivated and provides techniques for increasing the client's interest in participating in the process (Gold, 1990; Hepworth, Rooney, and Larsen, 2002). This characterization obscures the fact that embarking on a change process is complex. It is not unusual for people seeking help to have mixed feelings and motivations about change. While an individual's troublesome behavior and painful situations may cause great distress, the familiar may be more comfortable than the unknown and one may conclude that change is not possible or necessary as a result. Although the client may begin with the intention and expectation of change, both internal and external factors may mitigate against it. Change is strange and may involve loss. Skilled practitioners respect the anxiety and ambivalence that people face when confronted with their own self-defeating behavior. Many individuals experience fear and despair when they consider change in an interpersonal relationship, even one that causes great difficulty and pain. Furthermore, as noted in chapter 4, when clients are referred or mandated by others for service, they may not share the view that they need to change. In order to engage these clients, social workers search for ways of working collaboratively to find goals meaningful to the individual and consistent with the court order.

Understanding the processes that individuals go through as they change thoughts, feelings, and behaviors can provide practitioners with more complex ways of thinking about concepts such as motivation, resistance, and ambivalence. The extensive work of Prochaska and his colleagues (Prochaska, 1995, 1999; Prochaska, DiClemente, and Norcross, 1992) is useful to social workers since these researchers provide fresh insights for a theory of change and its implications for practice. For over twenty years Prochaska has studied more than three thousand individuals, some of whom were receiving therapy and others who were engaged in change on their own. Individuals in the studies were dealing with problems such as depression, marital discord, eating disorders, smoking, alcoholism, and compliance with child protection requirements. Regardless of familial and cultural background, the problem faced, or whether or not they were receiving professional help, the researchers identified six stages of change through which individuals progressed. These stages reflect different and progressive attitudes and behaviors over time about the presenting problem and about change.

An understanding of the stage in which the individual client is with regard to change can guide practice. Social workers can use helping processes, practice principles, interventions, and interviewing skills that are matched to helping the person progress through the stages. This perspective is more likely to increase participation than one that labels the individual as noncooperative, hostile, or resistant. These stages are labeled as follows: precontemplation, contemplation, preparation, action, maintenance, and termination.

BOX 5.1: STAGES OF CHANGE

STAGES OF CHANGE
- Precontemplation
- Contemplation
- Preparation
- Action
- Maintenance
- Termination

Prochaska, DiClemente, and Norcross 1992

Precontemplation. In this stage the individual does not intend to change the problematic behavior in the near future (for example, in the next six months). A number of reasons may account for this position. The individual may lack awareness that a problem exists or may not appreciate the consequences of his behavior for himself or others. For example, many couples present for couple therapy reporting a long period in which one party has identified a problem and was unable to gain the attention and agreement of the other that a concern was serious enough to warrant professional help. When individuals have tried to change on their own and have not been successful, they may feel defeated about the prospect of another attempt. For example, individuals faced with an addiction often have tried numerous treatment programs and still find themselves struggling to curtail their use of alcohol, drugs, or tobacco. Weight loss efforts are the same. Prochaska (1999) observes that people who go into therapy at this stage often do so because of environmental pressures. For example, external pressure can come from a marital partner who threatens to leave unless the spouse seeks counseling, an employer who makes continued employment contingent on cessation of alcohol consumption, or a court order that requires a previously volatile and threatening father to enter therapy before access to his children will be permitted.

Practitioners are advised to recognize that, despite attending a first session, the client may be in the precontemplation stage. It is important to assess the client's stage of readiness to change before assuming that discussing an action plan is in order. Direct questions that address the client's readiness for change can be useful. In the first session the social worker can inquire whether the individual thinks that any of his behaviors are a problem and when he intends to change those actions. Hubble, Duncan, and Miller (1999a) recommend "creating a climate in the interview where the client can consider, explore, and appreciate the benefits of changing" (p. 430). Observations and interpretations that gently raise awareness of difficulties are also recommended as an appropriate intervention at this stage (Lebow, 2002). The social worker can help the client become aware of the factors impinging on the problem and both the potential positive and potential negative consequences of change. It is not productive at this stage to provide a lot of information since the client is not ready to absorb it. A reasonable outcome of this stage occurs when the individual begins, albeit in a hesitant manner, to consider and express that perhaps change may be desirable.

Contemplation. Individuals in this stage state that they intend to change within the next six months. At this point people are more aware of the positives of changing, but also conscious of the drawbacks, the efforts and energy required. Ambivalence is characteristic here, and "yes, but" (Hubble, Duncan, and Miller 1999a, p. 414) is a frequent response. Moving back and forth in thinking about and planning to take some action is prevalent. Practitioners need to be patient and support the client as he considers the pros and cons of making a change. For example, practitioners who work with women living in abusive and destructive relationships are aware of the huge emotional, social, and financial costs as well as the potential benefits to women who separate from abusive partners. They understand that many women will need a protracted period of time in which to consider whether leaving or staying in the relationship is best for them.

A patient and supportive stance may be difficult for the social worker to maintain in settings that are limited to providing short-term contacts. However, when practitioners pressure the client to prematurely undertake an action plan it is likely that there is little follow-through on action steps or there is a rupture in the alliance and the client drops out and stops attending sessions. Prochaska (1999) recommends setting realistic goals such as helping individuals move out of a "stuck place" (p. 252). This can be accomplished through exploring both sides of the ambivalence, the positives to be gained from changing as well as the negatives, fears, and catastrophic expectations. Practitioners can offer a "space and place" where, through reflection and discussion, individuals sort out conflicting and competing motivations, wishes, and concerns.

Preparation. At this point the individual is intending to take some action, usually in the next month. Some small changes in behavior and thinking may be reported, along with some sporadic change efforts. Applying the stage model to working with families where there has been child abuse and neglect, Prochaska and Prochaska (2002) give examples such as parents in this stage declaring, "I have questions for my caseworker about taking care of my kids" ... "If I don't change, I will never be the kind of parent my children need" (p. 380). In comparison, when in the precontemplation stage these parents denied they had any responsibility for the presence of the child welfare authorities in their lives and resented their intrusion. In the contemplation phase these parents began to acknowledge they had a problem and needed to work on it.

If in the preparation phase the developing plan includes seeking professional help, the individual is now likely to be amenable to short-term intervention. It is at this point that the individual can be seen as a client or consumer of service. The practitioner can utilize the principles of preliminary joint planning, discussed in greater detail in the next chapter, to involve and engage the client. Some activities are identifying general and specific goals and determining the focus for change—the individual, the environment, or both. A crucial aspect of building a helping relationship at this point is reaching agreement about the tasks and expectations of both worker and client. Ambivalence is still a feature in this stage, and it is helpful for practitioners to point out the client's strengths and previous change efforts that have worked. Consistent with a collaborative approach, clients can be actively involved in choosing strategies through examining alternatives and considering their potential impact.

Action. In this phase the client is committed to change and is focused on taking action to alter his behavior, his environment, or the relationship between the two in order to modify the problematic issues. This stage matches with action-oriented intervention models that specify tasks for the client to achieve. (Processes and tasks of the middle stages are discussed in detail in chapter 7.) As observed earlier, change is difficult and can stir up ambivalence. Therefore this phase can be challenging and requires persistence and tenacity on the part of the client and support and encouragement from the practitioner.

Stage theories are presented in a linear fashion for purposes of explication. To better reflect actual experience, stages are conceived of as a spiral with movement forward and backward (Prochaska and Prochaska, 2002). The colloquial expression "two steps forward and one step backward" captures this phenomenon. Since fluctuation and uneven progress is a common feature of change efforts, it is useful when practitioners normalize this experience even before it occurs. When individuals experience difficulty maintaining progress, they may feel a range of emotions from anger, to embarrassment, to guilt and may become demoralized and lose hope in change efforts. An understanding and sustaining professional relationship remains crucial at this point.

Maintenance. In this stage the focus is on consolidating gains and building on strengths and successes. Meetings with the practitioner are less frequent and a longer time span between sessions helps the client evaluate whether new behaviors and attitudes are easily maintained in everyday life or whether particular strategies need to be further developed. In the interests of building the client's capacity to deal with future issues when counseling is terminated, this phase also includes developing relapse prevention approaches. For example, the client can be helped to anticipate what he can do differently in the future when experiencing environmental, social, health, or emotional pressures and distress.

Termination. At this point individuals no longer have any thought of engaging in the problem behavior that was the initial focus of change. They feel enough confidence that the changes that have been made are permanent and will not reoccur even when confronted with environmental and personal stressors. From his studies Prochaska (1999) found that only 20 percent of individuals who formerly abused alcohol or smoked were in this stage. He suggests that for many people the stage of maintenance may be more realistic. In the maintenance stage there is a continuous awareness of threats to retaining new adaptations and a conscious attempt to use new thoughts, behaviors, and supports to maintain these changes.

An understanding of stages in change from the client's perspective provides insights into an important dynamic that can affect outcome. Many models provide principles and techniques directly aimed at changing presenting and underlying problems. Less explicit attention is given to underlying, implicit, and potent dynamics about how the client perceives the need to change and the experience of trying, failing, and attempting to try again. Prochaska's work illuminates these dynamics and provides invaluable guidelines for practice. Box 5.2 summarizes practice principles suggested by Prochaska and Prochaska (2002) emanating from this body of knowledge.

Currently, in most social work and mental health settings the amount of time available for the client and practitioner to work together is dependent on the funding formula as expressed in agency policy. This contextual variable presents the most difficult challenge for practitioners, as most models have been conceptualized as if the client's needs and pace were the major determinant of the duration of the intervention—not the administrative arrangements with funders. Change generally does not happen quickly. More usually it is slow, with small steps taken. In a study that explored clients' perceptions of the change process, respondents reported that change was not associated with any clear or dramatic event in or out of the session. Rather change was perceived as incremental and gradual, with small, significant experiences (Christensen et al., 1998). The gap between what is known about how the change process actually evolves and what service systems will provide creates one of the tensions that bear on contemporary professional practice. In this context the need is great to define efficient and effective approaches.

COMMON FACTORS

The common factors phenomenon has already been referred to in chapter 2 in the discussion on evaluating progress and in chapter 4 in the discussion of the therapeutic alliance. To recapitulate, meta-analysis of outcome studies in counseling and psychotherapy has led a number of researchers to observe that outcomes are generally similar across the range of intervention models. Therefore, researchers argue that there must be factors common to all models that account for change rather than the specific activities of discrete approaches (Bergin and Garfield, 1994; Hubble, Duncan, and Miller, 1999b; Lambert, 1992; Wampold, 2001). These various conceptualizations of those common factors have been offered and are summarized in the following discussion. Readers can refer to the following for further elaboration of the factors: Frank and Frank (1991), Grencavage and Norcross (1990), Hubble, Duncan, and Miller (1999b), and Wampold (2001).

CLIENT AND EXTRATHERAPEUTIC FACTORS

Client and extratherapeutic factors refers to characteristics of the client or the client's social situation and environment that support the ability of an intervention to achieve its goals. That is, they are factors beyond the activities in the interview. Client factors refer to strengths of the client, for example, individual personality, including cognitive and appraisal skills, defenses and coping mechanisms, resilience, and temperamental and dispositional factors. The client's interpersonal skills and the capacity to give and take in interpersonal relationships, the ability to talk about a situation with another, and the ability to identify a specific area to work on are also important contributions brought by the client. Outcomes are also affected by individual and family history and development, the presence and impact of stress and trauma, and the severity and history of a problem or condition. For example, where there is long-standing addiction, persistent mental illness, or a history of severe childhood abuse these conditions will significantly affect the individual's growth and personality development, ability to achieve satisfying interpersonal relationships, and general well-being.

Extratherapeutic factors also refers to the client's social situation and environmental factors that can positively or negatively affect the impact of the professional help being provided. Lambert's (1992) interesting finding that these client and extratherapeutic factors account for 40 percent of the variance in outcome provides strong empirical support for the importance social work practice theory has always accorded to understanding and intervening in the environment. In both assessment and intervention attention is paid to three elements: (1) the client, (2) the relevant social environment, including family, friends, neighborhood, community, organizations, informal and formal networks and social supports, and work colleagues, and (3) the transactions between the two. These elements constitute the extratherapeutic factors that could be enhanced, supported, or brought into the intervention plan to facilitate the client's progress. Conversely, where the client experiences these relationships as exploitative, undermining, or troublesome the focus may then be to help the client separate from these systems.

THE HELPING RELATIONSHIP

The helping relationship refers to a relationship with a professional where it is expected that the client will self-disclose or confide important information and that the practitioner's involvement is for the benefit of the client. As elaborated in chapters 3 and 4, the relationship consists of a number of attributes; an empathic and available practitioner, a sense of emotional bonding between client and worker, and agreement on goals and tasks. Lambert (1992) found that 30 percent of the variance in outcome across models was accounted for by relationship factors. Other meta-analyses found a moderately strong relationship between the alliance and outcome in psychotherapy (Horvath and Symonds, 1991; Lambert and Barley, 2002; Martin, Garske, and Davis, 2000). The characteristics of these relationships mirror those described in the social work literature and include "caring, empathy, warmth, acceptance, mutual affirmation, and encouragement of risk taking and mastery" (Hubble, Duncan, and Miller, 1999b, p. 9).

The context of the helping relationship refers to the environment in which the professional activity takes place and that it is a setting viewed as responsible for providing helpful services (Frank and Frank, 1991). The nature of the institution confers an expectation that the work of individual practitioners with their clients will be productive. This notion fits well with practice in settings such as mental health clinics, family service agencies, and community settings that specialize in serving populations with particular issues. It does not fit with services that are mandated. Clients may initially perceive these institutions as intrusive, threatening, and with the power to remove their children or incarcerate the individual. Hence, this positive common factor, while applicable in many counseling encounters, is compromised in mandated social work services. As a result social workers must focus on developing the other significant factors to counterbalance the negative impact of court-ordered counseling.

BELIEF OR HOPE

Belief or hope refers to the client's expectation that the helping process and interventions offered will be effective and bring about change or at least provide some support or relief. When the client believes that the practitioner knows how to help and that the methods will work, there is a potent impact on change outcomes. In other words, the client experiences the helping process as credible and expects to gain something of value from it. This concept resonates with previous discussions in this text about the importance of understanding the client's worldview and beliefs about the problem situation and what is needed to bring about change. Especially when working in situations of diversity, if the client believes that the approach offered is deficient, foolish, or lacking an important component, then the factor of hope and confidence will be absent. The practitioner must also have a belief that the intervention he is providing is based on a rationale and is likely to be effective. A rationale provides an intellectual base to guide practice. A belief in the work can serve as an important aspect of self care as it provides a foundation that may protect practitioners from being overwhelmed, confused, and disheartened when confronted with the vicissitudes of practice. Of course, convictions and beliefs about the effectiveness of interventions should not be held so rigidly that alternate approaches are not tried when there is a lack of progress. Finally, it is likely that the development and maintenance of hope, belief, and expectation operates in concert with the alliance; as the work yields positive results confidence in the practitioner develops and both client and worker become more optimistic about making more progress.

PROCEDURES AND TECHNIQUES

Procedures and techniques emanate from the explanatory concepts and intervention methods associated with specialized practice approaches. Techniques provide the link between the concepts in the model and the actions and stance the practitioner should take in the actual work to bring about change. While the central point of the common factors analysis is that generally all models are effective, specialized models and their related procedures or processes are still viewed as playing a significant role. Procedures and techniques provide practitioners with a coherent framework that includes a rationale for their work based on ways of understanding human functioning and problems, processes for bringing about change or offering relief, and skills or techniques for bringing about that change. Procedures provide structure, focus, and a plan for the work, dimensions that have been shown to be important for a positive outcome (Mohl, 1995).

Some have suggested that models can be thought of as healing rituals. According to Jerome Frank, an early proponent of the common factors approach, "the success of all techniques depends on the patient's sense of alliance with an actual or symbolic healer" (Frank and Frank, 1991, p. xv). Hence technique is important, as it supports the working relationship and the expectation that the practitioner has special knowledge and is able to provide something of value to the client. Wampold (2001) elaborates on this idea stating that practitioners need to know and use specific techniques while remembering that "it is the healing context and the meaning that the client gives to the experience that are important" (p. 219). This explanation supports the importance of indigenous knowledge and healing practices in ethnocultural and religious communities.

Hubble, Duncan, and Miller (1999b) argue that models and techniques are useful insofar as they enhance the common factors that lead to change, the strengths and resources in clients and their environments, the relationship between client and worker, and the client's hope and expectation that the work together will result in a positive change. They conclude that clients are best served when the model chosen fits with the client's view of why there is a problem and how problems are changed, builds on and utilizes client strengths, and fits with the client's goals, hopes, and expectations.

This theme, that the approach used needs to make sense to the client and fit with her view of why there is a problem and what is needed to bring about change, has been presented earlier in this book. This point was stressed when discussing how diversity is taken into account; practitioners cannot assume that the client's worldview is similar to their own. They need to learn about the client's explanatory models and try to select approaches that are compatible with that view. Recall also the discussion of the therapeutic alliance in chapter 4 and the importance of agreement on tasks between the client and practitioner. The implication for practice is that since there are numerous models, practitioners are well equipped if they are relatively comfortable with a number of approaches rather than rigid adherents of only one. In discussion with their clients practitioners can both explore clients' explanations and expectations and explain their preferred ways of working. Where possible the model selected should be in some accord with the client's expectations and views. For example, some clients want to learn strategies for dealing with conflict in interpersonal relationships and will respond well to a behavioral approach. Others will believe that this approach is superficial and does not address the "real heart of the issue," which may be defined as stemming from old issues in the family of origin. With this belief a more exploratory model that links past and present phenomena would better match the client's view.

Practitioners who pay attention to the client's reaction to the approach used can consider whether procedures from other models should be included to supplement what is being offered. If the approach chosen is clearly not producing desired movement, thought needs to be given to whether other approaches should be tried as well or instead. This is the activity referred to earlier as reflection to evaluate the impact of the work. Through reviewing and planning with the client, collaboration is furthered when both client and therapist actively find ways of working together. In some instances collaboration is not made explicit in the communication that exists but still operates as one of the therapeutic ingredients or enablers. For many practitioners, however, making the process more explicit is seen as beneficial as it models communication and negotiation and clients can transfer skills to extratherapeutic important relationships.

STRENGTHS

In part as a reaction to the focus on dysfunction, disorder, and pathology, an approach to social work has developed that directs attention to resilience, competence, creativity, and the human capacity to overcome adversity. This philosophical and practice stance in social work is well articulated by Saleeby (1992):

> Individuals have survived.... They have taken steps, summed up resources, and coped. We need to know what they have done, how they have done it, what they have learned from doing it, what resources (inner and outer) were available in their struggle to surmount their troubles. People are always working on their situations, even if just deciding to be resigned to them; as helpers we must tap into that work, elucidate it, find and build on its possibilities. (pp. 171–172)

The importance of the client's strengths and contributions in achieving goals receives empirical support from Lambert's (1992) conclusion that client variables and extratherapeutic influences account for as much as 40 percent of improvement.

How do we understand the way in which client characteristics and strengths operate in the helping process to produce change? Collaboration between worker and client is emerging as a common value and principle in contemporary practice theory across philosophies and models. Such a stance recognizes that change comes about through a partnership between client and worker. A strengths perspective goes even further and views the client as the primary force of change and the professional as facilitator. Through supporting the client's efforts and providing focus in the discussion, the client's personal agency or self-healing efforts and abilities are elicited. In this formulation

> the relationship is helpful because it provides a safe, sheltered "space" in which clients can take a deep breath, consider their problems in context, brainstorm with another person, gain perspective, examine their "bad sides," make mistakes, generate new alternatives, re-experience old wounds and problematic issues, think, analyze, recover the strength to reconfront life, and try new behaviors. In all, the relationship provides a supportive structure within which clients' generative, self-healing capacities can optimally operate. (Tallman and Bohart, 1999, p. 102)

Recall that in the discussion of relationship and the impact of empathy offered by the social worker what was crucial was the way in which the client experienced the comments and attitudes of the professional. Similarly, the client's ability to take from the process that which may be helpful to him affects whether he perceives the encounter as useful. While the practitioner may intend an intervention to aim at changing behavior, the client might experience the interest and attention to his behavior as the important ingredient. In a study where clients were asked to discuss what had been helpful in the interventions received, respondents noted that suggestions offered by the practitioner were rarely followed. However, participants commented that the worker's advice stimulated them to think about possible actions, which helped them come up with their own solutions (Gehart-Brooks and Lyle, 1998). Therefore, it is useful to view the worker as a process expert and catalyst, one who can provide the opportunity, stimulation, and support to the client to mobilize and channel his own capacities to deal with or solve problems, take new risks, gain greater understanding, and make changes in his life. This point is consistent with the essence of Prochaska's (1995; 1999) conceptualization of stages of change, discussed earlier. Since individuals go through stages on their own to bring about change, when receiving professional help this self-change process should be taken into account. Searching for, honoring, and accentuating client strengths, along with increasing collaboration between the client and practitioner, means that part of the role of the professional may be seen as one of coach.

A strengths perspective ensures that in the assessment phase attention will focus not only on problems, needs, and gaps but will also include a search for examples of successful coping and of instances where the client gained successful mastery over a troubling situation. A strengths perspective should not be equated with giving the client a false and inflated view of self or communicating naive possibilities through "positive thinking." Rather, by eliciting information from the client about experiences where he was able to deal with a situation effectively, both participants have a common, specific, articulated understanding of the client's actual past successes. The worker then focuses on how he can help the client harness and amplify these internal strengths and resources to deal with the current situation at hand. The question becomes, how can the client's own resilience, ability, and competence be brought into the present and what role can the worker play to assist in that process?

Many authors have pointed out that change is to some extent a naturally occurring phenomenon and that professional help is only one factor in facilitating it (Hubble, Duncan, and Miller, 1999b; Prochaska, DiClemente, and Norcross 1992). This observation has implications for practice. Specifically, professionals do well to have a change focus, to inquire about changes that have occurred prior to the first meeting with the worker and to regularly inquire about change that occurs between meetings. When plans, tasks, or homework are agreed upon, it is important to follow up in the next meeting with a full exploration of the change and to specifically highlight the ways in which the client brought about that change. This is the essence of capacity building and empowerment, helping the client to recognize and use her ability and recognize her agency and power. When individuals recognize that they have the capacity to have an impact on their lives and their environments, they gain in self-esteem. They also see that whatever they were able to do in this instance they can do in other situations. It appears to be a corollary of human experience (Bowlby, 1988) that when insights such as these occur in the context of a caring relationship they are more easily internalized and can change an individual's self-concept.

Notions about change are incorporated in practitioners' thinking as they proceed to work with clients on a short- or long-term basis. At times the ideas presented thus far will fit well with the client's presentation and lead the social worker to feel confident about what is being offered and what is being achieved. There will also be other instances when the goodness-of-fit between change theories and the actual experience in practice is incongruent. It is from these exceptions that new ideas about the dynamics of change and the helping process are generated. When traditional notions do not serve us well in practice we are driven to create new understandings.

The following discussion about stages in the helping process was originally articulated in the social work literature before the more recent empirical findings about change, presented above, had been disseminated. These new empirical findings provide support for the stages and their related processes and tasks and increase our confidence in social work's repertoire of helping procedures.

STAGES IN THE HELPING PROCESS

Across most practice models the helping process is conceived of as one that is systematic and proceeds through stages, also referred to as phases. That is, the interaction between worker and client is not haphazard or random. The achievement of goals is the aim of the professional encounter. Hence, the dialogue and tasks undertaken are done so with a purpose. The stages and associated activities provide structure, direction, or guidelines in this regard.

As noted earlier, structure, focus, and a plan contribute to positive outcomes for clients (Mohl, 1995) and provide practitioners with an organized way to be intentional and purposeful in their practice.

Definitions and tasks of each stage vary according to specific models. However, social work practice texts generally group phases and tasks into preparatory, initial, middle, and end stages (Compton and Galaway, 1999; Hepworth, Rooney, and Larsen, 2002; Sheafor, Horejsi, and Horejsi, 1997). Box 5.3 presents these stages and their associated tasks.

All professional encounters are organized around a purpose and set of tasks. At the same time, and usually through the same behaviors, the social worker and client relate to each other interpersonally. The term *process* is frequently used to refer to the ways in which the participants interact as they work on the tasks and discuss the content or substance of the work. This includes underlying or covert messages that are inferred from verbal and nonverbal communication or may be observed from the way in which each person is behaving. All inferences are only educated guesses or hypotheses and ultimately can only be verified if examined and discussed.

Throughout all the stages these two threads are operating in concert: 1) building and sustaining a collaborative relationship and 2) working on task or content toward achieving goals. The two themes are interwoven, each affecting the other in a progressive and reciprocal manner. For example, as the client develops increasing confidence in the worker's interest and ability to help he may become more open and able to try behaviors previously experienced as too threatening. Conversely, if the client experiences the discussion in the sessions as irrelevant to his concerns, he may view the worker as not really listening or understanding and hence not interested in him. Practitioners pay close attention to both themes throughout all stages. The themes are artificially separated for the purpose of presentation in this chapter. In practice they both proceed at the same time.

Particular intellectual concepts inform each stage and the tasks, activities, and processes chosen reflect the practitioner's thoughts about what is necessary at specific points in time to bring about change. In discussing how professional knowledge is used by social workers, in chapter 2, the activity of linkage was introduced. Linkage refers to the way social workers identify and label knowledge that can potentially explain the practice situation and provide directions for intervention. For example, using concepts and practice principles about building a working alliance in the early stage of practice the social worker will actively focus on relationship development through listening attentively to the client, trying to convey a beginning understanding of what is being said, and exploring what the client expects from the social worker. Similarly, understanding formulations about stages of change, the social worker will try to determine what stage the client is in before moving on to joint planning and action strategies. Since the task of the early stage is developing understandings of the practice situation, various theories of human behavior and the social environment may be used interchangeably to develop potential ways of addressing the questions what is the issue, what is the nature of the client's situation, and why is there a problem at this time. In the middle phase, when the emphasis is on active helping and change, practice principles and models that offer change strategies are more likely to be used in linkage to provide direction for the practitioner's next responses.

Different skill sets are needed at different stages in the process. For example, in the early phase the worker may use more reflective listening, questions, clarification, and validation. In the middle phase skills such as exploring meanings and feelings in depth and challenging assumptions and beliefs may be more prevalent. The tasks of each stage provide focus for the work. Through differential use of interviewing skills practitioners maintain this focus. The following chapters will examine all phases and the primary interviewing skills associated with each.

While this discussion might suggest that there is an orderly progression through stages, in fact the helping process is more accurately viewed as iterative. That is, activities are generally not fully accomplished at one time. They are repeated through subsequent discussions, yielding increased understanding as issues are explored in greater depth. For example, information gathering and arriving at shared understandings of the issues is characteristic of the early stage of the work. However, as the client comes to know the worker better and to develop some trust in the safety and support offered in the relationship, the client is more likely to confide and share important information that was initially withheld. This new information may change the way in which intervention proceeds. Furthermore, through in-depth exploration, characteristic of the middle phase, new insights may emerge that will affect the earlier agreements about the goals and the direction of the work. It is useful then to view the stages as overlapping, spiraling, or cycling back and forth. A notion of stages can provide structure, focus, and guidelines; at the same time, it is important to remember that the helping process is fluid and flexible.

An understanding of the purposes and tasks of each phase provides this structure and direction. Practitioners can then use interviewing skills and techniques in an intentional manner to achieve the specific goals of each stage. The following chapters will present the purposes and tasks of each stage. Finally, the last section of the text will present interview skills and strategies for change.

Part II } THE PROCESS OF HELPING IN SOCIAL WORK PRACTICE

$\left\{6\right.$

THE BEGINNING STAGE

A professional practice is purposeful, goal oriented, and systematic. The worker's behavior is intentional, as she aims to achieve particular objectives. The beginning phase sets the stage for the subsequent work, and first encounters have a significant impact on the client's decision to continue to seek the services of the agency. The aim of the beginning stage is to develop a working relationship with the client and enough shared understanding, or an agreed-upon assessment, that initial planning and goal setting can occur. To achieve these aims the worker strives to provide a comfortable and welcoming environment so that the client can begin to share the salient aspects of the situation that he is confronting. The worker and client will jointly examine that situation in light of the agency's service to determine whether there is a good enough fit to meet the client's needs. Through these activities the client will experience what the setting provides, how the worker proceeds, and will gain a "flavor" of the helping process.

PREPARATORY STAGE

Given the importance of beginnings, workers spend some time thinking about and preparing for the first meeting with each new client. A number of factors impinge on the first interview and it is worthwhile to review those aspects that can be planned for in advance. The following discussion reviews these factors, which are summarized in box 6.1.

Presession preparation continues throughout each stage as the social worker reflects on, evaluates, and links her specific hypotheses and questions about a particular client to concepts, intervention models, and practice research that may help her to better understand and work with this client. As discussed in chapter 1, the ITP Loop provides an organizing framework for reviewing each session and preparing for the following interview.

PREPARING THE SETTING

A WELCOMING AGENCY

The client's early experience of the helping process occurs on the telephone at intake and when he comes to the agency for a first appointment. Social workers should be aware of the clients' experiences when they telephone for service. What is the reception they receive, are they able to speak to an employee or do they encounter a recorded message? Are appointments provided quickly or is there a long wait? Attention to the waiting room is also important. What messages does it convey? Does the reading material match the language of clients or is it only in English? Do the pictures on the wall reflect the population served by the setting? Is the waiting room well maintained and welcoming, or is it in need of a fresh coat of paint and new, comfortable furniture? These physical attributes of the setting convey powerful messages about respect for the people who are requesting service. If necessary, social workers can bring about changes in the organization to improve intake procedures and the physical aspects of the setting that will more positively affect clients.

CREATING A PRIVATE SPACE

Ideally, the worker and client meet in a setting that is comfortable, private, and conveys an atmosphere of calm. A calm and quiet environment helps create a space where a client can share important matters, engage in a dialogue, experience and share hitherto avoided emotions, and reflect on important factors. In actual fact many social work interviews occur in settings that are not private, quiet, or free from distractions. For example, social workers meet with clients in their homes, in a corridor in an institutional setting, in a kitchen in a foster home, a cafeteria, or in an open space in a community center. Regardless of the setting, the practitioner tries to approximate, insofar as is possible, the features of a contained and private space.

If the worker meets the client in an office, ideally the office has good lighting and ventilation, a moderate temperature, and comfortable furniture. A private and soundproofed office provides confidentiality. The area has enough space to accommodate all the participants in the interview without anyone being cramped or having their personal space invaded. The room is large enough to accommodate wheelchairs or walkers. Furniture is arranged so as to emphasize collaboration; desks do not appear to be barriers or symbols of power, nor are workers seated in chairs that are greater in height than those of the client. In some settings offices are shared and the worker must arrange in advance for a private interviewing room for the session. A welcoming stance can be furthered in those settings where a beverage is offered to clients.

When social workers find themselves in settings other than an office, they try to arrange the setting to provide some privacy. In informal community settings the worker may meet the client in a cafeteria or a lounge. While the setting may be comfortable, there is a lack of privacy and there may be frequent interruptions. A table in a corner can provide some degree of contained space.

Social workers in hospitals often meet with clients and their families in a hospital room where there are other patients. Curtains can be used to section off rooms, but voices can still be heard. Many patients are ambulatory or can be assisted in a wheelchair or walker to move to a more private area. Arrangements should be made in advance with the ward staff so that the social worker is prepared and not searching for assists at the time of the interview.

MINIMIZING DISTRACTIONS AND INTERRUPTIONS

Active listening and attending closely to what the client is saying are important interviewing skills. In order to maintain focus and concentration it is useful to attempt to minimize distractions and interruptions. Many social workers turn off the telephone during an interview or do not answer the telephone when it rings. If an extremely important call is expected and must be received, it is respectful to tell the client about that at the start of your meeting. When on a home visit a television is distracting, social workers can request that it be turned off or that the meeting take place in a quieter room. It is important to explain that this request is being made so that there will be few distractions from hearing and understanding the issues under discussion. When there are young children present in the home, it is likely that the client's attention will be divided between speaking to the worker and attending to the children. Depending on the nature of the service the agency offers, child care arrangements at the office or in the home will free the client up to be fully involved in the interview. This is a more useful alternative than trying to maintain focus while caring for the children.

INCLUDING CLIENTS' CULTURAL NORMS

A range of norms governs the way in which an individual deems it appropriate to interact with professionals. Behaviors will also differ whether the interview is conducted in an office environment or on a home visit. For example, sitting in a face-to-face position where direct eye contact is maintained is not uniformly comfortable. When receiving visitors into one's home there are different customs about appropriate dress, whether shoes are worn or removed in the home, and whether food is offered and accepted. In an interview in a home the worker is a guest and does not have the degree of control she has in her own office. Workers need to be open to clients' customs, which may be different from their own. Awareness and understanding of their own comfort and discomfort levels about a range of behaviors is important so that practitioners can include and respect clients.

ANTICIPATING LINGUISTIC NEEDS

Social workers know the nature of the population they are serving and the degree to which they are likely to meet individuals who do not speak English well enough for helping to be meaningful. In such instances, to provide equitable access to needed services requires the presence of trained interpreters. Therefore, it is important to know in advance of meeting a new client what the linguistic needs may be and arrange for an appropriate interpreter. Often in crisis or emergency situations a family member or staff member who speaks the client's language is enlisted as an informal interpreter. This arrangement is not ideal, and the client may censor the information shared.

Interpretation for social service and health interactions is challenging and both social workers and interpreters need to be skilled in its use. Interpreters need to be trained to understand their role as a valuable conduit between client and professional. It is important for interpreters to convey clients' communication, not their understanding of what the client has said. In other words, it can be challenging for interpreters to simply translate directly what the client has said, and they may be tempted, consciously or not, to insert their construal of the clients' situation and needs. On the other hand, they need to assist the practitioner to appreciate the nuances, context, beliefs, and values reflected in clients' content but perhaps not explicitly stated. Verbal and nonverbal communications need to be expressed. Hence the notion of cultural, not personal, interpretation in a meaningful way that goes beyond translation.

Interpreters must agree to maintain confidentiality with respect to the information they learn, and clients should also be informed that the interpreter is present in a professional capacity. Especially in a town or neighborhood where there are small communities of those who share linguistic and cultural backgrounds, ethical standards about the professional role and relationship of the interpreter need to be clarified and understood by all participants (Hepworth, Rooney, and Larsen, 2002).

The introduction of a third party into the interaction between client and worker will change the pace of the session dramatically, as all communications must be translated and some statements will require even further elaboration to be understood. As a result, when using an interpreter the worker should plan for a longer session and be cognizant of how much can realistically be covered. Priority should be given to conveying important information such as results from psychological testing, details about a medical procedure, or standards about child-rearing practices (Murphy and Dillon, 2003).

CONSIDERING SAFETY ISSUES

Interview space and location should be structured to provide safety for the worker and the client. Agencies should have procedures that ensure that workers and their clients are not at risk if they meet in offices after usual business hours or when entering and leaving the building. When working with clients with a history of violence, the worker should ensure that others are present in the setting. If the worker is concerned about the potential for violence, she may wish to sit close to the office door or conduct the interview with an open door. Social workers can find themselves meeting clients for interviews in locations that pose a safety risk. Examples of this are parks and restaurants in high-crime neighborhoods. While a client's apartment may be safe, elevators and corridors in some high-rise buildings are not. Social workers may find themselves vacillating between minimizing risks and being overly cautious.

Decisions about safety are usefully addressed with colleagues and supervisors. Agencies should have safety and risk management policies, protocols, and guidelines that personnel can use in determining what are safe and unsafe situations and when a worker should go with a colleague to an interview rather than proceed alone.

EXAMINING PERTINENT INFORMATION

Controversy exists about how much information helping professionals should have before their first meeting with the client. On one hand, there may be a wealth of useful information available that will assist with facilitating engagement and providing a service efficiently. On the other hand, the existing information may be incorrect or biased and lead the worker to an inaccurate perception of the individual and his situation.

Social workers employed in organizations are expected to review existing information in the agency records, from the intake worker and referring agents, and from any other relevant source, such as family or community members. In preparing for the first meeting with the client, rather than come to premature judgments based on this information, the worker is encouraged to maintain an open mind and critical skepticism about how the information was gathered, in what context, and what alternative meanings it may have. For example, clients who challenge the nature of a service offered may be labeled hostile or resistant when in fact the client may have taken the initiative to point out gaps in service and advocate for his own needs. When clients have already given information to intake workers they expect that the social worker will have that data and they will not want to repeat it again. Where the client is required by law to see the social worker, or where there is a referral from a member of a helping team, the social worker will need to learn whether the client has this information. Even when the client has been told about the reasons for referral, it is important to hear from him what his understanding is of those reasons. If the client does not have the referral information, the social worker needs to prepare for how she will share it with the client. Two guidelines are useful: first, the client will benefit from a succinct summary of what is already known, and, second, the worker should make it clear that she is interested in hearing the client's perspective on the issue. For example, a client in a maternity ward was referred to the social worker because the nurses observed that the client and her boyfriend argued loudly on all their visits. The social worker introduced herself and said that the nurses had requested she visit the client. She conveyed their concern about the client, especially regarding the tension they observed when her boyfriend visited. The social worker wanted to know how the client felt it was going for herself as a new mother on this service and whether she had a concern about her relationship with her boyfriend.

PREPARING THE SOCIAL WORKER

Social workers think about the information they have about the client before the first meeting, regardless of how minimal or extensive it is. They try to begin to get a sense of what the individual may be feeling in relation to the situation and to seeking help from a professional. Preparatory empathy through "tuning in" has been discussed by Shulman (1999) and refers to the process of trying to get in touch, on an emotional level, with the possible feelings and concerns of the perspective client. As discussed in chapter 3, empathy relies on the social worker drawing on universal dimensions of the human condition. In this respect it enables us to try to feel as another feels and anticipate possible reactions to a challenging situation. The limitation of the concept lies in the recognition that the emotional and cognitive meaning of events is not only individual but also informed by a range of cultural and societal factors. Differences by virtue of a range of characteristics, such as age, class, ethnicity, gender, sexual orientation, and ability, may make it unlikely that one can identify with another who is significantly different from oneself. However, if these limits of empathy are recognized, social workers can still use the concept as a beginning to bridge the space between worker and client. This is accomplished by considering any hunches about how clients may be thinking and feeling as purely tentative. When empathic comments are offered, it is the client's reaction that can lead to a mutual dialogue that will assist the worker to better understand the client's subjective experience. Empathy can be useful when it increases understanding and compassion; it is not useful if it leads to premature judgments, conclusions, and closure.

Social workers who specialize in practice with a particular population or problem may begin to discern a limited range of reactions to particular situations. Research studies that identify characteristic responses to a specific occurrence are also useful. For example, social workers who work with couples where one partner has discovered that the other has been having an emotional and sexual relationship outside of the couple relationship may find that the betrayed partner usually reports experiencing great emotional pain. These partners may feel enormous hurt and anger, find themselves ruminating about details of the affair, have difficulty sleeping and eating, and experience depression. Theorists and researchers have noted the presence of behaviors similar to post-traumatic stress in betrayed partners (Glass and Wright, 1997; Johnson, Makinen, and Millikin, 2001). Knowing that these behaviors are likely and typical, the social worker can link this information to a cognitive type of preparatory empathy. That is, she may anticipate that the client will experience some or all of the reactions reported in the literature. When the practitioner actually meets the client her tentative expectation may be confirmed or disconfirmed. She may find that the client describes her experience of these reactions, or that the client refers to some of them in an indirect way, or that these reactions are not present. There may be another set of reactions that were not anticipated. Used flexibly, this type of knowledge can provide a guide, a point for connection, and a direction for exploration. If used inflexibly, the worker will ignore or minimize the client's experience and this will interfere with the alliance building that is so crucial in the initial stage.

Just as the social worker tunes into the client, he also tunes into himself. In anticipation of meeting the client, it is useful to have a sense of whether there are any particular issues presented by the client that have a special meaning for the worker. If so, some time spent in reflection is a useful preparatory activity. Self-awareness is discussed extensively in chapters 1 and 2. As a preliminary step, thinking about similarities and differences between the client's and the worker's circumstances can be useful. The necessity of differentiating the worker's experience from the client's is underscored, while recognizing that the practitioner's familiarity with issues provides another resource for relationship building—one that moves from the "inside out."

Based on a range of personal factors, the events presented by clients will have a differential affect on the practitioner. For example, a young social worker who enjoyed riding a bicycle in an urban setting found her sense of safety challenged when preparing to work with a young male who was left paraplegic as a result of a motorcycle accident. Some situations will affect a worker more than others because they stir up sensitive or anxiety-producing subjects. Some reflection on potential issues can help the worker sensitize herself to her concerns, anxieties, and internal reactions. This process can help practitioners so that in their practice they can be mindful of their internal thoughts and feeling, centered in their professional role, and client focused.

As noted, beginnings are a crucial part of any interpersonal relationship and encounter with a service program. Impressions are formed in the first contact, which can have a lasting affect on the way the client perceives the practitioner and the service setting and will determine whether or not the client will continue to participate with the social worker. The objective of this phase is to develop enough understanding that a preliminary joint assessment can be made and some preliminary goals defined. As noted frequently, this understanding is gained within the context of the developing relationship. Cultivation of a positive rapport, or the beginning of an affective bond, is an important task of this stage (Tsang and Bogo, 1997).

Attention to these objectives guides the practitioner in the initial stage. In chapter 5 it was noted that the social worker will be working on two levels simultaneously, that of the process and that of the task. To recapitulate, the process refers to all the ways in which the client and social worker interact with each other and the task refers to the content and substance of the work. The point was made that these two aspects are interwoven and build on each other. They cannot easily be separated when in the actual interview. For example, one task is to understand what the client wants to achieve in coming to the agency. This information may be gained by the client's direct response to the worker's question, it may emerge in the discussion, or the client may not be able to answer the question directly. In the later case the worker will need to probe for the information. The client may not be able to put his goals into specific terms; he may simply be feeling upset and want some relief from a troubling situation. The way in which the worker asks for information, responds to the client's description of his situation and his feelings about it, and how this helps or hinders the client to proceed in the interview constitute elements of the process. This interaction, both the verbal and subtle nonverbal aspects of the *process*, will be perceived by the client to some degree as helpful or not helpful. In turn, it will affect the client's ability to gain greater clarity about what he wants to achieve—the *task* dimension.

The various aspects of the initial stage are presented in box 6.2. These activities incorporate both the task and process dimension in the helping process.

JOINING

From the first telephone call or face-to-face meeting with the potential client, the worker is concerned with conveying respect, interest, and a commitment to understanding the client's situation and determining whether the agency can provide a service. This stance is conveyed in verbal and nonverbal ways. Practitioners use their own natural warmth, friendliness, and a low-key caring and concerned attitude to begin connecting with the person who may become a client. The aim at this point is to clearly communicate the role of the social worker and the purpose for meeting. A warm-up stage can help to put the client at ease and can include some "social talk" along with a brief introduction of the worker and her role. The degree of formality or informality of these initial interchanges is based on factors, such as the nature of the problem, what is appropriate for the age of the client, and whether the meeting is client initiated or court ordered. For example, a different stance is appropriate when initially meeting an individual who is referred for help with a life-threatening illness as compared to a family where there is disagreement between parents and children about an appropriate curfew. When working with children and adolescents there may be a preference for the use of first names and some easy discussion about how they reached the setting, what they usually do at this time of the day, and their hobbies or favorite activities. In meeting an elderly client the worker should be sensitive to their age difference and inquire whether the person prefers to be addressed by their surname.

When clients are ordered by the court to meet with a social worker, it is wise to discuss the mandate explicitly and fully very early in the first meeting. In many instances clients do not fully understand why they may be referred for counseling. For example, an adolescent girl was ordered by the court to see a counselor after she was charged with shoplifting. The client could not easily understand the link between the two events. For the worker to join with the client it was necessary to address two issues: the client's perceptions and the court order. First, the situation needs to be examined from the client's perspective and the worker needs to validate her confusion. Second, the worker needs to clearly communicate what the court order consists of, what is expected, and what the consequences are of noncompliance. In this way the worker attempts to work with the tensions involved in mandated services, that of serving the needs of the client and that of responding to the court. The more direct the worker is in clarifying her role, the context of the service, and the expectations of all parties, the more likely the worker is to gain credibility in the eyes of the client.

ESTABLISHING THAT A SERVICE IS REQUESTED

As observed, frequently clients are referred to social workers and social agencies by other professionals or institutions. For example, in school settings the teacher usually refers a student and the child's family, in medical settings members of the team may refer the client to a social worker, and mandated services such as probation and child protection are almost always initiated through a referral. Hence it is of the utmost importance to begin by clarifying the potential client's understanding of the referral, the nature of the agency, and the service that can be provided. The social worker shares with the client information that is already known about her and discusses the services the agency and worker can offer. In this way the principle of collaboration is put into action early in the helping process. The two participants explore whether the client's needs and issues can be addressed by the program and the social worker's role and function.

RELATIONSHIP BUILDING

As discussed in chapters 3 and 4 an atmosphere of trust provides a crucial foundation for helping. To briefly review, the relationship that social workers aim to create is one that offers warmth and caring concern, acceptance, positive regard, respect, and a nonjudgmental attitude. Genuineness, empathy, and a commitment to understanding and working with diversity refer to facilitative attitudes and a particular type of stance in practice with clients. There are specific skills that will help workers convey this position, such as active attending and listening, communicating developing understanding of the situation, and seeking feedback from clients to learn whether these initial impressions capture the client's experience.

Relationship building and maintenance continues over each interview and throughout the process. Workers stay attuned to overt and covert indications about the degree of joining, connection, and understanding that is developing. Where there are ruptures, they need to be attended to directly or through some change in what the worker offers. Hence the relationship component is one that workers remain aware of throughout the process.

INFORMATION GATHERING THROUGH HELPING CLIENTS TELL THEIR STORY

The preferred means of working with the client is collaborative, as compared with a hierarchical stance where the expert professional proffers advice. From the beginning the worker invites the client to tell his story in his own words. The practitioner listens carefully and helps the client elaborate and explore through using open- and close-ended questions, clarifying and asking for more specific details, reflecting thoughts and feelings, paraphrasing and summarizing. These skills are fully discussed in the following chapters. Individuals can benefit simply from expressing inner concerns to another person. Through talking out loud, individuals report better understanding of what is troublesome to them.

There are many ways of gathering information, from highly structured interviews to those that are unstructured. For example, a social worker could administer a checklist or a set of specific questions in an orderly fashion. Or she could begin in an open-ended way, asking the client, "What has brought you here" or "Could you tell me about your situation" (Hepworth, Rooney, and Larsen, 2002). As the session proceeds the worker asks for specific relevant information that has not emerged. The social work practice principle of "start where the client is" puts into practice many of the values discussed regarding collaboration and prizing the client's view. This principle gives the client's agenda or immediate issue top priority. It guides the worker to follow the client's lead, to respond to what she is introducing.

Social workers are always balancing the issue of when to focus in greater depth and when to develop more breadth. At what point does the worker need to help the client expand her story to obtain a fuller picture of the client's life and the important contributing factors? To what extent does the dialogue need to proceed into more depth about the client's feelings, thoughts, motivations, and wishes about a particular matter? While definitive answers are not available, the following factors can be considered: client interest, urgency of the situation and available time, and agency mandate. Especially at the beginning of the process, prior to the development of a strong relationship, the topic that the client considers of greatest interest and concern needs to be addressed. Urgency and time available play a part in deciding on the issue to focus on. If the situation is a crisis and individuals' health and safety are at risk, these matters become the focus of attention. Where the issue is long-standing it can be examined at a slower pace. Finally, the agency mandate and role of the social worker frame the issues that will be addressed.

Following are two examples that illustrate how these different factors are used in guiding the interviewer's behavior. The first example takes place in a hospital setting. A single mother has been diagnosed with ovarian cancer and told that she will need an operation immediately. She is referred to the social worker, as she has stated that it is impossible to leave her two children for this procedure. The hospital worker begins with the mother's concerns about her children's reactions to a separation from her and listens to her discuss the individual personalities and needs of each child at some length. The social worker responds supportively to the mother's concerns about her children, however, given the quasi-emergency nature of the illness, the worker tells the client that they will need to change the focus of their discussion. She clarifies that she is involved to help her with a plan that will take into account both the children's care as well as mother's medical needs. She asks the client if they can move on to examine whether there are family members, friends, or neighbors that could help her with her children through this medical problem or whether they will need to explore using community services.

The second example takes place in a community-based senior's center where the social worker is involved with an elderly widow who inquires whether the worker can give her information about applying for assisted housing. The client has been self-sufficient and living comfortably in her own apartment for many years. Over a harsh winter she found it more difficult to get out as her arthritis was exacerbated by the weather. Currently she is feeling better but wonders about the future. In the initial interview the client takes great pleasure in telling the worker about her functioning in the community. The worker listens and provides feedback that reflects her understanding that the client is both satisfied with her current arrangement but also concerned about the future.

With a focus on these two themes, the interviewer can balance the interview to include hearing about the present, and gaining a fuller picture of strengths, needs, and supports, with clarifying what future issues and assistance may be needed and available to help this woman continue to live in the community.

INTEGRATING A DIVERSITY PERSPECTIVE

In the previous discussions about diversity in this text the point was made that individuals' attitudes, thoughts, feelings, and behaviors reflect their own unique identification with and internalization of aspects of their original culture and the other cultures they reference (Tsang, Bogo, and George, 2003). Following from Dyche and Zayas, (1995, 2001), the recommended practice strategy is one of a "cultural learner." This stance involves the practitioner listening to and learning from the client about factors that will impinge on the helping process: these are 1) relevant aspects of the client's culture in relation to the way she perceives the presenting problem, her current relationships, and life experiences, 2) internalized cultural expectations about seeking help from a professional, and 3) potential ways of dealing with issues. This is not an intrusive, unstructured, curious attempt to learn about another's cultural background. Rather it is an intentional activity aimed at linking cultural information and meanings to the situation that is the focus of attention in the professional meeting.

These authors describe a stance for professionals to take in an interview, one that conveys that the client is the expert about herself and that the worker needs to understand the client's views in order to be helpful. The interviewing processes promote dialogue through a back and forth interchange. The worker uses skills of active listening and attempts to convey what has been heard and understood, offers tentative hunches, requests feedback, and continuously offers reformulations and modifications based on the client's responses and reactions to the worker's comments. Clark (2003) studied a sample of experienced social work practitioners who were viewed by peers as committed to working effectively with clients from diverse backgrounds. These workers emphasized the importance of honoring and respecting their clients and saw the challenge not as one of difference but rather as one where workers lacked information and knowledge. They asked themselves and their clients, "What do I need to know?" in order to understand. They demonstrated a collaborative stance in predicting that they may not understand what the client tells them and requested the client to work with them to inform them of their mistakes.

They used questions such as "What have I not asked you that is important? What am I getting wrong?" (Clark, 2003, p. 111.)

There are some specific issues that practitioners need to attend to when practicing with clients whose country of origin is different from the worker. These issues are the meaning of help seeking from strangers, the way language is used to convey problems, how acculturation manifests itself in the client, and the client's history of oppression. Practitioners need to be attentive to the meanings associated with requesting assistance from strangers and from professionals. Help-seeking behavior and the pathways used to gain help vary; in some cultures extended families are expected to solve problems, and approaching professional helpers is the last resort. In other cultures the family doctor or the religious leader is respected and consulted when the family cannot deal with a difficulty on their own. Providing personal information to outsiders may be acceptable only in desperate situations. Problems may be minimized, based on a cultural belief that problems reflect poorly on the family or the community. Others may be reluctant to ask for help directly. The ways in which problems are identified and described varies. For example, in many cultures the symptoms of depression are described in physical rather than emotional terms.

Clients tell their stories in many different ways and practitioners need to be open-minded and flexible as they gather information and try to make meaning of it. After reviewing research on cross-cultural counseling, Tsang and Bogo (1997) concluded that clients who are not acculturated to Euro-North American cultures may present problems to professionals in ways that are unfamiliar to the practitioner. The practitioner will need to listen carefully and inquire at length to better understand the client's experience and the meanings they attribute to the presenting problem. As noted earlier, behaviors with professionals and strangers may be influenced by cultural norms unfamiliar to the social worker. The potential client may also be influenced by racist or prejudicial attitudes toward their community held by the dominant group and present in a guarded manner, not spontaneously sharing information until the worker has demonstrated enough genuine interest and respect that the client deems engaging with the worker potentially worthwhile.

Clients who have immigrated from societies vastly different from North America may be living in two worlds simultaneously. Questions aimed at comparing the differences and similarities between those two cultures can be helpful if linked directly to the issues under discussion (Waldman, 1999). For example, when child rearing and discipline practices differ, clients who become involved with child protection authorities often report considerable confusion between the values, norms, and laws in the new community as compared to their country of origin. Social workers can help clients learn about the current expectations and consider how they will respond to them in a way that prevents further involvement with the authorities but also enables them to experience continuity with their own culture and life history. Younger clients, who have been exposed to a global popular culture through the internet, movies, television, and music may not have the same sense of dislocation or confusion as their older relatives.

A multicultural perspective also pays attention to and incorporates an understanding of "invisible wounds of oppression" (Hardy and Laszloffy, 2002, p. 577). The aim is to take into account how structural issues of power, marginalization, and oppression operate in an individual's internal functioning, in interpersonal relationships, and in the way in which problems are addressed. Four types of oppression are identified that are important to understand in relation to the specific presenting problem and in relation to behavior with the worker. First, when others have persistently defined an individual's problems, one can learn to be voiceless or silent and have difficulty advocating for self, being self-assertive, or being able to define what one needs. A second feature may be a sense of psychological, social, or community homelessness in which one feels alienated and not belonging anywhere. Rage and an overwhelming sense of pain is another reaction to pervasive experiences of social injustice. Conversely, societal messages about lack of worth can be internalized as self-hate toward oneself, toward others who represent aspects of self, or toward both.

TOWARD DEVELOPING SHARED
UNDERSTANDING/ASSESSMENT

Life situations are complex, and it is difficult to clearly tell another about one's self, what issues have been challenges and struggles, and what are current concerns. Clients often begin with comments such as "I don't know where to begin." It is also a challenge in both social and professional contexts to truly comprehend what another is trying to convey and grasp her meaning and perception of her situation. Given these axioms of human experience, how can social workers adopt a position that recognizes both the advantages of active listening and empathic understanding as well as the human limits of ever truly knowing another? It is apparent that at least some amount of time is needed to have an appreciation of another's life. Premature problem solving and advice giving can work against developing an approximation of understanding. Instead, what is recommended is the opportunity for clients to discuss their story, issues, and concerns in some depth. A modicum of prolonged engagement is more likely to lead to understandings and directions that are shared between the client and the worker. Assessment and goal setting will more closely reflect the client's concerns and wishes. This principle is also consistent with the recommendations of Prochaska and his colleagues, who have pointed out that individuals may be in a precontemplation stage, not at all ready to engage in planning and action strategies to bring about changes in their lives (Prochaska, 1999; Prochaska, DiClemente, and Norcross, 1992). Prematurely introducing an intervention plan is likely to be ineffective or result in the client not returning. Instead a prolonged period of exploration with the client that focuses on the benefits and costs of change can be more productive.

While a professional stance respects the fact that our knowledge of another will always be partial, it also recognizes that help can be offered and received, even under these conditions. Practice research has demonstrated that, with a particular type of relationship, the provision of hope, and an expectation that the work will be useful, positive outcomes are achievable (Hubble, Duncan, and Miller, 1999). Perhaps it is more accurate to state that the worker strives for *sufficient* or *enough* understanding of the client's subjective experience, wishes, and goals so that they can embark on working together (Tsang and Bogo, 1997).

Assessment is an ongoing and continuous process that unfolds throughout the time the worker and client are together. All assessments are incomplete, hence the phrase "toward developing shared understanding" is meant to capture the fluid and partial nature of the activity where the worker and client engage in a process of clarifying issues and expanding explanations of why a problem exists and what should be done. For the purpose of providing structure, focus, and direction, most general and specialized models include a defined stage where information is collected, examined, and reviewed to answer key questions and provide a direction for planning and goal setting.

A perspective on human well-being and social functioning is presented in chapter 1. With these explanatory concepts in mind social workers can use an ecosystemic perspective to integrate personal and contextual factors in people's lives when conducting an assessment (Germain and Bloom, 1999). This perspective provides a useful preliminary organizing framework. Specialized models offer particular concepts to enable greater depth of exploration and understanding. Box 6.3 presents three activities that are undertaken to arrive at the assessment and plan.

GATHERING RELEVANT DATA

Using an ecosystemic perspective to guide data gathering. The data practitioners gather should ultimately provide them with the information to answer the key questions that emanate from their explanatory frameworks about why a problem exists. Flowing from a contemporary understanding of the *ecosystemic perspective*, the questions in box 6.4 provide a guide for data gathering in this phase. The client's ecological context is broadened to taken into account cultural and societal issues that may need to be addressed.

The worker seeks to understand the needs, problems, challenges, and barriers faced by the individual as well as the personal and situational resources, strengths, opportunities, and supports available. With regard to the individual, it is important to understand how he responds to stress and to what extent reactions are internal and to what extent they are externally directed. For example, some individuals will adapt to environmental demands and change behavior or feelings when confronted with challenges. Others may feel overwhelmed, experience a flood of negative emotions, and retreat from the situation. And others may focus more on changing their physical, relational, and social environment so that it may become more likely to meet their needs.

Germain (1991) drew attention to the way an individual's unique style of coping can make the initial situation better or worse. Stress typically leads to a range of subjective emotional experiences—including anxiety, energy, a desire to fight, or a desire to flee. Based on the situation, some reactions can promote problem solving and well-being and others can further exacerbate the precipitating issue. For example, when the primary bread winner in a family loses his job, he likely will experience stress. He may react to that stress with anxiety and energy that propels him to work tirelessly on finding another place of employment. Or, he may respond to the stress of the loss with great anxiety and profound feelings of demoralization. If alcohol is used to manage these feelings to the point where he becomes immobilized, a downward cycle of more stress begins. The dysfunctional reaction to the initial precipitant becomes a secondary and confounding problem.

With regard to the environment, the worker seeks to learn about the problems and potential strengths that exist at micro, mezzo, and macro levels. The micro level refers to the client's significant relationships, as, for example, in intimate relationships, among family members, in friendships and social activities, and in work settings. The mezzo level refers to the nature of the neighborhood and community, the expectations and atmosphere in the work setting, and the programs and services available through relevant social and health delivery systems. The macro level refers to the significant societal and structural forces that affect the client, such as health, education, or social service policy, and attitudes, barriers, and opportunities encountered by the client because of a range of individual diverse characteristics. Social workers are concerned with clients' life histories and whether they have experienced marginalization in their interactions with significant institutions.

The information gathered will provide a direction for intervention by separating out environmental and individual issues. The worker and client will consider the following questions in this regard. To what extent does the environment need to be changed to be more supportive and nourishing to the client? To what extent does the client need to change in order to adapt to the environmental demands? To what extent does the client need to try to change external factors and relationships or to leave situations that are emotionally and physically damaging to the client? Given the focus on transactions, systemic interventions that aim to change interaction patterns between clients and significant others in their environment are also included in change efforts. For example, in many presenting situations of child and family problems, family dynamics and interactions are the focus of change. The family is conceived of as the client. While it is somewhat artificial to separate the individual and the environment, this formulation provides some organizing guidelines for assessment and planning. Family therapists have used an ecological model to assess the various systems that adolescents and their families are involved with: families, school, neighborhood, and peers (Henggeler et al., 1998). They examine risk factors, protective factors, and strengths to pinpoint where interventions need to be directed. A substantial body of research supports their multisystemic treatment approach.

An ecomap was described by Hartman (1978; 1994) to provide a picture of the client and his significant relationships and context. It is a useful tool to ground the ecosystemic perspective and to help worker and client collaborate when gathering information. Clients see themselves and the key relationships, systems, pressures, and supports in their lives. The client and worker draw a map and place the client at the center in a circle. Squares or circles are drawn to represent relationships with partners, family, friends, neighbors, and relevant systems such as neighborhood, work setting, religious organizations, clubs, and so forth. Lines are drawn between the client and each system, with symbols to indicate whether the relationship is strong (_____), tenuous (- - - - -), or conflictual (+++++). Arrows are used to indicate whether the relationship involves the client giving to the other, the other giving to the client, or both giving to each other. This device elucidates the client's world and can be used to explore the sources and nature of nurturance, support, stress, and difficulty.

When conducting an assessment it is useful to make a distinction between issues that arise from a crisis, a transitional stage, or from an ongoing situation. Crises and traumatic events can incapacitate individuals who were previously functioning well. Short-term intervention can be effective when aimed at helping the individual regain his previous equilibrium and deal with the impact of the crisis. Stress can arise in trying to cope with the affects of transitions. For example, issues can arise from new developmental stages and roles, from relocations brought on through a change of employment, from voluntary immigration to a new country, or from moving to a new community. Interventions may need to be prolonged as individuals are supported to deal with the challenges of new circumstances. Ongoing problematic environmental pressures, long-standing difficulty in a significant interpersonal relationship, self-destructive behavior patterns, or addictions are also situations that may require an extended intervention.

How much historical data should a social worker collect? Given the time constraints of most settings, many contemporary models focus on the present and collect historical data when the client or the presenting problem deems it to be relevant. For example, clients who have chosen or were forced to leave their countries of origin may define current issues in relation to past experiences and make comparisons between what it is like coping in a new country with their earlier life. When clients define problems in current functioning in relation to having been abused as children or to difficulties they experienced in adolescence, the worker needs to be responsive and hear what the client chooses to reveal about these past significant events in his life.

Using multiple perspectives to guide data gathering. Clinical social workers keep, on average, eight conceptual templates in mind as they listen to the client tell her story and link practice phenomena to explanatory frameworks (Timberlake, Sabatino, and Martin, 1997). These frameworks help the practitioner identify aspects of the client's situation that are missing from the client's spontaneous narrative. These templates also guide practitioners to seek information that will help form a joint understanding or assessment between worker and client. As noted earlier, experienced practitioners integrate theory and practice through a looping process that links concepts with practice events, both during and after an interview (Bogo and Vayda, 1998).

A *multiperspective model* for assessment has been described by Weerasekera (1993), who also observes that mental health practitioners actively use numerous lenses for understanding their clients. Her model provides a systematic way of capturing this phenomenon. A grid serves to organize a comprehensive understanding of an individual in his systemic context along a number of dimensions. Depending on the presenting situation, the organizational mandate, and the time available, the grid can be assessed in its entirety or only selected dimensions can be addressed. Specialized theories can be used to develop greater depth in assessing any of the dimensions.

The first dimension of the multiperspective model consists of biological factors such as the individual's medical and psychiatric history and current health and mental health status. Although some social work practice models refer to a biopsychosocial paradigm (Turner, 2002), there has been less attention given to biological factors. With recent highly relevant research findings from the fields of neuroscience and neurobiology, a greater appreciation of the interrelationships between mind, body, and behavior is imperative for social workers (Shapiro and Applegate, 2000).

The second dimension directs attention to behaviors that are problematic and involves assessing their frequency and duration as well as factors that reinforce and perpetuate or serve as negative consequences of these behaviors. This perspective draws from behavioral theory and intervention and is useful in general for specifying sequences of behaviors that provoke and maintain problematic responses.

The third dimension consists of cognitive factors such as the individual's judgment, view of reality, attitudes, assumptions, and core beliefs about self and others. This perspective draws from an understanding of individual's cognitions—how the world is viewed and how information is processed. Ideas about self, others, and relationships are related to the discussion of attachment theory found in chapter 3.

The fourth dimension consists of psychodynamic factors such as the individual's feelings and thoughts about key relationships in the past and present, his ways of handling conflict, his experience of self, and his conscious and unconscious motivations. It is likely that the client and the practitioner will require a longer period of exploration and discussion to learn about and understand these elements. More specific psychodynamic theories can be used if the practitioner wishes to develop greater depth in understanding any of these factors. The contributions of contemporary psychodynamic theories, specifically self psychology, intersubjectivity theory, and relational theory are especially useful for social workers (Rasmussen and Mishna, 2003).

The fifth dimension consists of systemic factors and involves assessing the nature of the individual's central interpersonal relationships and networks, such as intimate adult relationships, current nuclear family, family of origin, and extended family, friendships and social networks, and school or employment relationships. The many contributions from family systems theory and models provide a wealth of concepts and interventions that are part of most clinical social workers' knowledge base (Hanna and Brown, 1999; Nichols and Schwartz, 2001).

The sixth dimension consists of social or structural factors and includes the identification of societal and cultural factors that play an important part in the person's life. This perspective is one that has been well articulated by social workers and is part of the discussion throughout this text.

Each dimension in the multifactorial grid is assessed with respect to four factors that are seen as impinging on the presenting problem and that can be a potential focus in intervention. These factors are predisposing or risk factors, precipitating factors that resulted in help seeking or referral, perpetuating factors that maintain the situation, and protective factors that social workers would label as strengths and resources.

Each agency, based on their mandate and particular circumstances, provides assessment formats to guide practitioners in gathering the most relevant data. The following psychosocial assessment format is presented as one example of the information that can be collected when working from a stance that integrates the ecosystemic framework and a multiperspective model. For additional guides see Jordan and Franklin (2003), for a thorough review of quantitative and qualitative methods of assessment in social work, and Cowger (1994), for a format for incorporating a strengths focus.

Based on the foregoing discussion, box 6.5 provides a guide that social workers can use to determine what data needs to be collected. The guide can also serve to organize the presentation of written information in an agency recording or in a verbal presentation to colleagues and team members. The interview does not rigidly follow any guide; rather the worker helps the client to tell his story, probes for more information in key areas, and over the course of the meeting aims to gather most of the information.

ANALYZING THE DATA

Analysis takes place in the session with the client as an active participant and is ongoing and cumulative. As the relationship develops, new information

BOX 6.5. BIOPSYCHOSOCIAL ASSESSMENT GUIDE

IDENTIFYING DATA

This section includes demographic information that describes relevant identifying characteristics of the client such as age, gender, sexual orientation, occupation, socioeconomic status, religion, ethnicity, family status, and health status. The type of information included is based on its relevance to the setting. For example, in a health facility a medical diagnosis is included, and where there is managed care funding a psychiatric diagnosis based on DSM-IV-TR is given.

PRESENTING PROBLEM

This section includes relevant information about the presenting problem and how the client came to the agency. It provides data to answer the following questions.

What is the problem, who is involved, and where does it occur?

What is the duration and severity of the problem? Is it pervasive in the client's life?

Why is the client coming for help now? What precipitated the problem? What maintains the problem?

If this is a referral, who is the referral source and what is the reason for referral?

Have there been previous agency contacts or is there any relevant history of professional help?

What has the client done to deal with the problem thus far?

What does the client think are possible solutions?

THE INDIVIDUAL

In order to understand the client's needs, strengths, and resources, as well as the obstacles and challenges, the following information is useful to collect. The purpose of the work, the time frame available, and the nature of the presenting issue will affect how comprehensive the assessment will be and how much information will initially be gathered.

What is the nature of the client's functioning in the past and currently in key roles, in relation to his developmental stage, to work or school, and in the context of cultural expectations?

Does the client have adequate housing, income, employment, transportation, nutrition, clothing, and recreation?

What is the client's health status—are there any significant health issues and is medication taken regularly?

What is the client's mental health status, including whether there is a psychiatric diagnosis?

What is the nature of the client's alcohol or substance usage?

What is the nature of the individual's cognitive functioning, judgment, intellectual and problem-solving capacity? What is the client's view of reality, attitudes, assumptions, and core beliefs about self and others in the context of his cultural and life experiences?

What is the nature of the individual's emotional expressions about the problem, about significant relationships, and toward the worker?

What is the nature of the client's interpersonal functioning with family members, intimate relationships, and friends? Does he seek to understand others' needs, give and take, and is confident about self and others in relationships?

How does the individual cope with stress and deal with conflict?

Does the client experience violence or the threat of violence in daily life in his relationships with family, peers, and neighbors?

Are there significant life experiences, such as abuse, trauma, forced relocation, imprisonment, that affect the client currently?

ENVIRONMENT (ALSO REFERRED TO AS SOCIAL SITUATION)

In order to understand the nature of the client's environment, the expectations it places on the client, the strengths, supports, and resources it provides, and the obstacles and challenges it presents, the following information is useful to collect. The mandate of the agency, the time frame available, and the nature of the presenting issue will affect how much information will be sought.

What is the nature of the client's environment?

Who are the key participants and systems—intimate relationships, nuclear and extended family, friends, work colleagues, neighbors, community, religious or spiritual organizations, other social networks, and the health, education, criminal justice system, and social service system?

What is the nature of the key and relevant interpersonal relationships along dimensions such as important dynamics, patterns, alliances, conflict and conflict resolution styles, decision-making patterns, and support?

What cultural and societal factors play an important part in the client's life?

What have the client's experiences been with key societal institutions and service programs? Has the client experienced situations of discrimination and marginalization?

ABOUT CHANGE AND THE HELPING PROCESS

What is the client's explanation of why there is a problem and what are her beliefs about how to change it?

will emerge that will provide additional insights and a more complex understanding of the client and his situation. Analysis also takes place after the session as the social worker reflects on the interview or discusses it in supervision or consultation.

In chapters 1 and 2 the ITP Loop Model was introduced as a vehicle to assist social workers and social work students to reflect on their practice. The loop guides the practitioner to examine subjective reactions and objective facts, to analyze these observations through the lenses of one or more set of concepts, and to plan interventions. The aim of the activity is to construct a "theory" or formulation about the client and her situation. It involves the worker in examining and analyzing the information collected and the reactions he had to the client in the interview in light of explanatory concepts. These concepts are derived from both formal models and from those ideas that constitute the worker's implicit opinions derived from experience. The worker weighs the respective influence of relevant factors and seeks general themes that occur across areas of social functioning. A search for connections between factors helps explain the links between the problem, the person, and the situation. The aim is to arrive at a working summary that explains why the client has the particular problem presented, given the client's biological, psychological, familial, and social circumstances. This explanation then provides the direction for planning what is needed to bring about change or provide help. Since the summary only represents what is known at a particular point in time, it is seen as tentative. However, it should logically lead to the identification of goals and a preliminary intervention plan.

An ecosystemic and multiperspective approach has framed the discussion of assessment and served to guide the worker in initially seeking specific types of data (presented in box 6.4) and in subjecting that data to analysis. A set of

BOX 6.6. QUESTIONS TO GUIDE ANALYSIS OF DATA

- What are the links between the individual-internal issues, interpersonal issues, and the environmental situation?
- To what extent is the current situation a result of the lack of environmental resources or supports?
- To what extent is the current situation and difficulty a result of: stress from current life roles, developmental tasks, situational stress, traumatic events, or experiences of marginalization or discrimination?
- To what extent is the current situation a result of the lack of fit between the client's needs or aspirations and the nature of the environment?
- What strengths, competencies, aspirations, and resources of the client and the environment are present to address the situation?
- What obstacles, challenges, and constraints exist in the individual and the environment that will affect efforts to change the situation?
- What are the client's significant cognitive, emotional, and behavioral responses to issues in his life? How do these factors operate to affect the current problem and the client's efforts in dealing with the problem?
- To what extent are these thoughts, feelings, and reactions useful in the client's life and to what extent do they limit or interfere with the achievement of the client's life goals?
- To what extent are significant interpersonal relationships (intimate, familial, social, and work) and informal networks available and able to change so that a better fit between the client's needs and the social environment can result?
- To what extent are there repetitious patterns of interaction between the client and significant others that maintain the problem?

questions serve to link the worker's analysis of the data collected to the concepts associated with these approaches. They are presented in box 6.6 and are adapted from Goldstein (1995). We recognize that there are innumerable theoretical and practice models, and it is likely that many reasonable ways of understanding and helping exist for any situation. Professional practice involves making educated choices among competing paradigms.

An important question to address at this point is whether the practitioner's current assessment can benefit from a review of the research literature. Two types of studies may be of use: 1) studies about the population and problem and 2) studies about empirically validated approaches for situations similar to that presented by the client. Studies about the population and problem can provide valuable missing information to the worker and can also guide him to address important gaps in his knowledge about a particular client. Studies about interventions can provide a good beginning point to consider whether the client would be receptive to a particular approach. If so, the worker must evaluate whether he has enough knowledge and competence to provide those interventions or whether the client should be referred to another worker, program, or agency that specializes in that approach. A systematic approach to seeking, evaluating, and using evidence for practice is presented in the work of Gambrill (1999) and Gibbs (2002) who argue persuasively for the importance of practitioners critically using the best available information in their decision making about intervention choices. Clients' active involvement and collaboration in this process is an appealing aspect of their approach.

Assessment and planning also considers whether interventions should occur with the individual alone or with intimate relationship partners or family members. Social workers embraced family systems thinking from its inception, and many describe either their primary affiliation, or at least aspects of their practice, as offering couple and family therapy. If using a couple or family orientation, most practitioners begin the helping process by meeting with all significant and involved persons. For those practitioners who begin by seeing the primary individual, relationship partners will be involved to the extent that a family systems orientation pervades the way the worker conceptualizes the presenting problem and perpetuating factors. If it is decided that others need to be included, they should be invited to attend as early as possible. In this way there exists the possibility of forming an alliance with all members of the family or relationship pair. If others are invited to participate after a more prolonged period of time of engagement with the client, then the other may feel that the worker is already allied with the primary client and cannot understand another perspective or position. Similarly, the primary client may have difficulty when others are included later on, feeling that the relationship with the worker has changed, that the bond has been lost, and the client may even experience a sense of betrayal. A referral to another practitioner for couples or family therapy can provide a needed new start for work that will focus primarily on the couple or family. The initial client may still choose to continue with individual work.

When the assessment reveals that necessary resources are lacking in the client's life, the worker will include plans to address these needs. Social workers are distinguished on multidisciplinary teams by their knowledge of services and their ability to help clients gain access. The plan must consider whether it is sufficient to provide the client with referral information or whether the worker will need to actively assist the client in receiving the service. Clients may require help to determine whether they meet eligibility requirements, to deal proactively and effectively with intake or bureaucratic procedures, and to present needs and requests in a way that will elicit a positive response. Entitlements are not always easily accessible, and social workers who know how to "work the system" can provide invaluable information and coaching to clients. In some instances social workers will have to make the links for the client, coordinate the service requests, and advocate for particular clients. The case management model, described in the following chapter, presents aspects of working with these external systems on behalf of clients who are not able to do so entirely on their own.

As noted above, in postsession analysis the worker reflects on his personal-professional reactions to the client and incorporates the knowledge and understanding he gains into the emerging assessment. Reflection also involves a consideration of potential countertransference responses he is experiencing and that he might anticipate will be activated through the work. Recall the earlier discussions of this concept in chapter 1. Are there possible "blind spots," areas of identification, or issues that will provoke uncomfortable feelings for the worker or make an easy connection possible? Planning can include arranging for supervision or consultation that attends to examining the worker's responses with the goal of gaining insights into alternative ways of interacting in the interviews.

PRELIMINARY JOINT PLANNING AND GOAL SETTING

The preceding activities of gathering information, reflecting on it and linking it to a conceptual framework, reviewing empirical literature, and developing enough shared understanding with the client will culminate in some form of joint agreement about the goals to be achieved and how the worker and client may achieve them. The social worker and the client will consider two dimensions. First, what are we trying to achieve in this work, that is, what outcomes should result from meeting together? The goals emerge from the shared understanding or assessment developed by the worker and client. Second, how will we work together, what are the client expectations, and how will the worker provide his input and expertise? In chapter 3 and 4 the literature on the helping relationship and therapeutic alliance was presented along with guidelines to help the worker and client discuss and explore these questions.

As noted, through the process of linkage social workers put abstract concepts and general principles into practice by forming individualized concrete goals and tasks. To continue our analysis, using the ecological-systems and multiperspective framework to set goals, some agreement is reached about the nature of the issues and the relevant systems that are involved. Goals might include bringing about change in the individual, in the environment, or in the interactions between the two. Referring to change in the individual, change can be with respect to thoughts and meanings, feelings and reactions, and behaviors. For example, a school social worker is working with an adolescent girl who has recently moved to her current high school from another part of the country. She has not covered the same curriculum as that offered in this high school and feels that she is falling behind in some of her subjects. The adolescent explains that she is so preoccupied with her concerns about her lack of friends that she is feeling too depressed to focus on her schoolwork. Previously an excellent student and also popular with peers, she feels lonely, ill at ease in school, and unhappy. The social worker can help this student examine her own perceptions of the values in the school, the various types of student groups and different norms they ascribe to, and validate the teenager's strengths and struggles in moving to a new school and new community. This type of supportive relationship can provide a safe place where the adolescent can examine possible changes she may want to make regarding her relationships in the school environment. Practitioners also help change the "goodness of fit" between the individual and the environment. In this example the practitioner can help connect the adolescent to peers that share her academic interests and values. Understanding the importance of friends and a peer group at this stage of development, the worker may focus attention on this goal. Working to improve the relationships with key systems may include meeting with the family or developing and offering groups to students dealing with relocation. Plans can also include referral to programs such as an extracurricular tutoring program.

Goal setting always begins with what the client hoped to achieve in approaching the social worker. Goals are often expressed in general terms, for example, "to feel better," "to be accepted by peers," or "to better handle the stress in my life as a single parent of two teenagers." Helping clients express statements such as these in specific and concrete terms may make goal achievement more possible. It is useful to ask what would be different as a result of meeting with the social worker and what small things would need to happen for the client to feel progress was occurring.

To achieve the identified goals, thought is also given to the tasks that need to be undertaken. Some of these tasks are easily identifiable and shared with the client. For example, a family member with primary responsibility for care of her elderly widowed father approaches a long-term care facility to inquire about placement of her father. Through the assessment the worker and client identify that she would prefer to continue to keep her father at home with her but that she needs some relief. The plan developed included ways to access home services and a referral for periodic respite care. To proceed with the plan the client's mixed feelings about being solely responsible for her father and attitudes about herself as a caregiver needed to be discussed so that she could use the services without feeling guilty or that she was letting him down.

In more ambiguous situations the tasks to be carried out to achieve the goals are less easily described to clients, and practitioners search for ways to convey the nature of the helping process. For example, a young adult, a male in his mid-thirties, is referred to the social worker in the mental health clinic for "counseling." A psychiatric assessment for depression has concluded that he is not clinically depressed but rather needs the opportunity to consider why he feels "bored with his life and unmotivated to do anything to make it better." In this situation the social worker describes the counseling process as consisting of "meeting together, trying to figure out what are the important issues in your life, and what we both think needs to change."

Goal setting is best seen as an evolving process with periodic and frequent points at which progress is reviewed and new objectives made explicit. Some workers include this activity in every session; others structure it at defined points. For example, one approach is to "take stock" every few weeks to evaluate whether the worker and client remain in agreement that the original goals are relevant. As new information, insight, and understanding is gained, goals may change and become more specific.

Throughout the work it is vital to remain client focused, to continuously attend to how the client is experiencing the meetings, what the client finds as helpful, and, if there is little progress, what are interfering factors in the client's life or in the help offered. A collaborative stance involves actively soliciting the client's participation. This can be accomplished through initially defining the work as collaborative, stating that the client's input is crucial, and then regularly seeking and using the information provided. Asking the client, "What else do I

need to know to help you" is a useful strategy. Referring to the practice of psychotherapy, Hubble, Duncan, and Miller (1999) provide a point of view that is
equally applicable to social work practice. They urge the practitioner to carefully
monitor "client's reactions to comments, explanations, interpretations, questions, and suggestions. It also demands a higher measure of flexibility on the
part of the therapist and a willingness to change one's relational stance to fit
with the client's perceptions of what is most helpful" (p. 418). If social workers
respect clients' diverse preferences, they must be prepared to substitute their
preferred approach to intervention to that of the client. For example, they will be
open to switch from a casual and informal position to one that is more formal
if that is the client's preferred personal or cultural expectation. Or, a preference
to work primarily with behavior or with meanings and motivations or with feelings will become secondary to providing what the client believes is necessary
for change to happen. Currently many mental health practitioners and agencies
prefer short-term, present-, and future-focused change interventions. However,
the practitioner may encounter a client who believes that events in her family
when she was growing up have a crucial influence on her current circumstances
and that she must understand the past in order to deal with present dilemmas.
Other factors that can be modified are the degree of directiveness, who should
participate in the session, whether individual or family therapy should be offered, and the location, timing, and duration of meetings.

While it is recommended that practitioners need to "bend and flex" to meet
client's preferred styles of working, this does not imply that the worker's knowledge and expertise is negated. Workers can share their power to direct the work
with their clients as part of a collaborative and unfolding process. Especially in
the beginning stage, when the relationship is not yet well established, workers
can use the principle "start where the client is" and forge a partnership in a manner that is more, rather than less, comfortable for the client.

As stated earlier, practitioners will confront a wide range of client expectations about seeking help from professionals. These expectations may be based
on cultural values that define what constitutes a problem, how and where to seek
help, and whether sharing personal or family problems with strangers is appropriate. Some clients will expect a professional to function as an expert and
offer solutions to their problems, while others may expect the helper to function
with a more shared approach. Past experiences with social workers and mental
health professionals will also have a significant bearing on expectations. Finally,
personal beliefs about change will affect what clients perceive as important.

BOX 6.7. EXPECTATIONS ABOUT PROFESSIONAL HELPING

- What does the individual hope to achieve, what goals are important?
- What tasks or activities does the individual expect will be engaged in with the social worker and by the client between meetings?
- What importance is given to emotional support, increased self-understanding, practical skills, and resources and information in receiving help?
- What is the individual's expectation and preference regarding the degree of direction from the worker and the degree of participation of the client?
- What is the expected time frame that the individual envisions will be needed to gain help?
- How will the individual and the social worker know if progress is being made?

When clients' hopes and expectations are not likely to be met by the service the social worker is able to provide, it is important to spell out what can and cannot be offered in the initial stage. Clients may attribute greater power and influence to social workers than they actually have. For example, social workers who screen applicants for admission to a long-term care facility often help family members develop interim community support strategies when there is a waiting list. The family may expect that if they cooperate with the social worker she will be able to have their elderly relative admitted earlier. Clients in child protective services who are ordered by the court for therapy may expect that if they attend their sessions regularly their children will be returned to them. That they must change certain aspects of their lives in order to be reunited with their children may not have been clearly communicated. The questions presented in box 6.7 can be used to discuss and clarify expectations about help seeking early in the contact.

Thus far the principles and practices of the initial stage of the social work helping process have been discussed. A wide range of interviewing skills provides the techniques and behaviors to put these principles into practice. The following skills are used throughout the stages of helping and are especially useful in the beginning stage. These skills are posing open- and close-ended questions, seeking concreteness, attending and active listening, restatement and paraphrase, reflection, summarization, and seeking feedback. They will be discussed at length, with practice examples, in the following chapters.

THE MIDDLE STAGE

BRINGING ABOUT CHANGE

}7

THE SOCIAL WORKER AS PROCESS EXPERT

The middle stage in direct social work practice has been described in a variety of ways, as treatment (Goldstein, 2001; Woods and Hollis, 2000), intervention, or implementation (Compton and Galaway, 1999; Hepworth, Rooney, and Larsen, 2002). These terms may be misleading as they conjure up an image of a practitioner "doing something" to a client, that is, treating, intervening, or implementing an action plan. There can be an implication that the professional "has answers" and it is simply a matter of helping the client learn those answers. Clearly, this is not the view of professional practice that has characterized social work.

A view of the social worker as process expert is proposed in this text. The social worker knows how to engage people in a relationship and a process that involves joint discussion and reflection. Together the client and worker participate in a continuous dialogue, or therapeutic conversation, where they examine the salient aspects of the client's situation. This position is consistent with contemporary social work practice theory in its emphasis on collaboration (Dean, 2001; Saleeby, 2002a, b). The social worker's knowledge and skill is directed to providing a supportive "space and place" for this dialogue. This metaphor is elegantly captured by Murphy and Dillon (2003), who characterize the worker as providing steadiness and thoughtfulness and "an invisible bubble of calm and focused attention" (p. 22). As noted frequently in this text, unlike relationships in everyday life the professional helping relationship exists solely for the client's benefit. It provides the focused attention of another person who listens, explores, and aims to increase understanding of the client's issues so that potential goals can be identified, change brought about, or a particular kind of support or concrete assistance offered. Providing premature advice, giving unrealistic reassurance, and "swapping stories" are typical reactions when one hears about family members' and friends' problems. These reactions are not offered in professional work; they are processed, understood, and then may be used in a purposeful manner or held back.

In this text the term *intervention* will be used, despite the earlier critique, to maintain consistency with the professional literature. Taking into account the contextual and collaborative stance presented earlier, intervention is defined as the social worker's actions that aim to prevent, support, or change something. The term also includes the methods and techniques used to bring about some desired outcome.

CHANGE AND SUPPORT

The goal of direct practice in social work is to provide a service that promotes an individual's social functioning. Change efforts aim to help clients take or continue some action. Since the ecosystemic approach is used as the primary framework in social work, practitioners are always cognizant of the extent to which structural, systemic, and interpersonal factors play a significant role in the client's current and past concerns and the extent to which they must be changed to enhance well-being. Change efforts therefore can involve many aspects of an individual's life, both external and internal. Any social work practice intervention attends to addressing basic needs. When lack of resources or services are part of the problem, the social worker directs her attention to helping the client access those resources, either through referral, supporting the client in his efforts to obtain a service, or advocating on the client's behalf. External change also aims to improve or change interpersonal relationships that are intimate, familial, social, or work related. If the goal is change in a couple or family relationship, specialized couple or family therapy models are recommended based on their demonstrated superiority over individual treatment for relationship problems (Sprenkle, 2002).

When personal change is a goal, the social worker and client will examine the relationships between the client's perceptions, meanings, feelings, and behaviors. This perspective, that all of these factors are important, was briefly introduced in chapter 1 as a core concept and is elaborated on in the presentation of change processes that follows. While the initial focus may be on the development of new perceptions and meanings the person has about himself and his situation, it may be necessary to help the client identify emotions that may previously have stayed largely out of awareness. Or the client may find relief from experiencing her feelings more acutely. Emotions and the understandings and meanings attributed to them powerfully affect behavior (Greenberg, 2002b). Through examining the links between the domains of thoughts or meanings, feelings, and behaviors, individuals may identify persistent patterns they wish to change. In order to bring about change, interventions will also focus alternatively on new ways of thinking, feeling, and behaving. The interactions of these domains can be illustrated in the following example of a client requesting help from a social worker to deal with his social isolation. The practitioner may initially focus on helping this client develop better understanding or insights into his perceptions and thoughts about himself in social situations and intimate relationships. They may identify that he is doubtful about his ability to be close to a woman, perceiving that he does not measure up when compared to his peers. Through exploring these thoughts, the client becomes more aware that in social situations he feels insecure, anxious, and uncomfortable. Furthermore, he recognizes that these feelings have led him to avoid situations where he might meet others or, when in such situations, to behave in a withdrawn and reticent manner. This behavior in turn leads him to feel unconnected and isolated, further reinforcing both his conviction that he is unattractive to others and his feelings of unhappiness about himself. In attempting to bring about change, all three aspects will be addressed. It would not be sufficient to develop new insight without supporting and even coaching behavior change. Similarly, strategies to change behavior would fall short if not accompanied by interventions that modify the individual's self-concept and related feelings. Changes to the client's self-concept might come about through understanding its derivatives, challenging the meanings and conclusions the client has developed through his life experiences, providing a new relationship experience in the therapeutic alliance, or any combination of these approaches.

Based on the assessment, there will be situations where social workers are not working toward change, rather they are supporting individuals in difficult situations. For example, in palliative care units social workers often meet with family members to provide support through the final stages of a terminal illness. In child protection services for foster children the worker assists foster families to provide an emotionally supportive and stable home to meet children's developmental needs. Finally, where highly vulnerable client populations have pervasive needs over a prolonged period of time interventions may focus on support and environmental change. The case management model for individuals with severe mental illness is an example of such a situation.

Some practice models have drawn distinctions between two types of interventions: 1) those interventions aimed at supporting the individual's personality and characteristic ways of feeling, perceiving, and approaching the world and 2) those interventions aimed at modifying personality characteristics (Goldstein, 1995; Woods and Hollis, 2000). In actual practice supportive interventions can create new learning for the client, especially about expectations of self, other, and relationships, and result in fundamental changes. Similarly work aimed at changing personality can be experienced as supportive, especially insofar as the client feels understood and gains relief simply by expressing and exploring concerns in the presence of an empathic practitioner.

While referring to a middle *stage* may imply a finite period of time, many social workers work with populations with ongoing situations or conditions where this stage proceeds over a period of time, even though it may be divided into segments of service. In many organizations programs are designed to meet a range of physical, medical, and psychosocial needs over a significant period of the life cycle. For example, families with children who are born with visual, auditory, or physical disabilities, children who become wards of the state, and adults who develop chronic illnesses that interfere with their ability to live independently are populations that may require social work interventions on a continuous basis or at significant times of transition. Families with a child with significant physical disabilities may need different types of involvement with the social worker at various stages in a child's development. Initially this may consist of helping the family gain the information they need to understand the medical and physical condition, to learn about services and government entitlements available to them, and to deal with their emotional reactions. The family may then call the social worker for help in decision making about the benefits of the child attending a neighborhood school or a special school. At a later stage vocational preparation and decisions about autonomous living arrangements may be the focus. Hence the middle stage is continuous, although divided into segments of service at particular points.

A supportive relationship that the client experiences as helpful knits these phases together. The client returns to the social worker at crucial times when he feels a sense of connection and understanding as a result of the help previously received. In this situation the therapeutic relationship has provided a secure base, a place in which the client in distress experiences a bond with someone he perceives to be helpful. Help may be associated with any number of activities: the opportunity to talk things out, think through issues, express strong feelings, gain better mastery of a situation, receive acknowledgment and validation, or arrive at a decision. Therefore, while the middle phase is presented as if it were discrete, time limited, and focused, in actual practice it can be more fluid, continuous even with interruptions, and less action oriented than the technical language used to describe it implies.

MODELS, TECHNIQUES, AND INTERVIEWING BEHAVIOR

In the middle phase social workers use a wide range of interventions to accomplish the tasks associated with change. To reiterate, the middle stage flows initially from the assessment, where preliminary joint understandings of the problem were reached. As the worker proceeds to introduce interventions, he and the client have the opportunity to test out their initial assessments and to determine the extent to which their explanations of why there was a problem were useful. Both successful and unsuccessful interventions provide additional data about the person and her situation, which in turn contribute to gaining more depth and complexity in understanding. New insights also can lead to choosing additional intervention approaches.

When a particular model of change is directing the work, practitioners have available to them interventions and the related techniques designed to meet specific goals. As presented in chapter 1, in actual practice social workers use a wide variety of concepts, principles, interventions, techniques, and interviewing skills that reflect their own integration of theory and practice. Some of these concepts and skills are generic to social work, others are shared with all human service professions, and some, while associated with a particular model, can also be used in creative ways without adherence to the original model. What characterizes direct social work practice is that practitioners choose, combine, and adapt interventions in an intentional and purposeful manner to achieve changes in clients' perceptions, feelings, and behaviors or to offer support to clients.

Social workers need to be conversant with the latest empirical findings to determine whether there are innovative approaches and techniques that may be useful in their practice with specific populations and problems. While the "common factors" analysis reviewed in chapter 5 demonstrated the limited role of specific models and techniques, it also acknowledged their contributions (Hubble, Duncan, and Miller, 1999b). Models can provide focus through two features: 1) they give a structure to the work by setting out what must take place and when and 2) they offer descriptions of intervention procedures and techniques. More challenging is the response to the broader questions—what structure and procedures to use and what areas to focus on.

The choice of models is a complex matter, and any practice encounter represents some negotiation between the participants, the social worker, the client, and the degree of flexibility the agency allows in the choice of approach and time frame. For example, many practitioners today are embracing postmodernism and a narrative model for practice. Concepts offered appear well-suited for situations of diversity where the worker is striving to understand the experiences of clients who are different from themselves by virtue of race, class, ethnicity, sexual orientation, and ability (Dean, 2001; Laird, 1998). Despite the lack of empirical support for narrative approaches, many practitioners embrace this perspective for its resonance with social work values, especially the commitment to more egalitarian and complementary styles in the working relationship. However, if a client asks the worker to provide more direction, specific strategies, and guidance, these preferences must be taken into account if the social worker is truly aiming at honoring and respecting the client's view of what is useful. Even when both client and worker prefer a narrative approach and a prolonged period of engagement, if the agency or managed care requirements limit the service to one that is short-term, the approach must be adapted to these parameters.

Practitioners are responsible for continuously and critically evaluating their own knowledge in light of the ever expanding professional knowledge base. Remaining current with intellectual advances in the field and with practice research can lead to revising beliefs or assumptions about what is needed to bring about change. It can also provide validation for long-held practice wisdom. With this background practitioners need to work in concert with clients to select models and techniques that are credible to them. Furthermore, it is the worker's responsibility to be mindful of progress and evaluate whether the approach being used is bringing about some change within a reasonable period of time. In chapter 2 a number of questions were presented to help workers stay client centered and change focused rather than model centered ("Reflective Exercise: Evaluating Process and Progress"). When practitioners are allied with a particular model, lack of change in clients can inadvertently be addressed by offering "more of the same" and perhaps seeking supervision or consultation. The assumption is that the approach works and that the worker only needs additional supervision to learn to use the techniques in a more skillful manner. However, practitioners have a wide variety of individual, interpersonal, and group models available to them. When change is not occurring it is wise to consider using another approach.

PROCESSES FOR BRINGING ABOUT CHANGE

The key concern of practitioners is how change can be brought about, what principles, interventions, and processes are available to the worker to achieve positive outcomes. In this text the research literature on the outcomes of various intervention models and the meta-analysis of those findings has been referred to extensively. Another type of research, clinical process research, shows promise for providing more specific guidance to practitioners as these studies identify client and worker behaviors and patterns in interviews that account for positive change. When conducting process-outcome research, the first step is to establish positive outcome in the participating client sample using traditional research methods, such as comparing a range of client variables before and after intervention. The second step consists of an intensive investigation of what actually occurred in sessions in cases where there was positive change. A number of approaches are used to systematically code or analyze themes, processes, and behaviors that transpired in the sessions studied (Greenberg, 1999; Woolley, Butler, and Wampler, 2000). Researchers have used process outcome studies to investigate experiential psychotherapy (Greenberg, 1999; Greenberg, Rice, and Elliott, 1993), couple and family therapy (Woolley, Butler, and Wampler, 2000), and recently to study cross-cultural practice in social work agencies (Tsang, Bogo, and George, 2003).

A review of studies of intervention models in related helping professions reveals a number of shared change processes that appear to work across these models and have been described as transtheoretical (Orlinsky, Grawe, and Parks, 1994). Many of these processes have also been discussed in the social work practice theory literature, although they have not received the extensive empirical validation found in related disciplines. These processes or interventions can be especially useful when selected with an appreciation of the client's stage with respect to readiness to change, as reviewed in chapter 5 (Prochaska and Prochaska, 2002; Prochaska, DiClemente, and Norcross, 1992).

In the following discussion change processes are presented in a sequential order. In actual practice they unfold in a cyclical or looping manner. Conversations are repeated, key themes and insights are revisited and revised, and new behaviors and related changes are attempted more than once. That change usually does not come easily or quickly is important for both clients and practitioners to remember. Box 7.1 presents a list of the key types of change processes.

DEVELOPING AN EXPANDED UNDERSTANDING

In this process the problem or concern that was jointly identified by the client and worker in the beginning stage serves as the initial focus for discussion and is examined from a variety of perspectives. Discussions often begin with telling stories about what has recently happened in our everyday lives. In the interview clients frequently begin in this manner and tell their worker about what has happened to them since their last meeting. Clients need to have the opportunity to expand on details they deem important. The practitioner listens attentively and links what the client is presenting to issues from previous sessions.

Practitioners balance clients' need for expression with a structured dialogue. Providing focus and direction is linked to positive outcome and helps to contain clients' concerns. The goals that were agreed to in the planning phase provide some direction. The practitioner has the responsibility to keep these overall goals in mind during each interview, while inviting the client to begin each session by setting the agenda with issues of paramount concern to the client. It is likely that the particular issue or narrative that is introduced is connected to the overall themes and goals that constitute the emphasis in the work.

The presenting problem or primary clinical focus is the catalyst for the worker to learn more about the client's values and beliefs, especially when practicing in situations of diversity. Information that the worker needs to learn is revealed through dialogue about the key events and experiences introduced by the client and through seeking more information in a number of domains. With a better understanding of the important aspects of a client's life, there will be an expanded understanding of the present problem and salient issues. For example, a lesbian client was extremely distraught in her session with a male heterosexual worker. She discussed her dread that she would be alone on the day of the gay pride parade in her city. The worker inquired whether she had made any plans to attend the parade with friends and learned of her many unsuccessful attempts to find friends or even distant acquaintances with whom to spend the day. As the worker explored this presenting issue, he heard about how important the sense of belonging to the lesbian, gay, bisexual, and transgendered community was to the client and that attending the parade had always been a celebration for her. Having recently ended a three-year intimate relationship, the client was now alone and feeling rejected and disappointed with the total cut-off from her former partner. The process of choosing to live in a loving lesbian relationship and of coming out to family and work colleagues had been a difficult one for this client, but one she felt she had ultimately handled successfully. However, anticipating the impending community celebration, and that she would not be in a relationship when she attended it, symbolized for her how much she had sacrificed in the past. It led her to reflect with sadness on the many family gatherings and work-related social events she had attended alone before introducing her partner into these important circles. The meaning of the presenting problem in that session, attending the parade alone, was expanded to a more complex understanding of the feelings engendered in the client—being alone and marginalized. Societal attitudes, as perceived in family relationships and in the workplace, had limited this client's participation in meaningful events in the past. In the present it was her single status that was interfering with her participation in a celebration she valued. This expanded understanding helped her recognize that it was important for her to attend, and she left the session determined to find a way to do so.

EXPLORING IN DEPTH

This process builds from the significant stories, events, and issues connected to the presenting problem that forms the content of the work in the early stage. The worker helps the client explore her environmental circumstances and social context. Thoughts and meanings, feelings, and reactions associated with significant aspects of the client's internal experience are examined. As noted earlier, external and internal phenomena and the dimensions of thinking, feeling, and behaving are interrelated. Hence links between these two domains can be usefully explored. The choice of an initial focus is related to the theoretical model used and the preferred style of the client. Regardless of where one begins, the essence of an exploratory process is to expand the client's self-awareness and self-understanding on an emotional and intellectual level.

Focus on emotions. Emanating from the experiential tradition in clinical theory, currently most practitioners acknowledge the crucial role of emotion in organizing our perceptions, attributing meaning to events, and affecting our behaviors (Greenberg, 2002a). Clinical theorists note the usefulness of helping clients become aware of these powerful emotions and learning how to talk about and reflect on them. By the very nature of emotions, that they are immediate and of a feeling nature, individuals are often not able to spontaneously identify, label, or reflect on them. Rather, we are often vaguely aware of a sense of turmoil or we are "caught up in our emotions," undergoing something in an intense way with little understanding or insight about what has triggered this state.

One purpose of focusing on emotions is to symbolize the experience in words. This enables individuals to gain self-awareness and self-understanding so that they are better able to increase their sense of control over those feelings that previously exerted a powerful influence on them; these feelings affected their beliefs about what they could or could not tolerate or do (Greenberg and Bolger, 2001). Emotional processing empowers individuals so that they are no longer a prisoner of their feelings. Awareness and understanding provide the tools to deal differently with one's internal experience and subsequently to act differently in one's external life (Greenberg, 2002a).

A useful distinction is made by Greenberg and colleagues between primary and secondary emotions (Greenberg, 2002b; Greenberg and Pavio, 1997; Greenberg et al., 1993). "Primary emotions are the person's most fundamental direct initial reactions to a situation. Secondary emotions are those responses that are secondary to other more primary internal processes and may be defenses against these (Fosha, 2000; McCullough, 1997). Secondary emotions are responses to prior thoughts or feelings or to a complex sequences [sic] of these—sequences such as feeling angry in response to feeling hurt, feeling afraid about feeling angry, feeling guilty about a traumatic event by attributing responsibility to oneself for the event, or feeling afraid by generating catastrophic expectations. Secondary emotions need to be explored to get at their more primary generators. Thus, accessing the healthy anger at unfairness that underlies the powerlessness of some depressions promotes adaptation, whereas accessing the shame and/or sadness at the loss of esteem that underlies rage can promote attachment in place of destructiveness" (Greenberg, 2002b, p. 171).

The client is helped to express, think about, and experience feelings deeply. This activity may elicit a range of emotions from anger to sadness, and also include confusion, ambivalence, and general distress. As the worker and client explore strong feeling states they can illuminate associated thoughts and meanings, and the interrelationships between thoughts, feelings, and behaviors become more apparent. In chapter 9, on interviewing skills, the specific techniques for working with feelings are presented.

Focus on cognitions. Focusing on cognitions may begin with examining client's perceptions, thoughts, and attitudes as an entry into understanding the related feelings and behaviors that result. When addressing thoughts and meanings, the worker and client examine the ways in which an individual processes information and makes meaning of her world. Internal working models about self, other, and relationships can be examined.

Cognitive therapists have identified a number of tenets that can be integrated into any approach to understanding and helping. In Aaron Beck's seminal work on cognitive therapy for depression and in his subsequent writings he identified modes of organizing reality as faulty information processing (Beck, 1976; Beck et al., 1979). These ways of thinking can become habitual responses to most aspects of one's life. While Beck articulated these modes with reference to people presenting with depression, they can be applied to ways of thinking in the general population. The following list of cognitive processing styles is based on Beck's work (Beck et al., 1979) and provides useful concepts for understanding the way in which a client goes about making sense of his world.

Arbitrary inference refers to drawing a specific conclusion in the absence of evidence to support the conclusion or when the evidence is contrary to the conclusion. It can involve *emotional reasoning*: that if one feels a certain way a conviction must be true. For example, an individual feels that his presentation in class was poor and that he is stupid. This feeling overrides the positive responses of classmates and his instructor.

Selective abstraction refers to focusing on a detail taken out of context, ignoring other more salient features of the situation and conceptualizing the whole experience on the basis of this fragment. This is a process where information is filtered, usually in a negative way, and positives are ignored. The student in the preceding example, when reviewing the anonymous written feedback forms for the presentation, remembers and focuses on the few critical comments and skims over the many positives. The critical comments affirm for him how poorly he performed.

Overgeneralization refers to drawing a general rule or conclusion on the basis of one or more isolated incidents and applying the concept across the board to related and unrelated situations. This tendency is seen when an individual frequently uses the terms *never* and *always* to describe another's behavior in a relationship, such as in "He never says a kind word to me" and "She is always critical of everything I do with the children."

Magnification, or seeing small things as the beginning of a major problem, refers to an error in evaluating the significance or magnitude of an event. For example, an employee who receives excellent yearly written job appraisals fears that she will be fired on the rare occasions that her employer gives her mild negative feedback. *Minimization* operates in the opposite direction in a similar manner. For example, the family who does not regard a child's lack of interest in eating and absence of weight gain as an indication of a possible need for a checkup.

Personalization refers to relating external events to self when there is little or no basis for making such a connection. For example, in couple relationships one partner assumes that the other's silence at breakfast means she is angry despite her having frequently stated that she is not a morning person. This also involves blaming self and taking responsibility for things that are not the individual's.

Polarizing refers to thinking in extremes with all experiences evaluated in one of two opposite categories, smart or stupid, good or bad, with no shades of gray.

Another aspect of understanding individuals' ways of processing information is to gain access to underlying belief systems. Cognitive theorists posit that, from previous experience, individuals develop beliefs about self, about others and relationships, and about the human condition and the social world. Also referred to as schemas, individuals' beliefs serve as filters in subsequent life experiences and influence an individual's perceptions, meanings, and interpretations of internal experience and external events. These cognitions influence one's feelings and behaviors, which in turn will produce experiences that may reinforce and confirm these cognitions or challenge and modify them. The goal in working with cognitions is to help clients identify and understand these underlying belief system and modify those that are self-defeating. In chapter 3, in the description of attachment theory and the helping relationship, the concept of internal working models was linked particularly to how thoughts about relationships influence individuals' feelings and behavior about self and about the social worker.

With these concepts as a framework, practitioners can begin an in-depth exploration, with a focus on client's perceptions, thoughts, and attitudes. This focus will provide important insights both for the client and worker and can also serve as an entry into revealing related feelings and behaviors. When addressing thoughts and meanings, the worker and client also examine the ways in which an individual processes information and makes sense of his world. For example, a middle-aged man, James, was fearful that his gay relationship partner, Armand, was unhappy in the relationship and likely to leave. James reported numerous fights and disagreements that left him feeling demoralized. Although Armand reassured him that he was quite satisfied in their two-year relationship and that conflict and anger were "normal," James remained fearful that the relationship would dissolve. Further exploration revealed that James' family of origin, described by him as cerebral, frowned on displays of emotion and James had a view of relationships that expected calm, reasoned discussion and negotiation of any differences. He believed that strong displays of emotion, especially negative feelings, indicated great conflict that would inevitably lead to the disintegration of the relationship. James interpreted Armand's behavior through this schema and, when processing their disagreements, used emotional reasoning, convinced that his reaction of fear when Armand expressed himself in strong language was a true predictor of things to come. Overgeneralization that a few disagreements meant the end of the relationship interfered with his ability to see that their relationship held many positives or to hear what Armand was saying, that angry disagreements reflected a difference of opinion rather than an end to the relationship. Magnification of the negatives led to pervasive anxiety and to the beginning of emotional withdrawal on James's part. Withdrawing behavior was experienced as rejection by Armand and had begun to fuel a cycle between the two of greater distance. This example shows how cognitive styles in information processing can produce feelings and behaviors that can make a situation more problematic and unfulfilling. Since James was uncomfortable with emotional expression, he found a focus on his emotional experience as more anxiety producing. Rather, the practitioner helped him identify the thoughts and cognitive styles that led to his feelings and behaviors, challenged those conceptions, examined alternative interpretations, and ultimately helped him think, feel, and behave differently in the relationship.

Identifying themes. Through exploration the worker and client can begin to identify recurrent themes, patterns, or responses in the client's life. This also broadens the definition of the presenting problem. "A series of difficulties often represents a repeating theme in which the details may vary but the core event is the same" (Fusko, 1999, p. 49). Fusko provides the example of helping a client identify a long-standing pattern of difficulty in getting along with authority figures and notes that helping the client with this theme will build his capacity to deal more effectively with authority figures in general as well as get along better with a current employer.

While it can be an oversimplification to reduce an individual's life to a smattering of recurring patterns, these patterns frequently capture some essential themes that operate in a number of domains over time. It can be liberating for an individual to identify, define, and label these continuing themes. Furthermore, while there are themes that are connected to pain and suffering, there are also themes about strength and resilience that can be called upon to address current presenting issues. Themes may be about a number of issues: individual, interpersonal, and developmental.

Themes relating to the individual. Themes relating to the individual refer to the response patterns that reflect the individual's dynamics; how various aspects of the personality work in somewhat characteristic ways (Woods and Hollis, 2000). These dynamics may be sensed by the client, but have not yet been put into words. For example, through an exploratory process an individual comes to recognize that when she is feeling anxious about a new project or responsibility at work, she will devote all her time to the task at hand. This may involve spending long hours at work, searching for information and new skills to help her with the particular project, and doing whatever it takes to master the demands of a new position. This makes her a valuable employee and she is satisfied with her promotions. On the other hand she recognizes that her life is not well balanced to meet other needs she has for recreation and socializing. Or, an individual may recognize that when faced with stress and anxiety about his work performance his characteristic response has been to avoid dealing with the situation. Withdrawal may take the form of leaving the job or numbing his feelings through the overuse of alcohol or drugs. Disappointed with the lack of progress and advancement in his work, he comes to recognize the ways in which his characteristic pattern of dealing with anxiety has not served him in the long run.

Themes relating to interpersonal relationships. Themes in interpersonal relationships are about the way an individual interacts with significant others, the way expectations and demands of others are dealt with, and how conflict is perceived and managed. For example, an individual may recognize that in her significant roles as worker, friend, family member, and relationship partner she assumes responsibility for the well-being of others. This way of handling situations has resulted in others valuing and cherishing her, viewing her as a person who can always be counted on. It has however, at times left her feeling emotionally depleted and that there is little energy left over to meet her own needs. A frequent response to conflict in interpersonal relationships is to feel flooded with negative emotions and to believe that the conflict is of such a magnitude that the relationship is doomed. This constellation of feeling overwhelmed in conjunction with a pessimistic view of the future has been associated with emotional withdrawal from the partner: a cascade of distance and alienation ensues (Gottman and Levenson, 1999). Or, an individual complains that he can never please his partners; they have always been too demanding and selfish in the end. Through exploration he recognizes that although he feels respected and understood at the beginning of a new intimate relationship, when his partner disagrees with him he reacts with anger that frequently escalates to physical threats. Reviewing his failed relationships, he begins to see the way in which he is threatened and feels insecure when challenged and that he lashes out aggressively in response. He recognizes his contribution to broken relationships.

Themes relating to developmental issues. Developmental themes refer to patterns that were established early in an individual's life and are repeated in the present even in the face of different external circumstances. In the long-standing social work model psychosocial therapy, attention to these past dynamics is "usually undertaken in an episodic way...certain themes being explored as it becomes apparent that factors in the client's development are blocking improvement in current social adjustment" (Woods and Hollis, 2000, p. 141). Relevant aspects of the client's past are looked at as they are raised in relation to the present focus. A wide range of past experiences, at societal, familial, and personal levels, can be important for understanding the meaning of current issues in a person's life. It can be helpful to identify the way that societal and cultural values and messages have been transmitted through the client's family of origin and through the generations. Also useful is gaining a more acute awareness of the way in which these messages have been internalized and operate in the present. Where experiences of marginalization, discrimination, and oppression have had an impact on the individual, these past and current episodes are discussed. These dynamics can be seen to be operating in the example presented earlier in the discussion of the first process of change. In this example the client is able to explore how meanings and attitudes in past situations about her sexual orientation led to positions and related feelings that still carry an emotional impact as she faces her current dilemmas.

When clients are helped to reflect on earlier examples of repetitive patterns in their lives it is helpful to distinguish between periods when these patterns were useful in managing conflict situations and periods when these patterns limited the capacity to grow and develop fully. For example, an adult who was the eldest child in a family with an alcoholic parent recognizes through an exploratory process that, ever since he can remember, he adopted a position of vigilance with respect to his father's drinking behavior and related anger and verbal abuse to his siblings. This client felt responsible for his younger brothers and sisters and tried to minimize the impact of their father's anger on them by keeping the children out of the way when his father was drinking heavily, trying to anticipate his father's requests and meeting them. This externally focused and highly responsible way of behaving protected his younger siblings and enabled him to feel positively about his ability to help others. Only in adult life, through reflecting on his overly responsible manner in the work place and in relationships, has he become aware that an exaggerated focus on the needs of others has left him less aware of his own feelings, unable to identify his own needs and pursue ways of having them met. A longstanding pattern that was highly functional in his earlier years is interfering with his ability to find fulfillment as an adult.

A process-outcome research study of clients' subjective experience of psychotherapy supports many of the change processes discussed thus far (Watson and Rennie, 1994). Participants in the therapy and in the research reported that ongoing dialogue with the practitioner helped them put into words their feelings, perceptions, beliefs, values, and needs in relation to their inner and external world. They came to better understand themselves as well as the strong reactions they had toward events and interactions in their external world. Through telling stories about these significant events some clients visualized themselves in the episode and reexperienced their feelings. The process of discussion with another person was deemed helpful. "In the act of sharing their experience and confessing their difficulties and disturbing material to another person, their problems became more concrete and real, so that their problems had to be confronted and given attention" (Watson and Rennie, 1994, p. 503). The respondents further noted that finding the words to describe and convey their experiences was not easy; they had to make a number of attempts to put their inner experiences into words. Further, they believed that through this process of finding the words to capture their feelings and thoughts they were helped to distill the essence of what they were struggling with; they valued moving from a vague and amorphous sense of disquiet to having a handle on significant issues. Practitioners assisted them through reflecting feelings, probing, and providing words or phrases.

Through the two preceding processes clients' achieve an expanded understanding of the presenting problem and the external and internal factors that have an impact on it. The client may become more aware of issues in his life, which Prochaska and his colleagues have referred to as consciousness-raising. They may then develop some greater appreciation of the relationship between internal and environmental interactions, defined as environmental reevaluation (Prochaska, DiClemente, and Norcross, 1992). Through the exploratory activities discussed thus far, some important intermediate effects may be observed. These are greater awareness of the self and the problem, including weighing the effect of various factors in the individual and in the environment, giving thought to when one should change individual patterns and when one should change aspects of the environment, including significant relationships.

IDENTIFYING STRENGTHS AND ADDRESSING OBSTACLES
Social work practice has traditionally been concerned with issues and strengths in individual's lives and in their environment. More recently, prac-

tice approaches that place strengths and solutions at the core have been developed. Traditional practice theory will first be reviewed followed by recent approaches. Using information gleaned in the assessment, in the middle phase the worker uses examples of the client's successful past coping and mastery as appropriate. Through examining areas of the client's life that are conflict free and satisfying, client attributes and skills are identified. These examples provide a rich reservoir of information that is used to better understand the client's internal strengths and resources. The worker also helps the client become aware of and appreciate these instances of success, resilience, and effective coping that the client does not see or does not view as positive or exceptional. These client abilities can be brought to bear on the issues at hand, an emphasis that can promote the client's self-image and self-esteem.

When individuals turn to others for help, they may be feeling overwhelmed and demoralized and not in touch with their strengths. Therefore when the assessment has established that the client has been effective in many situations Goldstein (1995) recommends discussing this with the client. The focus would be on identifying previous coping successes and wondering what is currently occurring that interferes with the client's ability to use those personal resources and what they would need in order to recapture those competencies.

Clients come for help because something is troubling to them and they are likely to present difficulties, problems, pain, and deficits to the professional. The principle of "starting where the client is" directs us to begin at this point and respond to the client's lead. However, the strengths perspective takes the dialogue away from problems, dysfunction, and pathology. Some clients will welcome and feel invigorated by reclaiming their own power. Others will feel that the practitioner is not giving enough credence to the pain and discomfort they face or view the practitioner as superficial and not having an accurate understanding of the client's situation.

Strengths in the natural and social environment in which the client lives are also identified. Among the significant environmental factors that affect an individual's well-being are the presence of supportive people such as families, friends, employers, spiritual advisers, and teachers. The availability of resources and institutions that provide not only for basic human needs but also reinforce and celebrate accomplishments merits attention. Schools, work organizations, community centers, and neighborhood organizations that enable people to learn, grow, and develop their strengths provide nurturance and the conditions associated with well-being. The case management model focuses primarily on locating these environmental resources and encouraging clients to integrate the services and programs they offer into their lives.

A focus on strengths does not avoid a realistic appraisal of barriers or obstacles to change that exist in the individual and in the environment. Individual client factors can assist or impede the formation of a working alliance. The approach presented here gives primacy to the nature of the relationship and the ways in which the two participants are able to develop a helping system. The nature of the two individuals, the worker and the client, are active ingredients in determining the nature of an alliance. Earlier we discussed the contributions of the practitioner and that ongoing self-awareness and reflexivity assist us in being client centered and intentional rather than reactive in our work. Similarly, the stance of the client influences both the relationship created and the ability to extract something of use from the meetings. For example, individual change can be assisted or compromised by people's willingness to risk engaging. When mistrust, skepticism, and hostility toward professional help are predominant, it may compromise the client's ability to take an active and collaborative position. Two extensive reviews of client involvement in therapy found the following client factors highly predictive of positive results: cooperation, personal investment, openness, and collaboration, rather than a dependent or controlling posture (Garfield, 1994; Orlinsky, Grawe, and Parks, 1994). Some clients may demonstrate these attitudes in the beginning stage as a by-product of their personal style, such as their reaction to vulnerability and the need to seek professional help. For clients who are ordered to see a social worker for counseling or therapy it is understandable that they may initially present with hostility or guardedness. The challenge for social workers is to help clients arrive at a position that is more likely to help them benefit from the meetings they are ordered to attend.

When individual change will affect a client's significant intimate relationships or family and extended kin systems, it is important to think broadly and take these systems into account. Family systems theory highlights that change in an individual will have an impact on others in the person's relational world (Nichols and Schwartz, 2001). Parts of a system may react positively or negatively to change in one member's behavior. This can occur in extended and nuclear families, in intimate couple relationships, between close friends, and in work groups. For example, a twenty-seven-year-old man has been working with a social worker to explore whether he is able to live on his own. He has lived with his parents who have helped him with many of his physical needs since he became quadriplegic after a diving accident in late adolescence. His parents may react positively to this move, supporting his independence and autonomy, or they may perceive this move to be unrealistic and, fearful for their son's safety, may discourage any further thought or discussion.

Social workers often work with the significant relational units in a person's life. At times this may not be possible, as the relevant family member is not willing to participate or geographically available. In other instances the individual client may not wish to involve others in the interviews. When forced to work with an individual alone regarding relationship issues it is important to "think systemically" and devote attention to the interactions and experiences of the primary client with the influential people in his life.

Naturally occurring networks, such as neighbors, friends, teams in work organizations, and colleagues in faith-based organizations can be sources of great help or present barriers to change. If these associations are experienced by the client as exploitative, undermining, burdensome, or problematic, the focus may change to helping the client reevaluate membership in these systems. For example, youth members of violent gangs must go against the prevailing gang culture if they want to complete high school and obtain a legitimate form of employment. Not as clear-cut are those situations where immigrant women, especially those who do not speak English, are living with physically abusive husbands. These women may periodically seek shelter, however they report that they risk losing acceptance and their position in their ethnic communities if they choose to call on the police or seek a legal separation from their spouses.

Client strengths and goals are compromised not only by small systems. Social workers understand that structures in society can systematically create barriers for groups of people, for example, women, people from visible minority populations, gay, lesbian, and bisexual people, the elderly, people with visible and invisible disabilities. Barriers take many forms and include lack of access to or availability of needed resources. Useful programs and services may not be present in an individual's community, there may be long waiting lists, or the eligibility requirements may exclude the client. Furthermore, social service, educational, and health policies and programs, designed with the intention of helping people, often include ideologies, regulations, and procedures that ironically defeat their own goals of enhancing the social functioning of their clients.

More recently a strengths perspective that places the client's resilience and abilities at its core has been proposed (Saleeby, 2002b; Weick, Rapp, Sullivan, and Kisthardt, 1989). These authors focus on collaboration with clients to discover the resources they have used in their lives. Saleeby (2002a) recommends that social workers attend to evidence of client interests, talents, and competencies when they visit clients in their homes. He also identifies the following five types of questions designed to focus on positives, coping, and possibilities rather than on problems and deficits. The first set of questions take into account the challenges clients have faced and inquire how they have managed to *survive*, what they have learned from those experiences about self and their external world. These survival type questions are followed with elaborations and summaries about special strengths, insights, qualities, or skills developed by the client through dealing with adversity. The second set of questions is related to identifying the sources of *support* in the client's life. The worker inquires about people, organizations, and groups the client can depend on and what specifically each of these systems or individuals can provide. Furthering questions inquire about how the client connected with these supports and what they may have responded to in the client. The third set of questions is related to the future and asks about *possibilities*, hopes, and visions the client has and how the worker can help the client achieve those aspirations or draw on his special abilities and talents to make those dreams a reality. The fourth set of questions is about *esteem* and draws attention to what others would say about the client's positive qualities, what gives the client self-pride, and what circumstances lead the client to have positive self feelings. The final set of questions is about *exceptions* and is similar to those discussed below.

Solution-focused therapists also seek to identify strengths and amplify them in the interests of assisting clients to meet their goals (DeJong and Berg, 1998; Shezar, 1985). Recognizing that much time in an interview consists of discussion of problems and difficulties, these clinicians use exception-oriented questions to ask about recent instances when the problem might have occurred but somehow did not. DeJong and Berg (1998) propose the following steps and questions to elicit exceptions to the client's problems. The practitioner begins by trying to establish what exceptions look like. "We've been talking at length about the situations that lead you and your partner to argue. Can you tell me what it's like when you are not disagreeing?"

When the client provides an exception, the practitioner then asks for details about it, "the who, what, when, and where of exception times" (DeJong and Berg, 1998, p. 95). They recommend that listening and responses should be geared to what is different in the exception as compared to the problem time.

The practitioner then uses paraphrase and summary to clarify what the client has said about the nonproblem times. "When the two of you are doing something you like together, like bowling or taking a walk, you aren't arguing."

When the exception has been described, the practitioner inquires how the exception occurred—who did what so that it happened. Clients may or may not be able to identify what circumstances or actions led to a change. A distinction is made between deliberate exceptions, such as "My partner asked me to go for a walk and even though I was exhausted from a long day of work and taking care of the kids, I agreed," and random exceptions where the client is not able to distinguish any precipitating events. Through encouraging the client to elaborate on the circumstances around a deliberate exception the client can become more aware of recent successes in relation to the concern presented and the desired goals. Successes are highlighted and used to engender hope for future positive changes. Client strengths are also uncovered when a client is able to illustrate what he did differently. DeJong and Berg (1998) recommend that practitioners always attend to strengths and compliment the client for any successes. "You seem to have anticipated that going for a walk would be good for the two of you. Even though you were tired, you went along with his suggestion for the sake of the relationship."

DEVELOPING NEW PERSPECTIVES

Through interaction and dialogue with the worker the client gains some external feedback, another perspective on self and the world. A fifth process comes into play that involves gaining some distance from the immediate situation, which in turn enables consideration of new perspectives, including new emotional and cognitive understandings. This process of consideration is about thinking through a range of issues. Tallman and Bohart (1999) point out how little attention is paid in most intervention approaches to what they term "generative thinking" (p. 112), the human capacity for thinking about issues, figuring out what is happening, what is important, considering alternatives, reviewing one's experience, and generating possible solutions and outcomes of each way of responding. They note that when in a helping context it is the role of the practitioner to elicit and support these naturally occurring processes.

There are many techniques to use to help clients in this regard so that developing new perspectives can lead to the next phase where action is taken. Social workers vary along a continuum in being more or less direct in providing feedback. Questions can be used to help the client examine assumptions that were previously seen as fixed and rigid. Explanations or interpretations, offered tentatively as hunches, can help clients understand how their recurrent reactions are indications of unacknowledged thoughts, feelings, expectations of self or others. Challenge, confrontation, and reframing are also ways of helping unfreeze rigid perceptions and thinking about new possibilities. Finally, offering information about resources, about psychological and social phenomena, and about relevant medical or mental health issues is another way to help gain new perspectives. These techniques are discussed in chapter 9 on interviewing skills. Since all these techniques are provided within the context of an accepting relationship, the client is likely to feel supported rather than judged. Clients are helped to see that what they do, feel, or how they relate makes sense, given their unique personal and family histories and the cultural values and sociopolitical forces they have experienced (Mishna, 2003a, b).

With better understanding of their motivations and reactions, clients begin to consider whether their typical ways of dealing with situations in their life are likely to meet their needs in a way consistent with their self-image, goals, and values (Watson and Rennie, 1994). When clients reflect on the origins of their behavior, they can separate out what was appropriate in earlier and different interpersonal relationships from what they can choose to do and to be in the present. For example, a client reflected on how homophobia in his workplace had led him to take a distant and isolated position with colleagues. He wondered whether with changed societal attitudes toward gay and lesbian people and a diverse work force in his current job he could be less vigilant about discrimination and allow himself to be known by and to know others with whom he worked in a more authentic way.

An important by-product of developing new perspectives is that it can lead individuals to feel differently, and more positively, about themselves. Attributes that might previously have been experienced as negatives about the self may now be understood as a reasonable or effective response to a difficult external situation. Areas of strength that were previously taken for granted by an individual may now be perceived as evidence of her abilities. Realizing that these skills or attributes can be applied in other situations can build self-confidence and self-esteem.

Social workers draw from the ecosystemic perspective and help clients sort out the contributions of individual, relational, and societal or structural issues to experiences in daily life. It is extremely helpful for clients to take responsibility for what they bring to difficult situations and also to recognize what is not their responsibility, what are burdens they experience from factors beyond their individual control. Providing information and education about issues that clients might not usually have knowledge about can be extremely useful in this regard. When clients recognize the impact of external forces, social workers can raise with their clients whether they wish to involve themselves in community or social action.

TAKING ACTION

From developing new perspectives, any combination of taking new actions, developing alternative thoughts and feelings may arise. That is, while all aspects of the feeling-thinking-behaving cycle are likely involved in lasting change, individuals can begin change efforts with any one of these components. Clients have reported a "surge of energy and an elevation in their mood" (Watson and Rennie, 1994, p. 504) with new emotional and intellectual insights. This in turn seems to provide the impetus for making changes.

Ultimately the client comes to consider ways that he may change, that the environment may change, or that he can better live with the situation. When aiming to replace old patterns in the client's life, the practitioner and client can consider new adaptive responses in situations between the client and others and anticipate and manage potential responses. For example, a man in his early sixties, who typically adopted a distant position in family, social, and work relationships, came to recognize how that pattern conveyed a message to others that he was not interested in them, leaving him feeling isolated and disengaged from others. As he tried to change this behavior with more proactive interpersonal initiatives, he observed that his efforts were not always well received. His children did not immediately respond to his overtures, perceiving them as out of character and "too late." His spouse resented his intrusion into areas of their life that had previously been her responsibility. His coworkers were suspicious of his motives to extend their relationships beyond fixed and familiar parameters. When clients experience reactions such as these in relation to their change efforts, constancy and encouragement in the helping relationship is crucial. The worker not only provides the support to continue making efforts but also helps the client consider the reactions and possible thoughts and feelings of others in his environment in relation to his new attempts.

When contemplating taking action, it is important to convey a realistic and positive vision of what the future might consist of for the client—a sense of hopefulness. Hope has been identified as one of the common factors across models that lead clients to expect a positive outcome from meeting with the helping professional. Research on hope has found it associated with individuals' thoughts about their ability to move toward their goals (Snyder, Michael, and Cheavens, 1999). These researchers identify two components: pathways thinking and agency thinking. Pathways thinking refers to one's ability to think about various ways out of a situation and agency thinking refers to one's appraisal of the ability to actually take action and proceed on some selected path. If an individual can not either see potential ways out of a situation or feels she does not have the ability or resources to move along such a direction, then she is immobilized and cannot easily bring about any change.

It is through the dialogue in the session, where the client and worker together, consider alternatives and the ways in which the client can proceed, that a potential direction is chosen. In such a dialogue the practitioner may offer information, suggestions, questions that begin with "What if," brainstorm with the client, encourage the client to imagine possible future scenarios, and use stories illustratively. When offered within a collaborative relationship, this type of dialogue stimulates the client to develop his own ideas about what he wants to do differently. With a clearer sense of the goal, the focus then shifts to what initial steps are needed, that is, what would be the pathway along which the client can begin to reach that goal. In addition, consideration needs to be given to what conditions are needed for the client to take those steps. That is, agency thinking needs to be taken into account and efforts made to identify and then support what the client believes he needs to increase his ability to take that action. Returning to the previous case example, the worker inquired, "What do you need to happen in order for you to continue to reach out to your adult children even though they are resentful that you were not there for them when they were younger?" Through exploration and discussion the client, with the worker's help, recognized that he needed to be persistent and reliable, to demonstrate to his children his sincerity and commitment to forging a better relationship with them. In turn, he believed that he needed the worker's support at this point to help him maintain his hope that, with his best efforts, his children would ultimately believe him and allow more connection with them.

Change does not occur easily and progressively. There are many instances of a process more akin to "one step forward and two steps backward." Individuals can momentarily loose hope when their new efforts are not responded to favorably by others or when there are unanticipated consequences of new initiatives. There are also unanticipated consequences of taking new directions when one encounters new challenges. For example, a single mother with two children had invested great time, energy, and hope in employment upgrading only to encounter new stresses with full-time employment, restrictions on day care availability, and her children's reactions to her increased absence.

When clients recognize situations of a societal or organizational nature that are beyond their power to change, social workers may wish to point out opportunities in the community where clients can join with others for social change that increases services or changes relevant governmental policies. Some clients choose not to identify themselves with social causes that have an impact on their lives and others gain a great sense of power and relief from working with others in similar situations. For example, a young mother of an autistic child was reluctant to join a group of parents who were lobbying the school board to provide special classes for her child. She felt that all her energy was devoted to caring for her daughter and providing extra stimulation. She was still struggling with the emotional and practical implications of the diagnosis and her fears about her child's future. She stated that becoming part of a group of parents in a similar situation "only makes me feel worse about the diagnosis." Contrast this with a young woman who has had two bouts of cancer and becomes a community advocate for special services for women with cancer. She asserts that "working together with others with this terrible condition gives me energy and hope for my future."

When clients decide to try a new behavior or course of action, the interview can provide the chance to rehearse through coaching by the worker, role-playing, or talking about a potential scenario from the point of view of each participant. Any of these techniques serves to make an idea or intention into concrete reality. Possible future conversations can be enacted, with the worker making comments that help the client rehearse alternative behavioral responses, such as "What might you say if your daughter tells you she is not interested in your feelings?" or "How could you respond to her so that your anger and hurt don't push her further away?" or that provide suggestions through coaching, such as "have you thought about telling her that you can understand her feelings?" It is usually worthwhile for practitioners to continue to draw links between client insight and emotions and the way in which new intentions take shape in everyday life. Unless the internal gains made in the interview are carried over into clients' significant experiences and relationships out of the interview, change will not take place where it is meaningful—in the client's life.

When a new course of action is discussed in a session or homework tasks are agreed to, it is crucial that the worker follow up in the next meeting with inquiries about what transpired and what were the results of what was done differently (Hubble, Duncan, and Miller, 1999a). When clients report successes, they should be explored and reinforced. Clients and practitioners frequently gloss over successes and return to a focus on problems. Solution-focused therapy has provided useful insights and techniques for amplifying those client actions that are exceptions to the problem, that yield success, and that can be usefully generalized to other aspects of a client's life (Shezar, 1985).

Planning next steps and conveying realistic confidence in the client's ability to take those steps, can facilitate mastery experiences for the client. When a client succeeds in a new action it is useful to reflect with the client on that experience after the fact. Practitioners inquire about how it was accomplished and the client's subjective experience of doing, thinking, and feeling differently and provide reinforcement for the client's efforts. The helping relationship provides the attachment context and hence the emotional support for risk taking and new learning to occur. What is crucial, however, is that the client recognize what he did to bring about that change and, in the interests of the client's self-development, that he identifies the impact of this new behavior on his sense of self.

ADDITIONAL PRACTITIONER ACTIVITIES THAT SUPPORT CHANGE PROCESSES

Throughout the middle phase the worker is attending to two dimensions: 1) the interpersonal work with the client and 2) the progress toward goal achievement. While these dimensions are intertwined, they can be conceived as consisting of a process component and an outcome component. The first component focuses on the processes of change discussed in this chapter and the worker's behaviors or interventions that facilitate changes. This component includes attention to the alliance—that the client continues to feel understood and accepted by the worker and that they are focusing on issues deemed to be relevant by the client. The second component focuses on evaluation and requires attention to outcome and goal attainment. This was referred to in the ITPLoop Model as that aspect of reflection specifically concerned with evaluating the affect of the worker's interventions on progress toward achieving the goals in each interview as well as between sessions.

It is important to remember that the work with the practitioner in the interview is always in the interests of providing a context, experience, and activities that will prompt, support, and facilitate the client's active engagement in change (Tallman and Bohart, 1999). As noted throughout this text, when individuals' external environments do not provide the nutritive interpersonal relationships to help them solve problems in everyday living or do not provide support and assistance, then professional helpers can offer a safe "place and space" where the self-healing processes of thinking-feeling-behaving can occur (Tallman and Bohart, 1999). The relationship with the practitioner appears to be the key element in this regard.

Recall the extensive discussion of the helping relationship in chapters 3 and 4 and the well-supported finding from extensive empirical research that the helping relationship is a potent factor in bringing about positive change—far more so than the techniques of particular models. Furthermore, it is the client's experience of the relationship that is associated with outcome, not the ratings of the worker or of observers. The practice principle emanating from this research is that practitioners need to stay highly attuned to clients' perceptions about the relationship and to actively inquire whether it is offering the ingredients that each client believes are important. When the client's nonverbal behavior or direct feedback indicates either that certain elements are missing or that certain elements are helpful, practitioners strive to incorporate those factors that the client conveys are important and that can reasonably be included. Relationship elements may be about pace, style, frequency and duration of sessions, topics for discussion, tasks undertaken, and so on. These elements reflect a range of factors from individual attachment, personality, needs, and motivation, to sociocultural norms and conventions, and to the client's location in a stage of change. The preferred style for practitioners is one that is flexible, accommodates the client's wishes when possible, and is professionally appropriate.

Studies also find some universal characteristics of practitioners that clients describe as helpful: "understanding and accepting, empathic, warm and supportive. They engage in fewer negative behaviors such as blaming, ignoring, or rejecting" (Lambert and Barley, 2002, p. 26). When faced with challenging clients, for example, those who are mandated to attend sessions and consequently may behave in a negative, attacking, or hostile manner, practitioners work hard at containing critical or defensive responses and maintain an engaged client-centered stance.

Throughout the text the collaborative nature of the relationship as well as the usefulness of a stance that promotes client collaboration have been emphasized. Initially the work is presented as collaborative, and this approach is demonstrated in the many worker comments that seek feedback, ask directly whether she has understood the client, and ask the client for his ideas about topics under discussion. Explicit statements about working as a team, "putting two heads together," brainstorming ideas and possible solutions reinforce this notion. In the middle stage the relationship can be enhanced with references made to positive experiences the client and worker have had, especially when they find themselves at a difficult point in their work. For example, a woman in her early sixties had immigrated twenty years earlier and observed that as she got older she missed her extended family network in India. She found herself feeling lonely, especially at times of family celebrations she was not able to attend. She expressed regret that she had agreed with her husband to leave her home country for the benefit of their own children. When family events back home occurred she felt overwhelmed and depressed. The social worker had initially seen the client at such a time and could draw on those earlier experiences together to remind her that she had faced such feelings before and they had spent time discussing her situation and reactions, out of which emerged a number of insights and decisions. She had recognized that her feelings were normal and expected, a product of having a close and supportive family, and that it was at these times that the client needed to be actively involved with friends in her local community who could be supportive and understanding. Her depressed feelings led her to withdraw, however, the client and worker had learned together that, while difficult to do, the client's initiative to seek support from these friends had ultimately been very helpful to her. Such recall helps the client acknowledge and draw upon her own previously successful coping strategies. It also strengthens the relationship bond, which in turn helps the client move beyond the demoralization that accompanies her depressed feelings and experience hope that she will get some relief through discussion of the issues in the sessions.

Even when a positive relationship has developed in the beginning stage, it too can wax and wane in the more challenging phases, when change efforts are actively pursued. Practitioners need to remain sensitive to strains and tensions and take the initiative to explore what might be operating but unexpressed by the client. Studies have found that clients will continue to attend sessions even when they report that they did not feel the worker really understood them or find the meetings helpful (Hill, Thompson, Cogar, and Denman, 1993). This observation leads to the recommendation that practitioners make explicit at the beginning and throughout the meetings that discussion of the relationship, including negative feelings, is expected and important (Lambert and Barley, 2002).

A model for conceptualizing and intervening in alliance ruptures and repairs in psychotherapy has been developed and studied by Safran and Muran (2000). They define a rupture as a negative shift in the alliance that can be experienced as a tension or breakdown in the relationship. Ruptures vary along a continuum from minor tensions to major issues that can threaten the continuity and progress of the work. To deal effectively with ruptures they recommend the worker first identify in which *dimension* of the relationship there is difficulty: is there disagreement about the goals, the tasks, or are their strains in the nature of the bond? Based on this analysis the worker can choose to intervene *directly* or *indirectly*. If there is obvious disagreement about the tasks, for example, with the client maintaining that she wants individual sessions and will not attend if the worker pursues involving the rest of her family, the worker may agree to this in a direct manner. If the client indicates nonverbally that he is distressed when the worker answers the telephone during the session by subsequently providing fewer and fewer responses to the worker's comments, the worker may respond indirectly by turning off the telephone and positioning herself in a more attentive stance. Experienced workers continuously and intuitively respond in indirect ways when they sense that the client is feeling misunderstood or uncomfortable in some way.

The second dimension of Safran and Muran's model refers to the *level* of repair-oriented interventions: targeted at a *surface* level of meaning or at an *underlying* level. In the previous example the client is an adolescent in her late teenage years. Her mother and stepfather have expected her to provide extensive caretaking of her younger stepsiblings. Her adamant refusal to have family sessions could be addressed at the surface level by providing a rationale for family work, since the issues are about her perception of the unfair division of chores in the home now that the younger children are also teenagers. If her refusal were addressed on an underlying level the worker would explore an important theme for the client—her perception that she must always share with her siblings. Her anger at the worker would be linked to her disappointment that the counselor would no longer be there exclusively for her.

Safran and his colleagues have recently reviewed relevant studies related to alliance ruptures and repairs and draw a number of suggestions for practice from this literature (Safran et al., 2002). Social workers may find their recommendations useful when they identify tensions and breaks in relationships with clients in clinical and direct social work practice. When clients spontaneously express negative feelings about the relationship or when they express these feelings in response to the practitioner's inquiry or probes, it is important to respond in an open manner. Although social work practice theory encourages direct expression of clients' negative or critical comments, it is human nature that practitioners may experience such comments in a personally distressing way. They may feel these comments indicate something about their personality or their competence and suitability for this type of work. Self-awareness and clinical supervision can assist practitioners to contain these reactions and remain attuned and involved with their clients rather than respond in overtly negative ways such as through becoming defensive or overly critical of the client. Subtle and covert negative reactions such as withdrawing emotionally, becoming guarded, passive, or relatively silent in the sessions can also occur. These types of reactions between the client and the worker, where they each contribute negative communication behaviors, can produce a nonproductive interaction cycle. When confronted with negative feedback from clients, it is more useful for workers to listen carefully and clarify the client's concerns, including the client's perception and interpretation of the worker's behavior. Although it may feel uncomfortable, it is important for workers to take responsibility for their contribution, acknowledge that with the client, and apologize for a mistake or hurtful comment. While practitioners may be surprised by clients' views about the interaction, workers can recover from these disjunctions in the relationship and manage their own feelings effectively. Through both exploration with the client and reflection and debriefing after the session, on their own or in supervision, they are likely to learn something of value about clients and about themselves.

MONITOR AND SUPPORT GOAL ACHIEVEMENT

Social workers keep focused on the goals of the work and attend to indications that there is progress or lack of movement toward achieving positive outcomes. Some of the outcomes that result from social work intervention are a change in the presenting problem, a change in the client's ability to relate, to understand the situation and circumstances that led to seeking help, a change in significant interpersonal relationships, such as with intimate partners, family members, and in social and work relationships. Clients involved in mandated services may meet the conditions of the court or the agency and also gain personally from the required involvement with the practitioner. For example, in child protection interventions the client may learn new parenting skills and also how to effectively work with the agency social worker so that the client can request support and resources if difficulties arise in the future. When the presenting problem is due to a lack of resources, a crucial outcome is that the client experiences a significant improvement in basic human requirements such as food, shelter, and housing. This may be as a result of the client's efforts, for example, successfully completing a training course and finding employment, or as a result of successfully linking with a service that provides the resource that was absent.

The social worker continuously reviews process and outcome to determine whether progress is being made. When there is less than optimal movement, given that the relationship elements discussed above have been taken into account, it is useful to consider whether the goals, methods, or tasks are appropriate for the particular client and situation. Was the client in a stage in the change process that was matched by the worker's interventions? Or did the worker assume that the client was more ready to take action then he actually was? When the goals are not being achieved it may be timely to reconsider the original goals. Were they realistic, was the client a full participant in defining the goals, and were they truly agreed upon? Did the goals sufficiently capture underlying feelings that may have affected whether or not they could be achieved? For example, a gay male client requested help to leave a homosexual relationship that he felt was no longer meeting his needs. After a number of sessions it became evident that he had mixed feelings about his partner and was confused about whether or not the best course was to work to improve the relationship or to leave it. In the initial sessions these feelings had not been explored, and when they surfaced it became clear that the client was still in a decision-making phase, not an action phase. The client and worker reconsidered the goal and decided that resolving his mixed feelings was the necessary first step. Conjoint couple therapy was agreed upon as a method to help the client determine whether the blend of independence and interdependence he wanted was possible in this relationship. It was only after a few months of conjoint therapy with his partner that he came to the conclusion that the relationship dynamics were too rigid to allow for the kind of changes he had hoped for. Through the conjoint work he achieved the clarity and conviction he needed to work on the initial goal of leaving the relationship. In this example the goal was redefined and the methods expanded to include couples counseling. As the nature of the presenting issues and goals were better understood by both client and worker another intervention approach was used, one more appropriate for the concern.

In other instances the initial assessment needs to be revisited and examined to determine whether the approaches and resources introduced are sufficient to meet the presenting needs. For example, when peer tutorial help did not assist a shy and isolated adolescent boy to improve his scholastic performance, the social worker considered consultation with the school psychologist to determine further the nature of the student's performance problems. This assessment revealed that the student needed professional tutoring where he could review the material systematically. While the peer tutor had helped the student develop social skills, and he thus felt more comfortable in the school environment and was happier, it was not sufficient to address his educational needs. Through adding a different type of resource the adolescent was able to meet his goals.

In the interests of goal achievement practitioners are responsible for ensuring that the interviews and the overall helping process is focused and structured. Social workers are expected to make effective and efficient use of time and resources regardless of the auspice of practice, an agency, managed care environments, or private practice. Maintaining both focus and a supportive relationship are characteristic of skilled practitioners and associated with positive outcomes for clients.

Despite the use of appropriate helping principles, change may not be forthcoming; experienced social workers recognize that facilitating change is not a straightforward matter. Shulman (1999) offers a useful perspective in this regard. He describes clients' mixed feelings about both change and participation with social workers as a likely aspect of the helping process. He attributes this to the nature of the process; stressful issues are discussed with related painful feelings stirred up; individuals must confront their own contributions to problems, long-held beliefs that might be impeding their own progress, and take responsibility for their actions. Clients show mixed feelings in various direct and indirect ways. Some clients tell the worker directly that she does not understand what the issues are or that the topic under discussion is too difficult. More indirect ways of expressing ambivalence are through changing the topic under discussion, going off on tangents, silence, agreeing in a half-hearted way with the worker's conclusions while giving nonverbal signals of disagreeing, and so on. It is important for practitioners to be sensitive to the many ways in which clients can express their ambivalence and recognize that this may be intentional or more likely is a result of struggling with a difficult issue.

Drawing on Schwartz's (1961) principle of the "demand for work," Shulman (1999) notes that the important role and responsibility of the worker is to keep the interview structured and focused on "what we are here for" (Schwartz, 1961, p. 23) and how we will work together. The point is made that the worker does not demand specific changes in attitudes, skills, or behaviors. The only expectation is that there will be mutual contracting and ongoing engagement with the topics agreed upon and their associated feelings. While the term *demand* may conjure up a confrontational and challenging stance, this is not the intent. A social worker's demand for work, when offered in a supportive manner within a caring relationship, can be experienced as a powerful motivator. For example, whenever the topic of complying with a restrictive diet is raised, the client, a severely diabetic young woman, adopts an oppositional stance and declares that the topic is a boring one. The worker acknowledges with the client how tedious the subject is for the client, some of the painful feelings they have already discussed about her eating behavior, and refocuses on their agreement to work to develop ways that would help the client maintain better health. Shulman (1999) makes the point that the worker's expression of empathy and genuine concern for the client must accompany a demand for work. A relationship that is characterized as accepting and nonjudgmental provides the context within which a practitioner can make demands, use confrontation skillfully, and maintain focus in the work.

CASE MANAGEMENT MODEL

Before ending this discussion of processes and stages of change it is appropriate to refer to an approach to practice, the case management model, that is frequently used by social workers and differs in some ways from the stages presented thus far. Case management refers to a service originally developed for highly vulnerable client populations to ensure that they receive the help they need so that they can live in the community rather than in institutions (Rothman, 2002). It was designed in the mental health field to serve those with severe mental illness and as a response to the fragmented service delivery system. While case management is used by a number of health and human service professionals, it is similar in many ways to earlier conceptualizations of social casework. Social workers have adopted the model to support clients with conditions and situations that are likely to be long-term and affect their social functioning and well-being. For example, case management is used with children, adults, and families where there is a chronic physical illness or with elderly people living in the community where multiple health and social services are required. It is also used in family preservation approaches within a child protection mandate.

The basic premise of the approach stems from an ecological systemic perspective that recognizes individuals can benefit from access to a wide range of social, emotional, and physical services. Since services are increasingly fragmented, many programs are difficult to access, and more so for those with limited interpersonal and organizational skills; practitioners address clients' concrete needs acting as referral agents, advocates, educators, and coordinators. The relationship with the practitioner is also used in a supportive and therapeutic manner so that the client develops enough of a bond to follow through on referrals and sustains involvement with the services. The supportive nature of the relationship provides a context where the client can experience structure, learn that help is available, promote cognitive and experiential learning, and enhance self-esteem through successful experiences (Walsh, 2002).

In their meta-analysis of studies in social work, Reid and Fortune (2003) found that the approach yielded positive outcomes for people with severe mental illness with respect to enhancing work and quality of life, ability to live independently in the community and avoid hospitalization, and increased competence in the activities of daily living. It has also been shown to be effective in family preservation programs in helping families stay together (Smith, 1995).

Practice principles in the case management model are presented here, as they especially emphasize work with the environment, which is useful for other aspects of practice. Many of the interpersonal processes with the client are similar in many respects to the generic principles offered in this text. The following discussion is based on Rothman (1992), Rothman and Sager (1998), and Walsh (2000), and readers can consult these sources for more information.

The initial stage in case management includes the processes discussed thus far in this chapter with specific, structured attention to problems, client needs, and services required. A case management model is used when the assessment phase reveals that there are multiple issues requiring the services of a variety of agencies. In other words, the problems presented by the client are such that the emphasis will be less on the work between the professional and the client in the interview and more on locating and coordinating external, environmental resources. The worker adopts a supportive and collaborative stance that aims for maximum client participation and choice in setting goals, reviewing and assessing the programs available, and, when choice exists, encouraging the client to decide what services to use. In the course of this early stage of work the practitioner may accompany the client to apply for services, for example, a special work training program, or to visit potential group homes. Accompaniment is supportive to the relationship and provides the opportunity to maximize the client's participation in making significant decisions about meeting basic needs.

Case managers are also able to understand clients' internal dynamics and those factors than are evident in their interactions with others. The client's personality style and consistent ways of dealing with stress, challenge, or threats in daily living will significantly impact his ability to use the external resources that the worker is finding and coordinating. While the counseling or therapeutic aspect of case management does not aim to change persistent personality styles, without some modification of styles that are problematic the best set of external resources may not be able to be used successfully by a client. For example, if a client persistently responds to requests to follow guidelines with resistance, anger, and verbal abuse, that client will not be readily accommodated in community-based programs, group homes, or shelters. Skilled social workers can develop and use a trusting and supportive relationship to help such a client learn alternative ways of understanding and responding to requests for compliance from the programs he wishes to access.

Effective case management also requires skill in information gathering, analysis of the goodness of fit between the client's needs and the service available, and referral and linkage so that the client and program staff engage successfully with each other. Professionals need to know the relevant information about programs, eligibility requirements, application procedures, changing practices, and exceptions to regulations. Crucial information about these matters is often gained through informal professional relationships with employees in these services. Hence the interpersonal and relational aspects of working with professional and paraprofessional colleagues in related settings cannot be underemphasized. Through these relationships social workers learn how to navigate through a complicated bureaucracy, realistically appraise potential resources as well as barriers, and gain little-known entitlements for their clients. The ingredients for successful relationships with colleagues include being respectful of staff at all levels and understanding their role and function and the organizational contexts and pressures under which they operate. Emphasizing collaboration, joint efforts at problem solving, and providing positive feedback about the affects of their efforts are likely to produce lasting informal networks that ultimately serve clients.

Case management may be short-term and intensive when the need is to locate, organize, and make successful referrals to numerous services. Or, it may be long-term, to set in place a number of services to enable an individual to live in the community. After the initial phase, regular contact over a long period of time may support a plan that enables an individual to remain in the community and can also provide for changing needs. For example, an isolated individual with chronic mental health problems recently discharged from an inpatient unit is helped to find housing, apply for a disability pension, arrange attendance at a community mental health clinic for medication and follow-up, and is linked to a drop-in center in the neighborhood where there are social activities. Periodic follow-up by the case manager reveals that this individual has poor self-care skills. A more intensive period of contact follows, one that focuses on linking him to a life skills program. Through a constant, respectful, and caring relationship with the case manager the client accepts this referral and, with her encouragement, regularly attends the program and benefits from it.

A wide range of helping processes have been described in the social work literature and in related human services fields. Practitioners are confronted with a multitude of models and techniques with varying support for the claims made about bringing about change or offering needed support to clients. This chapter presented generic processes gleaned from a review of selected contemporary approaches. Social workers practice in an interactive and iterative manner; they work with clients to find and fashion unique helping pathways. Theoretical concepts, empirical findings, values, and preferences are reflected in the processes they decide to use.

THE ENDING STAGE {8

THE NATURE OF ENDING

The ending phase is also referred to in social work literature as the termination phase; a number of processes occur that bring the active work of the middle phase to a close. The term *ending* suggests that there has been a beginning, a protracted middle phase, and work that is now finished. This characterization of helping may better reflect social work practice in counseling situations, where the worker and client have met within a time frame agreed upon by both of them or set by the agency. Due to funding arrangements through employee assistance programs, managed care, or other types of third-party insurance coverage, many settings offer only a limited number of sessions to new clients. These parameters serve to structure the process and should be clearly stated at the initial meetings and referred to during subsequent sessions. The processes of the termination stage that will be presented in this section are especially applicable to these types of planned endings.

As noted throughout this text, social work practice takes place in many contexts different from that of counseling. Based on the nature of the social work activity and the intensity of the helping relationship, termination processes will be more or less intensive than those expected in protracted counseling. For example, in the health field social work intervention frequently occurs in response to a crisis or transition point, and practitioners may make little mention of an ending phase in their work with clients. In acute care facilities social workers often work with clients to plan for discharge and arrange in-home services or transfer to rehabilitation or long-term care settings. Discussions about psychosocial adjustment to illness or disability are interwoven with the immediacy of obtaining necessary resources. In part due to the intensity of a crisis, a helpful and engaged social worker can have a profound affect at such a time. When individuals and their families are struggling with painful information, such as a diagnosis of a chronic condition that has major implications for functioning and well-being, or are given a diagnosis of a terminal illness, a social worker who is both supportive and understanding of emotional reactions as well as able to provide practical information and help obtain necessary resources is invaluable. While the helping relationship in such cases is in some respects different from the counseling relationship, where there has been an interpersonal connection attention should be given to the ending phase of that relationship. In contrast to the brevity of practice in acute settings is the long-term work of practitioners in the child protection field. It is not unusual for social workers to be involved in relationships over many years with children under the agency's care or with families where there is continued supervision. When these relationships must end as the young person reaches the age where the agency no longer is mandated to provide service, termination will likely have profound meaning for the client and also affect the worker. The processes of termination that are presented in the following discussion can be thought of as general principles or guidelines that social workers adapt based on the particular context of their work.

A number of processes in the final stage are similar to those used in earlier stages. For example, throughout the middle stage the worker and the client periodically review progress being made toward achieving goals and examine the factors producing change. This type of review is repeated in the termination stage and encompasses reflection about all of the sessions. Similarly, the interviewing skills that ground these processes in practice are the same. Practitioners continue to use skills of attending, questioning, seeking concreteness, paraphrasing, reflecting, offering summaries, responding to feedback, and so on. The difference is the processes and skills are used in the interests of ending. Practice wisdom has led social workers to value the importance of a "good" ending. A good ending provides the opportunity to review the progress made since the initial meeting and helps the client integrate and take ownership for changes made, anticipate the future, and bring closure to an important relationship.

THE TIMING OF TERMINATION

Ideally termination occurs when the client and the worker believe that the goals they have identified have been met, enough progress has been achieved, or there is relief from the presenting situation or problem. This can arise during the middle stage as the worker and client upon review, or spontaneously, observe that progress is being made. In this context the worker may raise with the client whether it is timely to space their meetings further apart with the intention of moving toward ending. Consistent with the stance of collaboration there should be an opportunity for the client to take an equal part in the decision about when to end. Clients who have had a positive relationship with the worker and who have made progress may feel strengthened and energized by their experience. At the same time they may also be concerned about losing the involvement with the worker. Often clients are concerned about becoming overly dependent on the worker and view termination as an indication of their ability to function independently.

Termination may also come about when there has been an agreed upon period of service and little progress has been made. The practitioner has the responsibility to point this out in an empathic and nonjudgmental manner and engage the client in exploring reasons for this, including the behavior of the worker and the approaches being taken. A change in approach may be advisable, a transfer to another worker or service needed, or a planned termination with the offer for service at another point in time. As discussed throughout this text, social work effectiveness is dependent on a range of factors including the nature of the problem, client characteristics, environmental demands and supports, and the relationship between worker and client. There are situations where, despite the best efforts of all involved, change does not come about. The work of Prochaska and his colleagues, reviewed in chapter 5 (Prochaska, 1999; Prochaska, DiClemente, and Norcross, 1992), helps to illuminate this phenomenon to some extent. Recall that in their research they found that there are stages of change and the first three, precontemplation, contemplation, and preparation, can proceed over a considerable period of time. When individuals are in these stages action-oriented change strategies are premature and hence not successful. Therefore, in agency settings where the number of meetings is mandated, it may be useful to frame the work as "episodes of service." The client may benefit from a period of time where he is helped to contemplate the many pros and cons surrounding change; this may be all he can do at a particular point in time. At a later point another series of sessions may help him move into an action stage.

Since student social workers meet with clients in their practicum, many terminations occur because the students' field experience is coming to an end. Students may feel guilty and disappointed that they have not provided enough help to the client and recognize that termination is premature and not in the best interests of the client. In consultation with the field instructor, a transfer to another worker may be recommended. Transfers can make the termination phase more complex for the client since he is saying good-bye to a relationship that has been helpful at the same time that he must develop an alliance with a new and unknown person. In such situations it is helpful to review and discuss with the client his perception of his progress, needs, and preferences. Depending on the extent to which the initial goals have been achieved, the client may prefer to terminate and reapply to the agency at a later point in time if necessary. When a client chooses to transfer to another worker, the student should arrange a meeting with the client and the new worker as part of the termination.

Finally, there are situations when endings are unplanned—for example, when clients announce they will not return or simply stop attending the sessions. It is important for the worker to try to explore the client's reasons for ending while respecting her right to do so. When the client does not inform the worker, the worker should reach out through a telephone call or letter to arrange a conversation where he may be able to assess what accounts for the client's decision to drop out. An unplanned termination may reflect the client's sense that the relationship with the worker is strained or that attending the interviews is unhelpful or too difficult. Given the opportunity to discuss this with the client, the worker may be able to repair the alliance and the sessions can continue. In some instances attempts at repair are not successful and the practitioner needs to respect the client's decision, highlighting any gains that may have been made. Client-initiated termination may also reflect factors not related to the sessions. For example, if the location and time of the sessions presents too great a burden for the client, an unplanned dropout can simply signal that fact. Client-initiated termination can also reflect positive client perceptions. Many practitioners are troubled when clients do not terminate in a planned manner and may feel they have failed the client. In studies, however, as many as two-thirds of clients who drop out report they have made considerable progress (Fortune, 2002).

Cultural conventions may also affect the termination phase. Once part of a network and perceived as a helping and caring person, some clients may expect that the social worker will be a permanent person in their lives. A formal termination phase may be perplexing and seen as rejecting. It is important for practitioners to understand the cultural norms surrounding endings, gift giving, and being invited to significant family events. In many instances practitioners accept that they will continue to occupy a place of importance in the client's life, even if they no longer continue to meet. When receiving small gifts, cards, and occasional telephone calls from the client are indications of appropriate cultural behaviors around transitions, practitioners can graciously accept them and not offer psychological interpretations about their meaning.

PROCESSES OF TERMINATION

As with processes in the beginning and middle stage, in the termination stage the following processes do not unfold sequentially but are intertwined and repeated. Box 8.1 presents a list of the key processes involved in the termination stage.

REVIEW PROGRESS

A useful way to introduce the termination stage is to engage the client in a reflective discussion about the period of time over which the worker and client have met. Together they can recall the presenting situation that brought them together and their initial meetings. They can review the way in which they initially understood the issues that needed to be addressed and how they went about working on them. Different or enlarged understandings and key themes they discovered should be highlighted. Consideration should be given to the progress that has been made, what has changed, and why it has changed. An observation about themes and topics that are still challenging, difficult, or problematic should also be offered to indicate that individuals are in a constant process of dealing with life's events and this "work" of improved social functioning is a lifetime project, whether or not the individual is receiving professional help. Hence it is extremely helpful when the review includes the client's and the worker's perception of issues that may reoccur

---

BOX 8.1. PROCESSES OF TERMINATION

- Review progress
- Consolidate gains
- Plan for next steps
- Process the emotional bond

---

or are ongoing. Furthermore, a discussion about what the client and worker have learned should include a realistic evaluation of the strengths as well as the vulnerabilities that exist within the client and in her environment. The best termination gift the worker can give to the client is helping her recognize the internal strengths and capacities she has to change situations in her life, on her own and in the future.

An important aspect of this review is a joint consideration of how the goals were achieved, with particular attention to what the client brought to the effort. With a focus on strengths and collaboration it is important to help the client identify his attitudes, competencies, and resources that affected the change. It is also useful for the social worker to hear from the client what he experienced as helpful inputs from the practitioner. Clinical research studies that identify the processes that are associated with positive outcomes in practice are helping the profession build an empirical knowledge base. The case-by-case feedback that clients give to individual social workers is invaluable, as it helps practitioners develop specific knowledge about their own practice; it represents the most useful "supervision" and continuing education that one can receive.

CONSOLIDATE GAINS

During the termination phase the worker, while reviewing progress made, focuses on helping the client identify and take ownership for what he or she did to bring about change. Recall that a goal of social work practice is to build client capacity for independent functioning. Hence it is useful to make explicit those strengths of the client or new ways of thinking, behaving, and feeling that have developed. This type of feedback and resulting ownership of progress by the client increases a sense of mastery and recognition of capacities that she can use in future situations. Through exploration clients can be assisted to distinguish between individual factors and those factors that are part of the environment. What changes are a result of the client's new thinking, feeling, or behavior and what changes are a result of contributions from significant social relationships and environments such as family members, friends, and work colleagues? Clients can then extrapolate and generalize to consider what factors and circumstances will be important for them to have in order to maintain their achievements. For example, a young man who had grown up in a neighborhood known for violence and had previously been involved with street gangs had been able to break out of what he identified as "bad, old habits" through addiction treatment. He was aware that loneliness could lead him back to his former peers and in the termination phase discussed the many strategies he had developed for avoiding being lonely, including returning to see the worker if he felt he was slipping. They also considered whether he was interested in taking a role in a new "peer modeling" program run by a neighborhood agency.

For many clients the stage of maintaining and consolidating gains will proceed over an indeterminate time long after they have discontinued meeting with the worker. Many intervention models for addictive behaviors state that attention to relapse prevention is a lifetime concern (Prochaska and Prochaska, 2002). It is useful for workers and clients to explicitly clarify the general principles the client can take from the intervention and use in a range of problems and situations in his natural environment. For example, cognitive and behavioral strategies for managing anger in an intimate relationship can be transferred to parenting and interactions at work. A client recognizes that he has a "short fuse" and can too quickly express anger inappropriately in a range of interpersonal and work related situations. This client developed a range of strategies to calm himself down, listen carefully, and think before responding through his work with the practitioner. This insight and the accompanying strategies (at the moment take a break, practice deep breathing, or count to ten, and, in general, limit alcohol consumption and ensure adequate sleep and exercise) served as useful activities that this client took from counseling and used in his everyday life.

The ecological systemic perspective has drawn attention to the importance of significant factors and relationships in the client's environment that can support new behaviors or undermine them. During the middle stage these factors will have been identified and changed, if possible, to support the client's goals. In situations where significant systems cannot be changed the client may have been helped to protect himself from their effect or deal differently with them. In the termination stage it is especially important to review these environmental conditions and how the client has learned to elicit support from them or to respond in a different way (Fortune, 2002).

To some extent the work with the professional can be seen as an episode in a client's life that facilitated some movement forward. This change is a process and will continue over time without the presence and involvement of the social worker. Change involves struggle, progress, and backward slips and is a natural part of the human condition. It is helpful to discuss this notion with the client and to reinforce this view of growth and change.

In many practice situations termination includes discharge planning or transfer to another agency that can provide resources or programs the client needs. Workers need to determine whether the client can easily access those resources on her own or whether unforeseen requirements and waiting lists will present overwhelming obstacles. For example, after a period of individual meetings to help a young family from Columbia, new to the country, with parenting issues, the worker and couple decide that, although they will terminate their meetings, the couple will join the local community center and enroll in an eight-session parenting group. If there is some concern that the plan, while agreed upon by all, may face obstacles to implementation, the worker should anticipate these and assist if necessary. The center may charge a fee for membership the couple cannot afford and they may not be aware they can ask for a lower fee, the classes may have a waiting list, or the couple may need help in accessing child care so that they can attend together. When clients are confronted with the regulations for eligibility for government retraining programs, financial assistance, home care, or a host of such services, they may feel defeated and overwhelmed by the "red tape" surrounding applications, long waiting lists, and less than welcoming attitudes of staff. Social workers should be able to work with these systems, to advocate for clients, to facilitate referrals and obtaining resources and entitlements. While the principles of self-determination and building the capacity of the client guide practitioners to encourage individuals to take these steps on their own, the reality of large government bureaucracies and their programs is such that a social worker may need to intervene to ensure that a discharge plan or referral is actually carried out.

When the worker persists in dealing with large systems, clients can learn useful attitudes and strategies through the model the worker provides. In addition, small encouragements from the worker can offer the boost to reinforce the client's desire and capacity to act. The importance of follow-up with clients is underscored. Social workers will learn whether the referral was successful and whether prolonged involvement from the social worker is still necessary to ensure follow-through. When follow-up reveals that the resource is not available or not adequate to meet the client's needs, the worker may have to become reengaged to develop alternate plans.

In situations where the relationship with the social worker was key and provided a degree of social support and interpersonal connection that was previously missing in the client's life, termination should occur only when those supports are present in the client's life. Through counseling, the client may have changed her behavior in social situations and developed the skills and ability to initiate and maintain relationships. When working with individuals who are isolated as a result of chronic mental illness, multiple losses as they age, or relocation and immigration, termination planning should include some form of volunteer or informal social support through home visits, accompanied recreational activities, or connection to social and community centers.

In situations where there is a planned termination and the worker remains with the agency or is still available in the community, the model of the "family doctor" has merit. Individuals see their family doctors for specific concerns and for regular checkups. Similarly, for many clients who have worked productively with a practitioner over a period of time and perceive that they are ready to terminate, knowing they can return if needed, for a "booster session" or a checkup, is reassuring. Indeed, when the helping relationship has been positive and the client perceives the worker understands her, the ongoing availability of the worker and the agency can reinforce the client's sense of having a "secure base."

PROCESS THE EMOTIONAL BOND

Throughout this text the emotional connection between worker and client in the helping relationship has been emphasized. While many clients "take endings in stride" (Murphy and Dillon, 2003, p. 284), it is not unusual for both client and worker to have a range of feelings and thoughts about ending and saying good-bye. It is helpful to clients when practitioners encourage clients to express these feelings and label as normal and healthy expressions of feelings such as pleasure, relief, ambivalence, and sadness about ending (Fortune, 2002). For the client the worker has become a person of greater or lesser importance in her life, someone she can rely on to provide a constant and available presence. Recall concepts such as transference, countertransference, and attachment theory introduced in the first part of this text. Since the relationship may have provided a secure base for the client to explore and change, endings may stir up feelings connected to a range of relationships; earlier significant relationships with caretakers, and current relationships with intimate partners and family. Feelings of loss are also understandably related to ending a real relationship with the practitioner, a person perceived as helpful. Feelings of loss and abandonment can be directly expressed or presented in a range of indirect ways. Clients may present new problems that will warrant continuing the meetings, miss or forget appointments, or appear indifferent to the ending. Any of these behaviors provides another opportunity to explore feelings and thoughts about central relationship themes for the client. If the concerns are handled in a way different from previous important endings in the client's life, new learning can ensue. The emotional meaning and immediacy of termination with the worker can offer the client a corrective experience of working through an ending in a way that leads to new internal working models of self, other, and relationships and, ultimately, to increased self-esteem.

Practitioners also experience a range of feelings in the ending stage. Depending on the way in which the work with the client affected the practitioner's experience of his personal self in the professional role, ending may be experienced in a positive manner and represent the effectiveness of his work. The client's progress may lead the worker to feel positively about his abilities and choice of career. Ambivalent feelings are normal, and the practitioner may feel that he will miss the client while simultaneously gaining personal and professional satisfaction from the client's ability to terminate and carry on in an independent manner.

For a variety of reasons clients may suggest that now that the work is ending they would like to have a personal relationship or friendship with the worker. The necessity of maintaining boundaries between confidential and structured professional relationships and fluid social relationships is clearly stated in the code of ethics of all the helping professions. It is the responsibility of the practitioner to avoid dual relationships and hence he cannot gratify the client's wishes. It is important, however, for the practitioner to discuss the client's request in an empathetic and nonjudgmental manner and to share the reasons for this professional standard. The unequal relationship, wherein the worker knows a great deal about the client and the client knows little about the worker, would create a set of power dynamics where clients can be exploited. Furthermore, if the client might benefit from follow-up or wish to return for counseling, the worker could no longer provide the help necessary. It is important to convey that the professions' position is not designed to reject clients but rather to protect them and ensure that access to their professional helper remains.

When social workers find that they would like to continue the relationship with the client, as in earlier discussions about self-awareness in this text, they are advised to pay attention to these feelings and understand what they reveal about themselves and their work. For example, is the worker concerned that despite progress the client still does not have enough positive relationships in his life? Is termination premature in this case—should more effort be directed to helping the client develop these relationships? Or does the worker feel regretful that more was not accomplished? Is he second-guessing his initial decision to go along with the regulations about insurance coverage in the client's plan and offer a limited number of sessions? Has he done all he can to apply to the funding authority for increased sessions? Or is the worker feeling a sense of attachment to the client beyond the relationship? For example, might the client represent the "good daughter" the worker never had? When the responses to these questions reveal that the worker is struggling with personal issues elicited by the termination, consultation or supervision provides a venue to discuss the matter and develop strategies to contain personal reactions so that the worker can respond to the client in a professional and ethical manner.

Ethical issues about continuing the helping relationship arise regularly for students when a client's termination or transfer is precipitated because of the end of the practicum rather than the client's needs. In a discussion of students' contact with clients after termination, Ringel and Mishna (2005) conclude that teachers in practice courses and field instructors need to navigate a delicate balance. On one hand, they need to provide a space where students can express their views and explore their feelings about such terminations. On the other hand, they need to be clear about ethical obligations to maintain appropriate boundaries that, if violated or crossed, put both the client and the student at risk. From students' anecdotes offered to these authors in advanced practice courses it appeared the students had approached field instructors about clients' desire to stay involved with the students and the students' desire to do so. Students reported that their field instructors reiterated ethical principles about boundaries in professional relationships, stated this was inappropriate, and directed students to terminate. In retrospect these students recognized that they needed to better understand their feelings about termination, which ranged from feeling their special understanding of the client would be of benefit to feeling guilty about leaving prematurely. Some students secretly continued to meet their clients after the practicum. They talked about feeling unsettled and confused, even though they did not define their meetings as a boundary crossing, but rather continuing in a helping role. Most students reported that these relationships became problematic because of the demands or needs of the clients. In their analysis Ringel and Mishna (2005) recommend that instructors orient students to termination issues, provide guidelines such as informing clients about ending in the initial meeting, and foster discussion about ethical issues and students' mixed feelings instead of simply stating the relevant standard of practice.

Social identity characteristics can enhance practice relationships or make them more difficult. When terminating with a client, these issues may or may not be significant. Working with clients who are different from the worker with respect to dimensions of ethnicity, race, religion, and sexual orientation can be experienced as energizing by some practitioners and challenging by others. The worker may feel that she has benefited tremendously from learning about the client's cultural group in a way different from reading or attending workshops. In the termination phase she is likely to thank the client for enriching her knowledge. Or the worker may feel that she was never able to address the way in which racism or sexual orientation had an impact in the client's life as well as in their working relationship. The worker may feel a lingering confusion and regret about whether she should have initiated discussion about this theme with the client.

Similarly, working with clients who are from similar reference groups as the worker can create comfort or discomfort, depending on the degree to which they both hold similar values as well as the way in which their individual personalities fit together. In termination with a client who shared many similarities, the worker may anticipate missing the easy connection afforded to him by virtue of their many subtle shared understandings. Or the worker may have felt uncomfortable with the client's assumption that since they shared significant social identity characteristics they also shared specific attitudes and beliefs.

In some instances social workers will be relieved when they terminate with clients. For each social worker there are clients with whom they find it difficult to work, depending on the practitioners' personal preferences and countertransference issues. Some workers may become anxious and preoccupied when working with suicidal clients: for others it may be clients who are verbally aggressive and hostile, for others it may be clients who are passive and dependent. Again, recognizing one's feelings and discussing them in supervision or consultation can be meaningful for the worker, lead to new insights and ultimately to more effective termination strategies with the client.

A "good ending" can be internalized by the client along with memories of the work with the practitioner and new insights and behaviors acquired. Hence clients and practitioners can review the elements in the relationship that made it special and clients can learn that important aspects of this relationship can be stored in their "hearts and minds" (Murphy and Dillon, 2003, p. 281). Murphy and Dillon (2003) recommend as part of ending that the worker and client talk about the relationship itself, discussing what it has meant to both parties. The worker can also give the client feedback about how the worker experienced and valued the collaboration and partnership.

Part III

INTERVIEWING
IN SOCIAL WORK
PRACTICE

INTERVIEWING SKILLS

{9

Interviewing skills are the behaviors or verbal actions that the social worker uses in the helping process. In the first part of this volume contextual frameworks were presented, and in the second part processes and tasks associated with the stages in the helping process. The skills are the bridge between these abstract concepts, change processes, and concrete activities and are evident in the practitioner's actual encounter with the client.

Interviewing skills reflect the many dimensions of practice discussed throughout the text such as the values of the profession, theoretical concepts, practice models and empirically supported procedures, and the context and mandate of the organization. Moreover, these skills are filtered through the personal characteristics and social identity of the worker and as such are demonstrated in a unique manner by each social worker. The challenge for practitioners is how to navigate the distance between general concepts and their specific actions to respond to the distinctiveness of each client. That is, since the components underlying interview behavior are generally expressed on an abstract level, each practitioner must develop her own way of transforming these principles into concrete behaviors in actual interviews. These behaviors must also be responsive to clients so that they experience their workers' comments as ultimately helpful. As a result, the particular constellation of interviewing skills used in any session varies according to the topics under discussion, the comfort level of the client, the purpose of the interview, and whether a particular practice model is guiding intervention. The primary factor that influences the selection of interviewing skills is the worker's intention: which skills are more likely to bring about some change or offer some relief for a troubling situation at a particular moment in time.

The links between concepts, self-knowledge, and practice are elaborated in chapter 1, especially in the discussion of the ITP Loop Model. The loop metaphor reflects the interrelated nature of these components as the worker strives to achieve specific goals. Since social work practice is grounded in a worker and client collaborative relationship, each participant contributes to its success and difficulties. In this respect the worker's interviewing behaviors represents her expertise as she uses intellectual frameworks in a purposeful or intentional manner.

Skills are presented in a text as if they are separate and discrete, similar to the way one might think about skills for playing a sport. This does not represent the reality of practice or, for that matter, the way any sport, tennis, swimming, or skiing, is played. While groups of skills provide a foundation or set of building blocks, they must be drawn together into a smooth, flowing, and natural performance (Ivey and Ivey, 2003). Furthermore, when carrying out the tasks and processes of the various stages workers draw on combinations of various skills. Change processes and skills overlap and circle back on themselves as themes and issues are revisited and reexamined. This reflects the nature of professional practice, which requires judgment in the selection and application of skills.

When students in the helping professions are first learning a new set of skills, it can be helpful to engage in the repetitive practice of a single skill, one by one, or of a limited group of skills with the sole intention of gaining some mastery. With this foundation it may then be easier to incorporate the new behaviors in actual interviewing sequences guided by the frameworks, practice principles, and change processes discussed earlier.

A final word about interviewing skills is needed. Through intensive analysis of audiotapes of workers and clients in our project on cross-cultural counseling, our team found frequent examples of interviewing behavior that was technically very effective (Tsang, Bogo, and George, 2004). The practitioners used the skills that will be presented here and the clients responded in a way that led to furthering their mutual understanding of the issues to be addressed. As a result engagement was successful and clients evidenced positive outcomes from the counseling. There were, however, many instances when the workers' use of skills was awkward or not well timed to respond to the immediacy of the client's presentation. Further examination of these instances demonstrated the importance of understanding the processes in and progress of an interview by analyzing it in its entirety. For example, there were instances where the client tried to introduce topics or issues for discussion in a subtle or vague way. The practitioner missed these cues, did not respond to or explore them, and continued with the worker's own agenda. Interestingly, the client followed the worker's lead, but from time to time would again introduce the topic. Where the worker finally heard what the client was trying to convey and responded to that theme, the engagement process was ultimately successful. In a number of interviews the worker picked up on the salient theme only in the last ten minutes of a one-hour interview. After analyzing many instances of this type of interview sequences, we concluded that for practitioners keeping focused on the *processes* that lead to successful engagement and change are crucial. With this focus in mind, even though there are episodes of awkward communication and lack of understanding, joining can occur, since the worker continuously tries to attend to, listen to, and hear what the client is trying to articulate and then respond in a way that conveys she has "sufficient understanding" to proceed. This analysis demonstrates that interviewing skills are only the tools used to carry out the helping processes and practice principles. Conversely, without some mastery of the interviewing skills the practitioner would not have the benefit of tools or techniques to use to ground or enact these general principles.

STARTING THE INTERVIEW

Many clients will spontaneously enter into conversation with the social worker and talk about why they are seeking professional help, what are the issues of concern, and what they hope to gain from the practitioner. It is preferable to encourage clients to tell their stories, also referred to as narratives, in their own way. This approach provides the client with some sense of leadership and control in the professional encounter. It also provides some insight for the worker into how the client organizes his experiences, what is most important for him, and what is his definition of the issue. The social worker approaches interviews in the beginning stage open to hearing and understanding the client's perceptions about his problems.

Some clients are less verbal and do not spontaneously offer full descriptions of the issues that have brought them to the social worker. They look to the worker to provide direction in the interview. Questions can help clients to begin, can help them focus and elaborate on their situation to move beyond details and to explore many aspects previously unexamined. The long-standing social work principle of partializing the problem guides the practitioner to ask about one aspect of the situation at a time and delve into facets that are relevant. Less pressing concerns can be returned to at a later time.

USING QUESTIONS

While the social worker listens to the client present his story, the practitioner draws on conceptual frameworks for assessment. In chapter 6 guidelines for assessment are presented in box 6.4, Data Gathering for Assessment, and in box 6.5, Bio-Psycho-Social Assessment Guide. While listening to the client, the practitioner refers to these frameworks to identify gaps in information. Hence questions are used for a reason, to pursue areas that are important for achieving joint understanding. Simply stated open-ended questions can be used as prompts to help clients expand in a general way on what they are offering or to help them discuss specific topics.

OPEN-ENDED QUESTIONS

Two types of questions are identified in the literature on interviewing skills: open-ended questions and close-ended questions (Hepworth, Rooney, and Larsen, 2002; Ivey and Ivey, 2003; Kadushin and Kadushin, 1997). Open-ended questions are similar to the prompts described above. They are questions that are phrased in a way that encourages the respondent to communicate information and focus on issues that he perceives as essential. By their unstructured nature, open-ended questions help clients take more of a lead in the interview. These questions provide possible directions for clients to elaborate on and explore thoughts or feelings that are expressed in a limited way, that they are only vaguely aware of, or that are hinted at or implied in their presentation of an issue. These questions assist in providing additional information and elucidating the depth and complexity that surround human situations.

OPEN-ENDED QUESTIONS THAT CAN BE USED AT SPECIFIC TIMES IN THE INTERVIEW IN AN INTENTIONAL WAY

- "What brings you here?" Used at the very beginning of the contact.
- "What are some of the things about this new job (any area the client identifies as a problem) that is troubling you? Used to help the client expand on the presenting problem.
- "How is it for you now?" Used to explore the problem in relation to time, the past, and the present.
- "How have you reacted to new situations in the past?" Used to elicit information about characteristic response patterns and potential strengths.
- "What else do you think I need to know about you to help me understand? Used to elicit important information, especially toward the end of a first interview.
- "What would you like us to discuss today? What is most pressing?" Used to begin interviews, especially in the beginning stage.
- "Have you any further thoughts about our discussions last week?" Used to draw links between sessions.

Given the recognition of the importance of emotional or feeling states in organizing our perceptions, attributing meaning to events, and affecting our behaviors, contemporary practice approaches aim to help clients process emotions and emotional reactions. This involves recognizing their emotions, understanding and clarifying what specific emotional states may convey, clarifying what triggers or stimulates specific emotions, and learning how to deal productively with emotions. The intention is not to encourage clients to vent as this has not been found to be effective in reducing distress (Bushman, Baumeister, and Stack, 1999; Greenberg, 2002b; Kennedy-Moore and Watson, 1999). In the beginning stage practitioners try to help clients access the emotions connected to significant events. Direct questions about feelings, such as "How did you feel when that happened?" or "How do you feel about that?" can sound hackneyed, especially if they are used too often. In later stages, when the worker is helping clients elaborate on and experience feelings in greater depth, these emotionally oriented questions are useful to begin the exploration process.

Another form of open-ended question useful for eliciting feelings is an incomplete phrase that ends with a question mark, such as in the following interchange. The client lives in an assisted living apartment building and is discussing her difficulties with her apartment mate. She tells the social worker about her efforts to help her roommate who has more limited mobility than does the client. However, when the client asks in turn for some assistance that she perceives her roommate is able to provide, her roommate is usually not responsive. The worker comments, "You've tried to be a helpful roommate... when it's not returned you feel... ?"

Another form of open-ended question occurs when the worker picks up on the feeling expressed by the client and repeats part of the client's phrase. Through the worker's use of a questioning tone at the end of the comment, the client is encouraged to elaborate.

Continuing with the previous example, the client relates that on the preceding day she asked her roommate to pick up her mail when she went to the mailboxes for her own mail, as she did every day. Her roommate did not respond to her and the client states that she felt angry and stupid for asking. The worker comments "You felt stupid... ?"

Open-ended questions are extremely useful for helping clients identify and reflect on the perceptions, thoughts, and expectations they use to interpret

- "What do you make of that?"
- "How does that make sense to you?"
- "What was going through your mind when your friend said that she didn't think you could succeed in that course?"
- "What were you thinking when your partner said he would try to control his anger next time?"
- "What are you hoping for?" "What would that mean for you?"

and make meaning of the situations in their lives and the feelings they experience. Similar to open-ended questions for exploring feelings discussed above, practitioners can use the technique of an incomplete phrase that ends with a question mark or repeating part of a client's phrase that includes a thought.

CLOSE-ENDED QUESTIONS

Close-ended questions are primarily used to elicit factual information. They are especially useful in intake and in the beginning stage to obtain the most pertinent facts about the client and the situation. They can be used throughout the helping process to clarify details and expand on missing information. When using close-ended direct questions, practitioners need to pose queries in a manner and tone that conveys respect, a nonjudgmental stance, and a genuine desire to understand the client and his circumstances. The direct question needs to also provide space for the client to explore and elaborate on the substance of the response.

Social work students observe that when they ask a number of close-ended questions they can fall into a pattern of "question from the worker/response from the client" that is more analogous to a Ping-Pong match than a collaborative dialogue. If workers use a series of closed questions to obtain a substantial amount of information, they can inadvertently define the helping process as expert oriented. This suggests that once they have amassed "the facts," they will provide "the answers." Furthermore, such a worker-directed stance reinforces the power differential between the worker and client, may leave the client feeling he has little control over the direction of the session or the process, and can encourage passivity on the part of the client. The helping model discussed in this text emphasizes a type of collaborative relationship where the worker and client proceed, as much as possible, in a joint effort at understanding and facilitating change. This approach has been associated with positive outcomes and empowerment for clients. Close-ended questions therefore can most productively be used judiciously and as one skill amongst others, such as open-ended questions, restatement, and reflections, that help clients provide information and elaborate on key topics.

Close-ended questions are also used when social workers are following a structured interview questionnaire that is required by the agency to determine such matters as eligibility for service, or diagnosis, or types of intervention needed. For example, in order to establish eligibility for home care services there are a number of questions about physical functioning, medical status, and the ability to carry out activities of daily living that must be asked at intake. In crisis situations social workers need specific information to evaluate the severity of the crisis and the social and environmental supports available to the client. In mental health settings social workers may administer standardized symptom checklists to determine appropriate referral and treatment procedures. When there is a perceived risk of suicidal behavior helping professionals ask directly about the presence of suicidal thoughts and plans. Similarly, when assessing for alcohol or drug abuse it is important to ask directly about the amount of the substance the individual uses on a daily and weekly basis. Topics such as suicidal ideation, substance abuse, violence in the home, or sexual abuse are emotionally laden topics and both clients and social workers may feel uncomfortable raising these subjects for discussion. Assumptions may be made or the discussion may be vague resulting in confusion for both the worker and the client. A series of close-ended questions are useful to clarify the nature of the problem and the frequency and duration of any number of behaviors. This information is necessary to assess the type and severity of a range of mental health and social problems and to determine what type of intervention may be needed.

Close-ended questions can provide useful direction when clients feel overwhelmed by their situations, experience the accompanying feelings of anxiety, and state that they "don't know where to start." A structured and focused set of questions can help clients contain a sense of disintegration and conveys that help will be offered. Such structure is also useful when the interview is appearing to wander or when the client's discussion veers into tangential topics that, while related, are less pertinent. In this instance questions offered in a gentle manner can steer the conversation back to the central issue. At times the social worker may need to offer a rationale for changing the topic. For example, a mother who is exasperated and exhausted by the demands of her adolescent daughter tells the worker about her own adolescence and her fear about disobeying her parents. She then begins to reminisce at length about more general aspects of growing up, commenting about tastes in music, clothes, and movies. The worker redirects the interview by drawing a link between what the client is discussing and the presenting issue—her relationship with her daughter. The worker then uses a question to refocus the interview. "It sounds as if your experiences growing up and your daughter's experiences growing up were very different, both in your family and in what was going on in the community and in the world around you. Are there any similarities between what you both experienced?"

CONSIDERATIONS IN THE USE OF QUESTIONS

There are a number of issues to consider in using questions, both close-ended and open-ended, in interviewing as their use may interfere with building a climate conducive to a collaborative relationship. As a general guide, one should try to use questions that are simple, clear, and fairly short. Practitioners are advised to refrain from stacking questions, that is, asking a number of questions before the client has the opportunity to answer the first one posed. For example, "How many children do you have, and are they in school and living with you?" Asking a question and providing a number of possible responses, akin to the multiple choice question, is not a useful way to gather information. For example, "When your partner threatened to leave did you feel angry, or relieved, or did you worry about how you would manage?" While asking questions that begin with "why" may help the client respond with information about his own motivations or that of others, or his explanation for why a situation has occurred, it has been observed that these questions may make clients feel challenged and put on the defensive (Collins and Coleman, 2000; Hill and O'Brien, 1999). Instead, questions that begin with "how" or "what" are recommended. For example, "Can you tell me what was going on for you that led to leaving the house after that argument?" has a softer ring than "Why did you leave after that argument?" Frequently social work students are reluctant to appear intrusive and avoid asking questions about topics that appear overly personal. This can inadvertently send a message to the client that certain subjects are to be avoided and hence limit the potential for comprehensive understanding.

We observe that it is a social convention to use close-ended questions as a manner of speech to express a preference or to lead the other in a particular direction. For example, based on the tone used, a question such as "Do you want to come with me to a movie?" can convey that the listener wants the responder to answer in the affirmative. In a professional interview this type of leading question can also be used. For example, when the worker asks "Shall we talk about the trouble you are having at work?" she may be actually asking the client to set the agenda or she may be directing the conversation. An open-ended question such as "What aspects of your situation do you feel we should pursue right now?" would help the client take the lead.

Pacing, which guides the pursuit of information gathering, is an important dimension in interviewing. Pacing refers to timing: when particular topics are introduced within an interview and when they are introduced into the overall intervention process. The concept of clients' preparedness with respect to change (Prochaska, 1999), discussed in chapter 5, provides useful information about how to assess clients' readiness to focus on thinking about change as distinct from planning for change or taking specific actions. When practitioners pay attention to pacing, it is with the aim of introducing topics for exploration and discussion in a way that is sensitive to this notion about client's readiness to engage meaningfully with the subject. Asking too many close-ended questions can create a pace that is inconsistent with providing time and space for clients to express themselves.

Tracking the client through open-ended questions or prompts is an important skill in conducting interviews. Tracking includes responding in a way that conveys to the client that the worker is following the narrative offered, is striving to understand it, and is communicating to the client the worker's developing grasp of the situation. Questions that are relevant to the client's concerns indicate the worker's involvement. Questions that are tangential or change the subject under discussion abruptly or prematurely can break the flow of the client's narrative and distract from clarifying the information the client is trying to share.

SEEKING CONCRETENESS AND ASKING FOR CLARIFICATION

In social conversation we often express ourselves in general terms that can be vague or unclear. In contrast, in the social work interview we are aiming to achieve an understanding of another's internal states and external circumstances, which requires a level of precision in communication that is not commonly used. Individuals vary in their ability to recall and report details of a situation. Furthermore, when we must communicate in a language other than our primary one, it is even more difficult to convey and understand nuances of emotions and the worldview, values, and working models that affect our perceptions, the meanings we attribute to others' behavior, and the feelings that are aroused.

The concept of concreteness refers to communicating in a specific manner by using words that explicitly describe events, behaviors, experiences, perceptions, and feelings (Hepworth Rooney, and Larsen, 2002). The related skill is seeking concreteness by asking for clarification of material that is presented in a vague, confusing, or abstract manner. It has also been referred to in the literature as the skill of clarification, which is defined as bringing vague material into sharper focus (Brammer and MacDonald, 1999).

Developing sufficient or enough joint and shared understanding of the client's situation has been identified as a key goal of the beginning stage (Tsang and Bogo, 1997). In the absence of clear information such understanding may be hampered. Rather the work may proceed on the basis of false assumptions or poor comprehension by the worker of the client and her situation and by the client of the helping process.

Simple, open-ended questions can be used to encourage the client to offer more concrete information, to clarify what they have presented, or to explore any issue further.

Some further techniques that can assist clients to provide a more textured and complex description of important issues are 1) obtaining specific and detailed examples of sequences of events that provide a broader context for understanding and 2) linking these examples to feelings and thoughts. Clients

---

QUESTIONS THAT SEEK CONCRETENESS OR REQUEST CLARIFICATION

- "Can you tell me what you mean when you talk about respect?"
- "Can you tell me exactly what happens when you say that you feel threatened in your relationship?"
- "You said that you feel uncomfortable with your roommate…uncomfortable, in what way?"

---

frequently share examples of situations that are representative of key themes or issues in their lives. It is worthwhile to inquire in some detail about these examples, specifically asking the client to describe the sequence of events including what was happening before the incident occurred, the incident itself, and the reactions of the various participants in the situation. In this way a pattern of reactions and counterreactions can be established. Descriptions of behaviors that refer to the issues under discussion can help concretize the meaning of emotionally meaningful terms such as in "My teen-agers don't show me any respect," "My life is a struggle," "My partner and I are not close," "I am alone in my pain," or " I have a real problem with my temper." Another way of gaining a sense of what the issues are is to ask the client to help the worker get a picture of what has happened, for example, "If I was watching you and your sisters having a fight, what would I see?" or "If I was doing a home video of what happens when you open the door to your house when you come home from school, what would be on the video?"

Second, when gaining a picture of significant events and behaviors, it is useful to ask the client to describe and clarify the way she was feeling in the example under discussion, the perceptions she had of the situation, and what information she used to draw those conclusions. This line of exploration will clarify the interrelationships between internal and external dynamics and can assist the client in developing better self-understanding. For example, the client tells the social worker that she "feels like a failure as a mother, my daughter has no respect for me." The worker uses open- and close-ended questions to gain concreteness by guiding the client through a description of a sequence of events that demonstrate "no respect" and by clarifying the feelings and perceptions related to these presenting statements of concerns. Through helping the client clarify the details of these components it became clear that the client expects her adolescent daughter to respond positively to her requests for help in the home, especially since the client is recovering from a recent operation. Her daughter's reluctance to help is interpreted by the client as meaning that the daughter does not respect her mother's wishes. In this example respect would be manifest by compliance on the daughter's part. Furthermore, the mother associates lack of respect with evidence that she has not been a good mother and has been remiss in teaching her daughter "good" values. Her expressed feelings of depression and of being disheartened about her mothering are connected to her perceptions and appraisals of the current interactions between herself and her daughter.

As clients describe the concrete details of a situation they often disclose accompanying feelings and begin the reflective work that leads to gaining a better understanding of their perceptions, feelings, and reactions. For example, an adolescent client reveals that when she loses her temper with her younger siblings she threatens them with "things I don't mean, and afterwards I cry and feel bad for doing it." When describing her high school as tough and one where there are a lot of people who pick fights, she volunteers that she feels scared and is very careful to avoid people who might start up with her. She describes feeling "all stopped up inside" when she leaves school, and, as she is talking about her angry outbursts at home after school, the client draws the link between her aggressive behavior at home and her avoidant response to potential aggression at school.

ATTENDING AND ACTIVE LISTENING

Asking questions is only one part of the worker's activity. At the same time, she is engaging with the client in a nonverbal manner through a range of behaviors, gestures, and expressions. Furthermore, the worker is listening carefully to what the client is saying and how he is conveying information. An important step in moving toward understanding another is the ability to listen in an active and open manner that conveys interest, attention, and engagement with the person and the material being shared. Listening relies on the worker's ability "to quiet your own frame of reference and listen more carefully to who and what are important to your clients" (DeJong and Berg, 1998, p. 23).

Attending and active listening are two terms that are used in the literature on interviewing in helping professions (Egan, 2002; Hill and O'Brien, 1999; Murphy and Dillon, 2003). The term *attending* refers to the nonverbal stance that practitioners use to orient themselves to their clients (Hill and O'Brien, 1999). The term *active listening* refers to a reflective type of listening and hearing that is attuned to the totality of the client and her experience. That is, the practitioner is listening for more than the facts that the client is presenting. Active listening involves hearing and striving to understand the verbal and nonverbal substance of the client's messages. The practitioner attempts to grasp both the specific and more general essence of what the client is trying to communicate by incorporating the client's feelings, meanings, and the context in which the situation occurred. Attention is paid to what the client says, how it is said, and what feelings are expressed, directly or indirectly, in relation to whatever is shared. This type of listening begins to build toward identifying themes and patterns. Attending and active listening are used throughout the helping process and are especially important in the early phase in the interests of building an effective relationship. Recall that in chapters 3 and 4 the qualities of helping relationships were presented. These qualities include warmth and caring concern; acceptance, positive regard, respect, and a nonjudgmental attitude; empathy and genuineness; and respecting diversity. Without these values, attitudes, and stance on the part of the worker, the behaviors associated with active listening may appear stiff and inauthentic.

Attending and conveying that one is listening begins with nonverbal actions and refers to a range of behaviors such as the following. Body posture can convey openness and interest through the way we sit, whether we lean toward or away from the client, whether our body position is relaxed and open, whether our arm and leg movements are distracting, and whether the distance between ourselves and the client is comfortable, too close and potentially experienced as intrusive, or too distant and potentially experienced as uninterested. Facial expressions such as occasional smiling can be interpreted as encouraging, and frowning may be interpreted as passing a negative judgment. Much has been written about eye contact and its reflection of social and cultural norms. Generally a natural gaze where eye contact is made, but not in a prolonged stare that engenders discomfort, is recommended. Head nods are also recommended as a natural way to indicate acknowledgment of what the client is saying. The worker's tone of voice can convey meanings such as warmth and concern, surprise and judgment, or aloofness and lack of interest. Some nonverbal behaviors that impede building a relationship have been identified by Okun (2002). These are looking away from the client, scowling, a tight mouth, yawning, rate of speech that is too slow or too fast, distracting behaviors, and acting rushed.

Note taking can also distract from attending to the client and can communicate that the worker is focusing more attention on writing a record than hearing the client. As a general guideline it is preferable to record information after a session, allowing full concentration on the client during the interview. When the worker is collecting complicated information that is difficult to recall, an ecomap or genogram can be a useful device to collect information (Hartman, 1995). These tools engage the client and the worker together in a joint effort at describing and documenting the important systems in the client's life, the nature of the relationships, and the history of the client's family relationships.

In many settings the pressures of workload make it necessary for social workers to write notes as the client speaks. In this event it is helpful to explain why the worker is doing this. For example, an intake worker in an assisted living residence for seniors stated, "The team at the home will want to know about you as we help you to settle in when you move here. I'm going to take some notes as we talk so that I don't forget some of the important information." When taking notes the worker can still maintain a stance of active listening by offering frequent nonverbal indications of her interest and involvement, such as head nodding and eye contact.

There are also verbal acknowledgments that can be included under this general category of attending behaviors. These include simple comments such as "I see" or sounds such as "uh-huh" or "mmhm." Generally these comments are used to indicate that one is listening and to encourage the client to continue talking about a particular topic. These comments indicate that one is following or tracking the speaker and serve as a facilitating response in place of a comment that addresses the issue directly. These comments and accompanying nonverbal gestures such as head nods serve as furthering comments; they encourage the client to continue to disclose aspects of the situation under consideration. Voice tone, whether it conveys warmth and interest, and speech rate and volume also communicate attending and interest. For example, if the client struggles with understanding English or hearing, a worker who adjusts the speed of her speech and enunciates clearly indicates her desire to have a meaningful interchange with the client.

Nonverbal social conventions and expected behaviors are learned from childhood through socialization in the family to the norms of their culture. These early lessons are incorporated in personal styles and will be apparent in the interview, both on the part of the client and the worker. There is an abundant literature that presents rules of nonverbal behavior in a number of countries and cultures. This literature may describe dominant trends that can usefully serve as a backdrop or reference point for the practitioner. For example, in some cultures and languages the word *yes* does not signal agreement but rather indicates that the listener is hearing and following the speaker. Misunderstanding can occur if this simple attending behavior is not understood correctly when speaking with clients who use this social convention differently than the worker. Since practitioners cannot be conversant with the multitude of nonverbal conventions that exist, it is useful to be aware that there may be differences and learn whether different social conventions and norms manifest with each client through observing the nonverbal interactions. For example, if the worker observes that the client averts her gaze when he tries to make prolonged eye contact, this may indicate a cultural or an individual preferred style of interacting. Clients should have the opportunity to choose how close or how distant they would like to be from the worker.

Special needs of clients must also be taken into account. Clients with visual impairments may be able to see and "read" the worker if he sits at an angle to the worker rather than in a face-to-face configuration. Clients who are totally blind will likely depend on their hearing acuity to determine whether the worker is speaking directly to them. When working with clients who use a hearing aid, practitioners should ensure that they face the client and speak directly to him, rather than raise their voice. Many social workers encounter elderly people in their practice who have some degree of hearing loss, vision loss, or both. It is useful to ask clients about these conditions and to request their guidance and suggestions to help the worker find the best positions and ways to talk with them.

DEVELOPING AN ATTENDING STANCE

Perhaps the greatest challenge when learning to develop an attending stance that conveys active listening is to find behaviors that are personally authentic, comfortable, and relaxed while at the same time are respectful of the clients one works with. For example, a relaxed, somewhat slouched posture that is in tune with that of an adolescent client may convey interest to the client. However, if this posture is uncomfortable for the worker and feels contrived, then it will take away from his comfort and natural demeanor. Similarly, the worker may be comfortable with a relaxed posture, but it may convey a lack of respect to a client who is older than the worker or from a culture that associates a more formal posture with a professional stance. The overriding principle that guides the use of nonverbal behaviors is that the worker needs to find a balance between the client's preferences and the worker's capacity to be flexible in meeting them.

An understanding of one's self is crucial and affects the worker's ability to truly attend to the client and be present and grounded in the interview rather than reactive or preoccupied with one's own issues. Self-awareness was discussed at length in part 1, especially in chapters 1 through 4 and is useful to review for this discussion. Self-understanding is a work in progress and one that is never finished. Rather, what is recommended is a self-reflective attitude where we are mindful and attuned to our own feelings, attitudes, and reactions and where we attempt to reflect on these factors and understand them so that our interactions with clients are not impulsive, reactive, and potentially destructive or, at the very least, unhelpful to clients. Practitioners change and develop and hence constantly learn more about themselves through new experiences in their professional and personal lives.

Recall in earlier chapters the discussion of the many factors that can diminish the worker's ability to be attentive. Some factors may be idiosyncratic personal issues not connected to the practice issue presented, such as the worker's preoccupation with her sick child at home. Factors may be connected to countertransference reactions that are stimulated by similarities between the client and her situation and issues in the worker's life. Countertransference reactions are also present when aspects of the client's situation, while not similar to the worker's, have potent meaning for the worker.

In chapter 6 aspects of the setting that have an impact on the social worker's ability to attend to and focus on the client were presented. Contextual features such as a comfortable and safe surrounding, a private space with minimal distractions and interruptions, and an environment where clients' cultural norms and linguistic needs are anticipated and provided for was presented as an ideal. The process of "tuning in" to the possible feelings of the client were discussed as potential aids to being fully present and receptive to whatever the client may present. Preparatory empathy may provide a useful starting point, but hunches are always subject to confirmation by the actual experience of the client. In an attending stance the practitioner is open to learning about the uniqueness of each client.

In the contemporary work environment many organizations have been affected by downsizing or managed care and have insufficient or diminished human resources to meet the needs of clients. Still, expectations about the quantity of work produced continue to grow exerting pressure on workers to handle cases efficiently and quickly. These demands can distract practitioners from therapeutic processes and produce a greater focus on meeting instrumental and administrative needs rather than working through a collaborative and empowering client relationship.

Videotaping actual or simulated interviews and reviewing them has proven to be an effective way to raise awareness about one's nonverbal behaviors and styles that may facilitate or interfere with the worker's verbal messages. Students can review these tapes and focus on two dimensions. First, they can identify their own behavior along the dimensions suggested by Egan (2002): posture and gestures; eye contact, gaze, and movement; facial expressions such as frowns, twitching, smiling, rolling one's eyes; voice-related characteristics such as speed of speaking, tone, volume, silences, stumbling, and repeated use of hackneyed phrases such as "OK," "I see," "Wow"; and the distance or space between the student and client. Second, it is useful to examine the affect of these behaviors on the client and whether or not they seem to make a difference. Obtaining feedback from a colleague or the person who plays a simulated client in a role-play is important as we may evaluate negatively a behavior that was viewed positively by the client or had no impact on them.

RESPONDING

Throughout the entire process the worker is focused on two tasks simultaneously: 1) assessment-intervention and 2) building and maintaining the working relationship. Assessment-intervention involves gathering information about the facts, the context, and the cognitive, affective, and behavioral aspects of the client's concerns and situation, so that sufficient joint understanding develops in the initial stage and throughout, and carrying out effective interventions. The interpersonal level includes developing and maintaining enough of a connection and relationship bond with the client so that he perceives that help may result from the meetings. The latter involves connecting with the client's emotions in a way that leads the client to experience the worker as empathetic. When these two conditions are met, the client is more likely to return for subsequent sessions (Tsang, Bogo, and George, 2004). It is useful to review the discussion on empathy, presented in chapter 3, and re-examine the crucial values, attitudes, and stance that are encompassed in this concept. As noted earlier, interviewing skills provide the techniques to ground this concept in actual behaviors in the interview. The skills are powerful only when they are used in conjunction with the more nebulous qualities of the empathic helping relationship.

Pacing and tracking the client so as to proceed at the client's pace was briefly discussed with respect to the use of questions. Similarly, when offering any of the responses that follow, the practice principle of going at the client's pace is demonstrated when the client perceives the worker's comments as relevant to his substantive concerns and that the client's messages were understood (Hepworth, Rooney, and Larsen, 2002). In the interaction between client and worker the client will give the worker some sort of feedback that indicates whether the worker is in tune or is missing some important aspect of the client's story. Practitioners welcome and encourage a conversation that provides them with this type of information and they use it to refocus and direct the dialogue so that it remains client centered. Active listening and attending behaviors are other ways for helpers to stay oriented to the client's issues and agenda.

RESTATEMENT OR PARAPHRASE

Restating or paraphrasing the client's comments refers to a verbal practice where the worker tries to understand the speaker and converts the original content expressed by the client into words that are expressed in a succinct and clear manner. Typically, a restatement is offered after the client has presented a significant amount of information. The terms *restatement* and *paraphrase* are used to refer to the content or meaning of what the client has said. The term *reflection* is used to refer to the same process when it is directed at the feeling conveyed. In order to paraphrase, the practitioner uses active listening, tries to understand what the speaker is conveying, and then formulates comments into the practitioner's version of what was said. This version is offered to the client in a tentative manner, inviting his response and feedback. It is through many series of such interactions that the dialogue progresses to a point where the worker may offer a summary of issues and point out connections between aspects of the situation, relevant dynamics, and pertinent themes.

Paraphrasing and restatements serve a number of purposes in the interview. They are a simple and nonintrusive way of keeping the focus on a relevant topic and serve the same purpose as questions or comments that seek concreteness. That is, they encourage the client to provide more information, elaborate on the message, or explore the particular subject further. When the client experiences the paraphrase in a way that conveys he is understood, he may also feel supported and connected to the worker. Furthermore, the process of "talking out loud" can of itself be helpful; when one hears himself repeating stories and issues he can obtain some clarification. When another person also responds, the experience is similar to what has been called having a sounding board. Simple feedback can further assist in clarifying and making sense of our experiences, feelings, and responses. When the helper's paraphrases do not fully and accurately grasp what the client is trying to convey, the client has the opportunity to clarify her message as she gives feedback to the worker (Hill and O'Brien, 1999).

Students often comment that when using paraphrasing they feel as if they are simply parroting what the client has told them and this leads to a sense of "going around in circles." Since the goal is to elicit various aspects of the situation—the facts, the context, as well as the relevant thoughts, feelings, and behaviors, paraphrase used alone is not sufficient. It needs to be used in conjunction with questions, seeking concreteness, and reflection of feelings. For example, a young man identifies with his social worker that his characteristic reaction to criticism in interpersonal relationships is aggression, which in turn leads to more difficulty in those relationships that he values and wants to keep. He wonders why people have to question what he is saying. The worker paraphrases, "You think the other person does not believe what you're saying." The client then goes on to discuss how angry he gets, introducing the feeling dimension of these interactions. The worker might then probe and use an open-ended question to further understand those feelings, saying, "What is it about another person questioning you that leads you to feel angry?" or the worker might seek concreteness: "Could you describe a recent example of someone questioning you and you feeling angry in response?" A rich repertoire of interviewing skills, used interchangeably, leads to a flow in the interview that more closely resembles a dialogue than a stilted set of responses.

REFLECTION OF FEELINGS

Following the literature, a distinction is made between interviewing skills used to address content and cognitive aspects of the client's message, such as the skill of paraphrasing and restatement, and interviewing skills used to address feelings, such as the skill of reflection (Hill and O'Brien, 1999; Poorman, 2003). This is an academic point, and, while useful for presentation in a text, in actual practice the worker's behavior when addressing content, cognition, or feelings may appear similar. The important feature in using these interviewing skills is the intention of the worker and her purpose in offering a particular comment. That is, is the purpose to clarify the events, to paraphrase and explore the thoughts, perceptions, and meanings the client draws upon, or to elicit and identify feelings experienced by the client?

The literature defines reflection of feelings as the worker repeating or rephrasing the client's communications about her feelings or putting into words feelings that are implied by the client's nonverbal behavior or by the content of the material under discussion (Hill and O'Brien, 1999). Reflection is used to help clients focus on a specific feeling and begin to explore it in greater depth. When practitioners use the skill of reflecting feelings, they are specifically directing clients to attend to the range of emotions that are stirred up in relation to an event or situation and to become aware of, or in touch with, those feelings that likely act as a powerful influence on the client's thoughts and subsequent actions. In order to offer reflections, practitioners use the stance and verbal and nonverbal behaviors referred to as attending and active listening. Through listening to the metacommunication about feelings and observing the way the client displays feelings or struggles to control the overt expression of feelings, the worker gains the insights that are captured in his reflection of the feelings. Directing attention to feelings, often sore spots or sources of pain for any individual, requires sensitivity, support, and empathy. Once again, the importance of the developing relationship cannot be underscored enough. In the early stages of relationship development, reflection of feelings needs to be offered tentatively as the bond between client and worker is only beginning to grow. On the other hand, when the worker does not connect with the client's emotions, the client may not feel heard or understood and decide not to return. In our analysis of the processes of engagement in first sessions we found that clients continued in counseling when their workers connected to their feelings, through furthering comments that encouraged discussion of feelings and through reflecting feelings that were conveyed directly or implied (Tsang, Bogo, and George, 2004). In contrast, when the worker did not respond to the client's feeling comments but changed the topic or offered a cognitive response, the client did not continue in counseling (Tsang, Bogo, and George, 2004).

When the worker has progressed beyond the middle stage, the worker and client may have more knowledge about the client's characteristic emotional responses to particular situations. Reflection of feelings still remains important as this process is often the entry point into greater in-depth exploration of any issue. Caution needs to be exercised that in this stage feeling-oriented material is not intellectualized and experiencing feelings replaced with talking about feelings.

The important processes that involve working with feelings were discussed in chapter 7 and acknowledgment made of the crucial role of emotion in organizing our perceptions, attributing meaning to events, and affecting our behaviors (Greenberg, 2002a). Hence skills such as the use of questions and seeking concreteness can also be used to assist clients to recognize their emotions and the role they play in their life. Practitioners often talk about the importance of helping clients "get in touch with their feelings." This refers to the notion that often individuals talk at length about the details of a situation and demonstrate emotions in nonverbal ways, through an agitated presentation, blushing, crying, discomfort, and so on. When asked directly about the feelings that are connected to the topic, individuals may or may not be able to label their emotions. In some instances the individual is aware of general feelings of confusion, being overwhelmed, or distressed, but has difficulty being specific about these feelings, the situations that elicit them, and the accompanying perceptions and meanings attributed to them. In other situations an individual may respond to a query about his emotions by talking about what he thinks about a situation, giving a cognitive or intellectual response rather than an affective one.

When practitioners use the skill of reflection of feelings, it is crucial to remember the distinctions drawn between primary emotions, those on the surface and readily accessible, and secondary emotions, those less obvious but perhaps more painful and more important. It draws our attention to the need to reflect not only the feelings that are on the surface, for example, anger, but also the underlying feelings that may fuel them, for example, hurt or vulnerability. Many of the change processes discussed in chapter 7 include working with the client's emotions. The skill of reflecting feelings is a basic skill in this activity as the worker uses it to help the client put the feeling he is experiencing into words.

The following example illustrates how the practitioner used reflection of feelings to help the client identify the various feelings producing her confusion about whether or not to remain in a relationship with a partner.

The client is discussing her annoyance with her partner's reluctance to be spontaneous. Her anger is heard and acknowledged by the worker, leading the client to elaborate, "I feel controlled by him, I have to do what we plan to do . . . if something interesting comes up that I'd like to do, I have to do it alone." The worker builds on the term *alone* and says, "What is that like for you?" The client becomes tearful and speaks at length about her years as a single parent and how busy and involved she was with her children. Now that they are young adults and in their own lives she has the time to spend with her new partner.

The worker reflects, "You're aware of feeling lonely, missing the close connection with people in your life." The client then elaborates on how much she misses her children and her struggle to recapture some of that closeness in her life. The worker reflects, "You feel a void when Jim (new partner) can't provide the closeness you want."

Note in this example that the reflections offered have three characteristics: 1) they stay close to the client's original expression and incorporate the client's language, 2) they link the feeling to the context, in this instance the client's relationships, and 3) they are succinct and, from reviewing the tape of this interview, are offered in a gentle tone and with a questioning manner at the end of the reflection. The later conveys the tentative nature of the worker's impression and provides the space for the client to disagree. These guidelines can be used when students are first learning to offer reflections. Later in this chapter methods for developing interviewing skills are presented. Some suggestions are provided for achieving competence in using the skill of reflection.

Social characteristics have a profound impact on individual's comfort in expressing and sharing feelings in general and with a stranger. In some cultures enduring negative feelings is valued and the expression of feelings is a reflection of immaturity and brings embarrassment to the individual, the individual's family, and the person who witnesses the emotional display. In other cultures emotions and private information are readily shared. For example, popular television programs in North America provide a model where the most intimate details of people's lives are disclosed and displayed. Age and generation also impact on internalized norms about expressing feelings. Many older individuals subscribe to a value on privacy and suppression of feelings. As noted earlier, generalizations about people on the basis of variables such as ethnicity, gender, and age can only serve as broad themes and possibilities. Social workers must assess the uniqueness of each individual client and the degree to which these cultural norms apply. When a client does not readily respond to reflection and discussion of feelings, practitioners need to give thought to whether this reflects a personality dynamic, such as being reserved, frightened, or uncomfortable with feelings, or whether this reflects an internalized social norm.

SILENCE

In the interview social workers think about when to allow silence and when to use questions or responding skills to further the session. Beginning practitioners often notice that silence feels uncomfortable and the tendency to fill it up with talk. As comfort sitting with silence develops, thought can be given to when allowing the silence to progress will be a helpful interviewing strategy.

Silence can be helpful when it is apparent that the client is thinking about the topic under discussion. Individuals vary with respect to how much time they need to form responses, continue a line of discussion, or manage strong feelings that are elicited. When the worker responds too quickly, he may subvert the client's desire to think something through. On the other hand, some people find prolonged silence uncomfortable, anxiety provoking, and immobilizing. They benefit from the structure and focus the worker provides through guiding the session. In other situations the practitioner may become aware that she is taking too much of a leading role in the session and decides to provide more space for the client. When a silence arises in this context the worker may wish to sit it out and nonverbally or with minimal prompts encourage the client to take the initiative. Finally, patterns of silence can vary based on different cultural meanings being ascribed to them, such as respect for the other person, or a signal that the topic is too private and the other is not comfortable to discuss it. As in the use of all interviewing behaviors, practitioners develop and use their clinical judgment to decide when to allow a silence to proceed and when to fill it.

Throughout the interview the practitioner offers paraphrases, restatements, and reflections that can be thought of as testing out whether the worker has grasped the salient components of the presenting problem and the client's situation as well as the essence of the relevant discrete thoughts, meanings, and feelings. The next step involves the worker and client in putting these separate components together to link them and to identify themes. Summary statements provide structure to the interview as they integrate many aspects of the client's story. Summaries can also refocus the discussion and prompt the client to elaborate on specific ideas.

Summary statements are generally offered in a tentative manner that invites the client to provide feedback, additional information, and qualifying comments. Through this type of dialogue the worker will revise her summaries so that a joint understanding emerges. Summary statements provide the client with information about the degree to which the worker has connected with him and appreciated his circumstances and concerns. To the extent the client ends the interview with a sense that the worker has this type of understanding, or at least is committed to developing it, it can be said that the client and worker have achieved enough of an engagement so that the client will return.

There are two types of summaries; those that take place periodically throughout an interview and those that are used toward the end of a session. Periodic summaries link a number of factors, for example, information given at an earlier point in time with new information; the connections between the client's concerns, feelings, perceptions, and behaviors, or connections between any two of these; interrelationships between significant persons in the client's life and the presenting problem. The following example of a periodic summary comes halfway through the first interview. The client, a twenty-one-year-old female, and the social worker in a mental health clinic have traced the client's recurring experiences of feeling "depressed" in relation to her presenting concern that she is once again feeling low. The worker offers the following summary. "It sounds as if, if we look back over the past few years, that when you were depressed before you always had reasons for it, like fights with your friends or your Mom's illness. Now you don't really feel there is any reason for it, and that's confusing for you."

Summaries offered at the end of the interview are used as an entry into goal setting and planning and are comprehensive. They aim to highlight the key issues to be addressed. In this respect they provide focus and direction for the interventions in the next phase. These summaries can also be used at the next session to provide continuity over time and structure to the beginning of the interview. As the work progresses, the concluding summary in each session will change to reflect new information and perhaps new directions. Continuing with the above example, in the last quarter of the interview the client revealed limited information about an experience when she was harshly scolded for childhood sexual play. The client believed this event was influencing her current feelings of being stuck, trapped, and uncomfortable when she starts to get close to a potential boyfriend. The worker summarizes as follows,

> It sounds as if you're saying that while you feel confused about why you are feeling depressed, you think there might be some connection with your being uncomfortable as you get close to a new boyfriend and this experience when you were much younger. These are all really important things to explore and this counseling process will give the chance to do that. You started to talk about that experience with a counselor last year, but you felt too scared about it and stopped. You think that it's something you want to try to look at again now and we'll have to talk about what we need to do in this counseling so that you can continue with it.

The client responded with relief, saying, "That's the main reason I came here in the first place, I think I need to figure everything out."

ELICITING AND RESPONDING TO FEEDBACK

The importance of working in an interactive and collaborative way has been underscored throughout this text. The process of helping unfolds largely through dialogue, and practitioners are most concerned with the client's response to their comments. Therefore all comments made by the client can be conceived as including an element of response to the worker. When the client responds with further elaboration or indicates that the dialogue is helpful, the topic relevant, new ideas gained, or new actions planned, the worker can probably assume that the interview is progressing well for the client.

Feedback that indicates the client is not being helped can arise in a variety of ways. First, the client may simply correct the worker's impression with a direct clarification, disagreement, or refocus. For example, when interviewing a mother about her adolescent daughter who was skipping classes and where there was great frustration on the part of the mother, the worker drew attention on a few occasions to positive similarities between the mother's descriptions about herself and about her daughter. The mother gently refocused the worker, saying, "That may be so, we are alike in many ways, but I am very frustrated about how different we are in our ideas about her future, and that's what I need help with—how to get her to attend her classes." This information helped the worker attend to the problems as well as the strengths that the client wanted to discuss. It is human nature to want to avoid misunderstandings, however this type of client feedback gives the practitioner an opportunity to learn more about the client.

Clients can also provide feedback indirectly. For example, in a second session the worker inquired whether the client had any further thoughts about their discussion in the first meeting. The client said that she actually could not remember what they discussed. Further clarification revealed that this client had a learning disability and "if I just talk about something it doesn't sink in." This information led to her suggestion that she and the worker end each meeting with some written notes about what she would do or think about between meetings. Missed appointments and hesitancy in arranging subsequent meetings may also suggest that the client is not finding the sessions useful.

Finally, a worker and client can have a prolonged discussion about a particular topic and the client appear to be fully engaged. Subsequently, when the worker inquires if their conversation was helpful, the client informs the worker that, while "the discussion was helpful, it wasn't about what I really wanted to talk about." This example reveals how complex it is to assess another's experience. Despite the appearance in the session that the client was actively participating and seemingly receiving something of value, in fact the client would have preferred to be discussing another issue. The client did not give feedback at the time, so that the agenda could have been changed. In this example when the worker requested feedback the client could provide the worker with useful information. Together they then considered ways in which the client could more actively set the agenda. The worker suggested that each meeting begin with some thought given to what the client considered most pressing to discuss.

OFFERING SUPPORT

Social workers provide support to clients in many different ways. Their knowledge of resources enables them to quickly assess the gaps in services in a client's life. Using relationship, communication, and advocacy skills, they are often able to work with a range of agencies to secure resources. For example, social workers in medical settings develop a network of relationships with community agencies that provide services in the home including nursing, occupational therapy, and basic personal care. When a client is facing discharge from a hospital and needs assistance to return to independent living in the community, the social worker's ability to organize these services provides a level of fundamental support that is invaluable. Moreover, social workers are skilled at dealing with complicated eligibility requirements that can appear insurmountable when clients feel desperate and overwhelmed.

Support is also provided through the medium of the relationship where the client experiences the social worker as available, attentive, respectful, and committed to understand and help. As noted throughout the text, this stance is, in and of itself, nurturing and reassuring; it is also a crucial foundation from which change may occur. In chapters 3 and 4 the concept of a supportive relationship is presented and the notion that practitioners offer this relationship through displaying a set of values, attitudes, and behaviors in nonverbal, subtle, and verbal ways. The client is more likely to reveal and discuss a wide range of feelings, wishes, and thoughts as she learns that she will not be humiliated, misunderstood, or judged negatively. When these conditions are present the helping relationship is perceived as safe, and trust or confidence in the potential usefulness of this process may develop. In summary, the interviewing skills presented thus far are the interviewing skills that practitioners use to demonstrate their warmth, genuineness, and empathy. Questions, paraphrases, reflection of feelings, summarizing, and sensitive responses to client feedback can be experienced by clients as supportive when used in the context of building a beneficial relationship.

Validation refers to an extremely powerful process that many clients experience as supportive. It occurs when the practitioner confirms the client's subjective experience of the situation he is describing. It is akin to "bearing witness," conveying that the story shared is difficult or challenging or painful and that the client's feelings and reactions are understandable. Validation creates a feeling that someone appreciates the impact of the situation. The actual feeling the client describes may be painful, and validation will not diminish that discomfort. Rather it can offer enough support that the client can tolerate the pain and explore in more depth or elaborate on the feeling and the situation.

Recall the case example presented to illustrate the skill of summarizing. The client had struggled on and off over many years with a vague feeling of being low or depressed. She had a sense that in some way it was connected to a childhood experience of sexual play and a harsh parental response to it. When in an earlier attempt at counseling the previous worker had prematurely suggested that her parent's response was the issue, the client felt uncomfortable—"I don't want to blame my mother for my feelings"—and had discontinued. Still troubled and preoccupied seven months later, she initiated a request for counseling at another agency. She waited until more than half the session had transpired before disclosing these issues and her discomfort around thinking and talking about them. The following response of the worker demonstrates the skill of validation through her understanding the client's struggle with competing feelings. It also conveys that the worker and client will work together in this counseling experience. "I think it's courageous of you to want to look into these things. On the one hand, it is scary and it's understandable that you feel sort of hesitant. When you tried it before it didn't feel OK. On the other hand, you feel that it's going to be in your best interest to sort out all these questions, these feelings. I think that it will help you, and we both have to figure out how we can talk about this in a way that makes it not so hard for you."

SHARING IMPRESSIONS

The social worker is guided by the tasks of the beginning stage to arrive at enough or sufficient joint understanding with the client that they can productively agree to meet again and work on some topics or goals. In chapter 6 the tasks of this stage are outlined in box 6.2, The Initial Stage, and frameworks for assessment are presented in boxes 6.4 and 6.5. As noted, developing an understanding takes place with the client as an active participant in the interview and through the worker reflecting on the situation both during and after the interview. The worker shares her impressions about factors internal to the client and factors in the environment that contribute to his situation and encourages feedback about those impressions so that some agreement about what needs to be addressed and how it can be addressed is reached. Practitioners share these impressions through restatement, paraphrasing, reflecting feelings, and offering periodic summaries.

At the end of the first interview impressions are shared as summaries that suggest potential intervention plans. When the organizational context requires a plan that adheres to a limited number of sessions or involves a definite time frame, impressions form part of a more formal summary. In turn this summary is used to assess progress and determine next steps. For example, a family has met with the worker as agreed upon for six sessions to develop more effective approaches to helping their ten-year-old son with school adjustment issues. The worker observes that the family has started to make good use of the meetings and have followed up on suggestions. They have not yet held a meeting with their son's teacher. The worker summarizes, "It seems that you are saying that you've benefited from our meetings, and I would suggest that we schedule another four sessions and space them further apart than our weekly meetings. Let's consider how you can move ahead more quickly to set up a meeting with his teacher; I think that's an important thing to do and is still missing." As the work proceeds through the middle stage the practitioner continues to offer her impressions in an ongoing way in the course of discussion about any relevant issues.

SETTING GOALS

From the mutual conversation and the initial impressions of the worker, preliminary goals emerge that are expressed in general terms, for example, "trying to understand what these feelings of depression, which come and go, are about" to very specific terms, "I want to get and keep a job." The skill of seeking concreteness is very useful in helping clients define their goals in clear, behavioral terms and can be used to focus on the future, much the same way as the strengths-oriented questions presented earlier.

There are many situations where clear goals will only emerge through exploration and discussion in the helping process. When the agency provides opportunities for more prolonged work, there is less pressure to define goals specifically however it is a useful process and should be kept in mind. It helps clients clarify vague and abstract feelings and thoughts in terms that may make them more accessible to discussion, reflection, and progress. The social work principles of partializing the problem and setting priorities can be applied equally to goal setting. This notion involves breaking down a large issue into its component parts and determining which goal needs most attention at the outset. For example, the goal of getting and keeping a job can be broken down into filling out the forms for vocational rehabilitation, attending the retraining program regularly and punctually, and working with the job placement officer. The client may feel that these goals may not be able to be achieved until he feels more confident that his medication will help him remain stable in his mood and behavior. This goal may take priority over the others or the client and social worker may decide to focus on it as well as begin the vocational program.

When clear goals are present it is easier to identify the tasks or steps the worker and client need to take to ultimately reach those goals. For example, to enact a successful referral the worker may need to obtain necessary papers that the client must complete and the client may need to sign an agreement with the agency to attend a program regularly. When the goals are about internal or interpersonal dynamics, the only tasks at the beginning phase that may be identifiable are to attend sessions and to give some thought to the matters discussed. At a later point in the process the tasks may include the client's putting some insights derived in the interview into action in the client's life.

PROVIDING INFORMATION

Information, in the broadest sense of the term, is offered in many ways. Earlier we discussed the stance of active listening and the process of eliciting and responding to feedback. In the interview the worker and client are continuously involved in this cyclical interchange of listening, commenting, listening, and so on. The worker's comments can be conceived of as providing information in subtle ways. For example, when highlighting strengths, the worker is "providing information"—he is saying, in effect, "Even though you are telling me about the difficulties in your life, I see that you also have many positives and the ability to cope with tough situations."

Workers also give information about the client's situation in a direct manner. While the helping process has been discussed as a collaborative one, clients expect that social workers will offer something to them. Expectations will vary and are affected by factors such as the services the agency offers, how clear the client was about her goals when initiating the process, or whether the service request was a result of an agreed upon or mandated referral. If the client was self-referred for counseling, she may be more or less clear about what the problem is and what type of help she wants. In the beginning stage, therefore, the social worker offers his impressions in a tentative manner that invites comments. The practitioner's impressions may expand the definition of the issues to be addressed or may focus more specifically on a particular topic. For example, a single mother approached an agency serving adolescents for help with her daughter's poor school attendance and failing performance. Through an interview with the daughter and mother, their tense relationship was identified as an area that interfered with their ability to deal with the school issue and was also a source of strain and disappointment for both. The worker shared this impression, which led them to discuss and recognize that as a family who had recently immigrated they both wanted a closer relationship and were disappointed with their estrangement. Throughout the interview the worker used the preceding interview skills and introduced her impressions through reflecting feelings and offering summaries in a manner that invited reflection and dialogue. This process led to an expansion of the issues to be addressed.

The following example is one where a more focused intervention plan came about during the first interview. The client had recently been discharged from an inpatient psychiatric unit and was referred to the social worker for help in discharge planning. A thorough assessment revealed that the client was stable in most areas of his life and his primary goal was finding and keeping a job. The social worker conducted a comprehensive scan of the client's world, using an ecological framework to guide the interview. However, the client kept returning to his concern about employment. Through attentive listening to the client the social worker concluded that the most helpful intervention he could offer was a successful referral, with follow-up, to an agency that specialized in vocational rehabilitation for former psychiatric patients.

INFORMATION ABOUT THE SERVICE

Since most social workers offer service within an agency context, they must be clear about what the agency can provide, what the duration of service is, what problems they can address, and what is expected of the client. Some clients will also want to know about the professional qualifications of the social worker and something about his role or function in the setting. Especially when clients are mandated by the court to attend, Shulman (1999) recommends that the session begin with the worker describing the purpose of their meetings and the role played by the worker. He recommends that the language used should be simple.

In our analysis of first sessions in a wide range of settings we found that the workers did not begin the first interview giving this type of information (Tsang, Bogo, and George, 2004). Rather they asked open-ended questions about the client's decision to attend the agency such as "What brings you here?" or "What prompted you to contact the agency?" Some workers began with some preliminary comments about their understanding of what led to the meeting with the social worker. For example, "I understand that the staff on the floor thought it would be a good idea for you to see a social worker since you were leaving the hospital. What do you think about that?" "I see on the intake form that you are concerned about feelings of depression, is that why you came in?" It was only at the end of the session that the workers in this study offered information about how they might be able to help the client. The information was offered after the worker developed some grasp of the presenting situation, conducted a preliminary assessment of the client's significant relationships and issues, and arrived at some joint agreement about what needed attention. All their comments were related to the specific needs of the client: for an adolescent and her mother, the worker proposed joint counseling and also informed them that she could facilitate a meeting with the school; for an adult female client who wanted counseling about relationship issues and was depressed and potentially suicidal, the worker informed her that he would continue to meet with her as well as refer her for psychiatric assessment and provide her with information about the crisis team should she feel unsafe.

These interviewing behaviors in positive outcome cases lead to the recommendation that information is most useful when offered at a time that it will be meaningful for the client. Usually this happens toward the end of the interview as part of a general wrap-up, summary, and plan about the next steps. Any policies about attendance, cancellation of meetings, fees, and limits to confidentiality can also be explained at that time.

PSYCHOEDUCATION

Social workers use an educative function when they link clients with environmental resources. Educating about a range of issues and expectations related to individual and social functioning can be incorporated in the helping process and is referred to as psychoeducation. This approach is frequently used in groups where information is presented in a formal manner, group discussion and exercises take place, and individual members share their own thoughts and experiences regarding the topic. Psychoeducation can be integrated in the individual counseling process, although it should be offered in a way that does not elevate the worker and diminish the client. For example, social workers working with children and their families know about milestones in child development and can share this information in an appropriate way with parents whose expectations may be unrealistic. Social workers practicing with the elderly and their families also know about the components of healthy aging, indicators that lead to considering community-based supports, and usual reactions to decision making about moving to a care facility. When an elderly person decides to enter a residential setting and then expresses highly ambivalent feelings about having moved, social workers can help family members by providing information about reactions to relocation and suggestions about how to best respond. Social workers in the health and mental health field know a considerable amount about the conditions of their clients and can provide invaluable psychoeducational information to the identified patient and to families about such things as when an individual might reach a point when they can resume normal activities of daily living, feel less tired, have more motivation or whether these are realistic expectations and goals.

NORMALIZATION

Related to imparting information is the process of normalization or universalization. This occurs when the social worker uses data from research studies or numerous practice experiences to convey to the client that a particular reaction he is having is one shared by many others. For example, a woman had been receiving medical interventions for infertility and was informed by the physician in the clinic that she was terminated from the program, as it was not producing the desired outcomes. The social worker on the service met with the client and listened empathically to her feelings of disappointment, discouragement, and anger. She told the worker that even though she had agreed to the protocol, actually hearing that the interventions were not working was devastating. The social worker had met and worked with many women in such situations and could honestly convey that the client's reaction was similar to that of other women who had heard this information. For many people learning that others have had similar reactions and feelings is validating and helpful. Others, however, may feel that hearing about someone else's reaction trivializes her own or that she has nothing in common with these other women and such information is burdensome, tangential to her current needs, and not useful. When using normalization the practitioner needs to be sensitive that her comments do not minimize or diminish the client's experience of the uniqueness of the situation.

PROVIDING SUGGESTIONS

The approach presented in this text emphasizes collaboration between client and worker and building the client's capacity to think through issues, arrive at solutions, and take action. Similarly, social work practice theory generally recommends helping clients think through issues and make their own decisions about what to change and how to go about it. Reflecting on this stance, Woods (Woods and Hollis, 2000) observes that the official position of reluctance about telling clients what to do has probably been more extreme than what actually occurs in practice. She suggests that experienced social workers are likely to give some direct advice to clients and offers guidelines in this regard. Woods (Woods and Hollis, 2000) comments on the degree of directiveness in the worker's suggestions and draws a distinction along a continuum based on the nature of the topic under consideration. Especially when there are situations of urgency or where safety is an issue, the worker might insist the client take particular action or actively intervene. For example, if the client tells the worker of a suicide plan, the worker might insist the client go to an emergency department and the worker will accompany the client. If the client remains unwilling to do this, the worker might contact the relevant authorities. When the situation poses less risk but appears inadvisable, the worker might strongly urge the client to take a particular course of action. For example, a young adolescent girl tells her social worker that she has becomes sexually active with her boyfriend. The worker learns that this client has little knowledge of or interest in birth control. The educational information that she provides about attending a planned parenthood clinic and choosing a method of birth control is not given in a neutral manner; she strongly urges the client to do so.

There are many situations where workers provide suggestions or encourage clients to consider alternatives when deciding on a course of action where the risk is not as blatant as in the examples above but where the client may benefit from the worker's advice. For example, a teenaged boy was concerned that his poor record of attendance at school had left him so far behind in his studies that there was no hope of catching up. He sought counseling at a community agency and found the social worker supportive and understanding. In the course of talking about his school year he felt that his only option was to drop out. The worker asked whether he had considered other options and, when the client responded that he had not, what did the worker have in mind, she suggested that they might arrange a meeting with his teachers to work out a plan, the agency might arrange a volunteer tutor, or he might consider switching to an alternative school that would provide some credit for work he had already completed. In this instance the worker provided a number of suggestions the client had not considered and was not aware existed. Since a positive alliance had been established together, they proceeded to consider the advantages and disadvantages of these options.

When offering suggestions it is generally advisable to first ensure that there has been some exploration of the issue with the client and that he is truly "stuck." Too often, unable to tolerate the difficulty that the client is experiencing, interviewers rush in prematurely to offer suggestions only to find that the client has a reason why each one would not work. If enough time and space for exploration and reflection have not transpired, the client may not yet be ready to hear what the worker is proposing. An additional element in offering advice is the manner, tone, and stance of the worker. Within the context of a strong relationship and offered in a manner that invites dialogue and consideration, many clients will be open to the suggestion and view it as new information. Recall that in a study on helpful aspects of psychotherapy clients noted that suggestions made by practitioners were almost never followed (Gehart-Brooks and Lyle, 1998). Rather, clients reported that suggestions, followed by the give and take in the interviews, stimulated the clients to come up with their own new perspectives and behavioral, emotional, and cognitive changes.

Relationship issues and tone are important to keep in mind when offering suggestions. An authoritarian, opinionated, and definite manner on the part of the worker may divert the client from the issue under consideration. Rather, the client may become preoccupied with the worker and wonder about the consequences to their relationship if he agrees with or disagrees with the worker. The working alliance may be ruptured and a hierarchical power dynamic reinforced.

The goal of in-depth exploration is to expand the client's awareness and understanding of phenomena that have a significant impact on her thoughts, feelings, and behaviors. While specific models emphasize different components, promoting emotional experiencing and developing cognitive understanding or insight are effective helping processes across models. Contemporary change theory recognizes the interrelatedness of domains and encourages practitioners to adopt integrative approaches (Greenberg, 2002b; Hubble, Duncan, and Miller, 1999; Wampold, 2001).

IN-DEPTH EXPLORATION OF FEELINGS AND
PROMOTING EMOTIONAL EXPERIENCING

One can think of sharing and working with feelings as an experience involving levels that proceeds from the surface to ones of greater depth. It would be unusual to expect anyone to share her deepest feelings about an issue in a first encounter. Exceptions to this occur when an individual's sense of self and integration is threatened, such as in situations of trauma or crisis, or as indicators of forms of mental illness. Hence, when the worker decides to embark on a direction that will include exploring some aspect of the client's feelings at a deeper level, he will proceed in a progressive manner, moving through levels, and with sensitivity.

The skill of reflecting feelings, presented earlier in this chapter, provides a good beginning point from which to proceed to more in-depth exploration. As the worker considers further probing, the following factors are relevant. Since depth exploration can produce painful feelings, thought should be given to the relationship and degree of bonding between client and worker. Has the alliance developed to the extent that the client experiences the worker as empathic, supportive, and nonjudgmental and expects that sharing difficult feelings will lead to a validating or encouraging response? If the sense of attachment in the relationship is a positive one, the experience of exploring and expressing difficult or previously unacknowledged feelings and being understood and accepted can have extremely positive effects. Workers can express acceptance and give permission to clients to acknowledge, identify, and experience feelings and "allow them to come to full expression" (Cormier and Hackney, 1999, p. 135). Phrases such as "It's OK to feel what you are struggling with," "It's important for you to let yourself cry" can provide enough support so that the client can continue to explore and also tolerate the discomfort associated with the topic. Where a connected relationship exists, it provides a holding environment, and clients do not feel overwhelmed by these explorations. For example, in the early interviews a father who left his son when the boy was two years old and currently seeks a closer relationship with the twelve year old became tearful when discussing his reasons for leaving. He attempted to contain his tears and changed the subject. During later sessions the topic was approached again and the worker consistently offered nonjudgmental responses to his disclosing what he termed his "selfishness." Thereafter he could return to exploring his feelings of sadness about what he had missed in his son's life, his guilt and self-loathing about abandoning the boy and his mother to seek a more exciting relationship with a new partner.

Thought must also be given to the individual, familial, and cultural meanings attached to expressing feelings. If in all three domains the client has learned that this is not valued or seen negatively as a self-indulgent process, the client may experience this type of expression as one that stirs up anxiety and is not initially helpful. Beginning with exploration of cognitions or external phenomena may be a more productive direction. Or practitioners may want to make the discussion of feelings an explicit topic and ask clients what they have learned about talking about feelings. They can discuss what the client thinks about these norms and expectations and whether these cultural or family values currently fit for the client. Prevailing cultural mores may be perceived by the client as helpful and reasonable or as oppressive and leading to few options. A worker who both respects the impact of culture and can also be nonjudgmental when raising these issues provides a rare opportunity for the client to explore various aspects of her feelings. For example, a middle-aged woman from a Middle Eastern country was referred to the social worker in a family health clinic when her moderate depression was not relieved with medication. Through exploration this client was able to discuss her unhappiness in her long-standing arranged marriage and her feelings of being trapped in it with no alternatives. When exploring cultural norms, she stated that even though her parents and husband would not approve of her talking in this way, she felt such a pressure from these feelings that this discussion was helping her think more clearly.

Depth exploration of feelings is accomplished by using a variety of basic interviewing skills while maintaining a continuing focus on feelings. Probes and open-ended questions are useful to elicit feelings that may be relevant to the situation but are implied, hinted at, expressed in a nonverbal way but are not verbalized. A universalizing comment can be a helpful preface to such probes. For example, a client is discussing her instrumental needs if she plans to leave an abusive spouse and appears distraught. The worker says, "Many women who have left abusive men feel scared and uncertain when they are thinking about such a big move. What are you feeling about it?"

Seeking concreteness can be used in exploring feelings that are expressed in vague and general ways. Asking for specific nuances helps the client further express dimensions of the feelings. Some people find it useful to use metaphors to describe their feelings. A client contemplating the power imbalance in her spousal relationship frequently stated she felt small. The worker asked, "What does this feeling look like to you?" The client thought for awhile and then responded, "I feel like a little miniperson with him, that when I am standing next to him my eyes come up to his belt buckle." This graphic description vividly conveyed to both the client and the worker how diminished, insignificant, and powerless this client felt.

Evocative responding has been described as a way of illuminating and heightening the emotional experience of a client. "The therapist attempts to vividly capture the quality and the implicit elements of this experience, tentatively expanding such experience, often by the use of evocative imagery. This then helps the client to construct this experience in a more differentiated way" (Johnson, 1996, p. 45). The purpose is to take clients more deeply into their emotions and, by using a rich vocabulary, highlight the most poignant aspects of an emotional or physical response, desires, longings, and conflicts. The aim is not to offer an expert summary, rather, through the use of powerful and vivid language, to guide clients to the "leading edge of their experience and invite[s] them to take another step in formulating and symbolizing the experience" (Johnson, 1996, p. 46). The following are examples of evocative responding. "When you say that there is a catch in your voice, like it hurts so badly to even have to put that into words, that you may not be the person she wants in her life." "You're trying so hard to get on with your life and you feel a heavy weight pressing down on you . . . the gloominess when you realize that she may not come back to your relationship."

That an individual may experience opposing emotions toward the same situation or person is well recognized. Hence practitioners expect to hear about clients' ambivalent or mixed feelings, and it is helpful to normalize that conflicting emotions are often a corollary of human relationships. For example, a teenaged boy attending an inner-city school has been accepted in an enriched program based on his aptitude, motivation, and achievements in courses and extracurricular activities. The program is in a high school in another part of the city where he knows no one. On one hand, he is excited at the chance to pursue studies that may lead to a scholarship to a top college. On the other hand, he is afraid of being lonely, anxious about whether he will be accepted in the new school and how his current friends will view him, and concerned that he might not succeed. These mixed feelings are paramount in affecting his decision whether or not to accept the offer of admission. By exploring these seemingly contradictory feelings he was able to recognize how important a sense of belonging with friends had been to him throughout his life. During highly conflictual times in his family, his friends had provided a stability he valued. Through recognizing the issue at the core of his ambivalence, he could consider ways in which he could attend the new program and still maintain his close connections to particular friends.

IN-DEPTH EXPLORATION OF THOUGHTS AND BELIEFS

It is useful to refer to the discussion about exploring cognitions presented in chapter 7 when considering the skills of in-depth exploration of thoughts and beliefs. To review briefly, cognitive theorists provide concepts that help practitioners and their clients identify and understand how ways of processing information affects the meanings given to and feelings associated with personal events in an individual's life. Concepts also provide explanations for how current experiences, feelings, and perceptions are filtered and interpreted through cognitive schemas. When preparing to explore thoughts and beliefs, practitioners recognize that many factors will affect the client's ability to engage in reflective discussion. Factors include the client's intellectual functioning and the degree to which he can engage in formal-operational thinking and use logic, abstractions, flexibility, and reasoning (Brems, 2001). To work with cognitions in the interview the client needs to be able to reflect on and talk about events, relationships, and situations even when they are not occurring in the moment. Based on a client's ability to engage on this cognitive level and think about alternative explanations, interpretations, and meanings of a situation, cognitive interventions can be useful. It requires some ability to symbolize one's experience through language and a degree of openness and flexibility toward considering different ways of viewing and appraising events. Rather than rigidly interpreting most events in a fixed manner, there needs to be some willingness to consider whether one could interpret events in another way. The more flexible and open, the more likely the individual will be to use new information gained through the helping process. Intelligence, educational level, and age do not predict the ability to be reflective, to think abstractly rather than concretely, or to be flexible rather than rigid in one's beliefs.

When considering cognitive patterns and beliefs, it is always necessary to understand the degree to which they reflect sociocultural mores and values. As noted throughout the text, the meanings given to a range of personal and interpersonal events is highly influenced by cultural belief systems. Social workers need to actively listen for and inquire about the links between individual schemas and these larger belief systems. The point has been made repeatedly that families interpret these beliefs in their own ways when bringing up their children and individuals also have unique individual interpretations and affiliations with these systems. In-depth exploration of thought and beliefs aims at helping the client elaborate on these various aspects of their meaning systems and whether there is dissonance and contradictions in particular areas.

The basic interviewing skills of asking open- and close-ended questions, seeking concreteness, paraphrasing, and restatement, and offering summaries provide the beginning point for more in-depth exploration and elaboration of cognitions. The aim is to elicit the underlying thoughts, schemas, and beliefs that affect the client's feelings and behavior. This process leads to summarizing themes or patterns that reflect a more textured, deeper, and comprehensive understanding of two interrelated dimensions in the client's life: 1) significant internal factors and external systems and 2) the ways in which his feelings, thoughts, and behaviors affect his relationships with external systems and are affected by them. Throughout this process the worker maintains the focus of the sessions, ensuring that the client is fully involved in the exploration and identification of themes and patterns and that a joint understanding has evolved.

REFRAMING

Family therapists introduced the concept of reframing into the helping literature as a technique that offered a different way of thinking about a situation or story the client has shared (Watzlawick, Beavin, and Jackson, 1974). Their aim was to identify contextual factors that influenced the way in which the presenting problem was attributed to one individual in the family. These theorists proposed that by providing a different viewpoint, perspective, or meaning to a problem new attitudes and options emerge. For example, a family sought help for their ten-year-old son, whom they described as aggressive with his younger siblings. As the therapist gained more information about the family dynamics, she relabeled this child the peace-keeper, since his challenging behavior brought his parents together to develop ways of handling him and diverted them from the marital conflict that threatened the stability of their family. With this new view of his behavior the parents could consider ways in which they might manage their relationship and contain the acrimony between them. The practitioner might support their desire to protect their son from such a heavy responsibility as taking care of the family and reframe efforts to interact more positively with each other as an example of their concern for their child.

While the technique of reframing developed out of working with families and reflected a belief in a systemic understanding of individual difficulties, it can be used effectively when working with individuals. Reframing, or relabeling, generally challenges individuals' perceptions and, if effective, facilitates a shift in characteristic and patterned ways of appraising behavior. Again, with expanded meanings given to an event there are more potential opportunities for action. For example, an eight-year-old boy described by his mother as wild and oppositional after the school day is referred to by the social worker as bright and active, thriving on stimulation and activity. Rather than focus on strategies to discipline and contain the child, the focus moves to ways to provide activities where he can be physically active in a structured and safe environment.

To some extent reframing has similarities to the concept introduced earlier of working with underlying emotions that fuel surface affect and behavior. Recall the discussion based on Greenberg's work on primary and secondary emotions (Greenberg, 2002a, 2002b). He points out the importance of helping clients recognize, relate to, and express the softer emotions underlying aggressive or hostile stances, the pain that underlies anger, the hurt that underlies hostility and withdrawal. Especially in work with couples, practitioners use reframing to help clients recognize that an aggressive attack on the partner may reflect the individual's feeling of being abandoned and unsupported by that partner (Johnson, 1996). When partners can recognize the underlying feelings of need for connection and fear of rejection, they can soften their re-actions, become more empathetic to the other, and respond differently to the initial angry attack. In these instances reframing helps clients interpret others' feelings and behaviors in more benign ways. Working within an emotionally focused approach, the practitioner uses attachment theory and a conceptual understanding of emotions and emotional experience to formulate the re-frames.

Reframing can be used not only in relation to specific problem behaviors but also more generally in relation to clients' experiences. Social workers can reframe clients' problem-saturated stories, when they are filled with examples of coping and survival, as stories of courage, determination, and persistence in the face of great odds. When narratives are given a different form, new ways of experiencing past and present events are created. Positive reframing rede-fines negative or hopeless situations in an affirmative manner that may identify overlooked aspects of the self and hence enhance self-esteem or create poten-tial for change. This stance is consistent with the work of social work theo-rists who emphasize the need for a strengths perspective that illuminates and amplifies clients' resources and thereby offers hope for the future (Saleeby, 2002b). It is also used liberally in solution-focused work that changes the em-phasis from the problem to the solution (DeJong and Berg, 1998).

Formulating reframes rests on the ability to understand that many mean-ings can be attributed to a situation or set of behaviors. Where a problem or pattern has persisted over time, it is likely that individuals will develop fixed and rigid interpretations of the particular behaviors. As one develops an ap-preciation for the complexity of human functioning and the recognition that there can be multiple meanings to events, practitioners find they can "see" and then use new language to describe the problem clients are presenting or the relevant behaviors and feelings. Practitioners who use this skill note that there must be a ring of truth to the relabeling. It must make sense to the worker for her to have some conviction when offering it. It must make sense to the client and reflect in some way a part of his experience that he can relate to if it is to have some impact. When reframing is used as a technique to highlight strengths or provide alternate explanations that have little or no basis in the client's reality, he may perceive the practitioner as off base, not empathetic, and misunderstanding the essence of the issue. In these cases the reframe is likely to be rejected or ignored by the client.

Interpretation is another technique that practitioners use to offer clients alternative ways of understanding their internal and external worlds. The term developed in psychoanalysis and psychodynamic therapy and referred to the practitioner's use of this specific conceptual framework to explain, or interpret, aspects and themes in the client's life. Interpretations originally focused on links to early experiences and transference to the therapist and brought unconscious material into awareness (Crits-Christoph and Gibbons, 2002). In contemporary social service and mental health practice practitioners from most theoretical perspectives use a form of interpretation or explanation to assist clients in gaining insights and alternate perspectives. The practitioner goes beyond what the client has said or recognized, makes connections between aspects of the client's internal world, for example, between events, themes, patterns, causal relationships, and gives alternative meanings or explanations for persistent issues, reactions, and feelings (Hill and O'Brien, 1999). When interpretation brings about new understandings for clients they can feel empowered, liberated, and energized. New ways of thinking and feeling can lead to more confidence and esteem and a readiness to try new behaviors.

Murphy and Dillon (2003) discuss this concept using less technical language that is closer to a collaborative stance in working with clients. They describe practitioners helping clients develop new perspectives by "sharing ideas or hunches about content, affect, themes and patterns, or relationship dynamics of which they may be unaware" (p. 159). They note that these hunches are only guesses or working ideas and must be offered in an exploratory and provisional way. Within the stance of collaboration the metaphor for offering interpretations is one of two people putting their heads together to come up with some useful ways of thinking about and acting on a challenging situation. The worker, through the dialogue, based on his empathy and developing understanding of the particular client, and his professional knowledge and clinical experience offers tentative explanations, interpretations, or hunches in a way that invites response and dialogue from the client. Practitioners can use questions or statements to convey the interpretation. For example, the worker might express the following as a statement, "Your father wasn't around when you were little; your partner didn't help out much when you had your first child . . . with your second baby due soon you are feeling very anxious that you will be on your own again with no one to count on for help." Or the practitioner might offer this interpretation as a question and begin with the phrase "Do you think that since..."

Reviewing the research on the impact of interpretations on outcome in short- and longer-term psychotherapy, Crits-Christoph and Gibbons (2002) note that there is support for the helpfulness of interpretations that accurately address aspects of clients' central interpersonal themes. There is indication however that high levels of interpretations of transference can lead to poor outcome for clients with significant relationship issues. This body of empirical work supports social work's interest in interpersonal processes. Interpretations can help clients understand the nature of their interpersonal relationships, the links between individual experience and external experience, and the similarities between the client's relationships. While they emphasize that interpretations need to be "accurate," a collaborative and interactive view of practice, as presented in this text, gives more emphasis to the practitioner's stance that invites dialogue and discussion of the interpretation she offers. It is not "accuracy" but the practitioner's commitment to arriving at joint understanding that appears to lead clients to experience the process as helpful.

From their review of studies Crits-Christoph and Gibbons (2002) note the importance of a number of factors that affect whether an interpretation is received in a positive or negative way by the client. Practitioners need to be sensitive to timing when offering interpretations. If the client is not yet ready to hear the content of the message, the interpretation may be unhelpful. Recall the discussion of a young woman in our study who told her current social worker that she had stopped attending counseling when her previous worker had linked her discomfort with sexual activity with a boyfriend to her parents' reactions to discovery of her sexual play when she was a child (Tsang, Bogo, and George, 2004). This interpretation was obviously not well timed; the client was not ready to consider this and reported that it increased her discomfort to suggest that her "parents were to blame." When the client has a firm alliance with the worker, the client may be able to provide feedback about an interpretation and disagree with its content or let the practitioner know that the ideas presented are too troublesome to consider further. Practitioners who are "tuned in" to their clients' reactions in the sessions can handle the discomfort by retracting the interpretation, inviting the client to offer her own interpretation, comment on the troubling emotion, or offer support. Even when interpretations are not well timed, when offered in an empathetic tone and manner and where there is a solid working relationship the client and worker can discuss the disjunction and recover. If the worker thinks that the content of the message has merit, she may reintroduce it at a later time, when she believes the client might be able to consider it. Cautions about use of interpretations appear to be related to the way in which they are delivered; when offered in a critical tone and experienced by clients as harsh and confrontational they can lead to poor outcome (Coady, 1991).

Given that social workers aim to develop clients' capacity in a range of areas, it is useful to encourage clients to develop self-reflective cognitive skills. These skills will help the client in the future to think over situations, to get in touch with the feelings and reactions that are stirred up, to examine them using the knowledge gained about self, others, and society, and to plan what they want to do in specific circumstances. Hence workers might be more helpful when they refrain from offering their own interpretations and focus more effort on assisting clients to draw their own observations and conclusions. Comments within the interview such as "What do you make of this?" "What are your thoughts about this recurring theme in your life—I can only depend on myself?" give clients the opportunity to develop their own insights. Practitioners can also end sessions with an explicit suggestion that the client give the matter under discussion some further thought and begin the next meeting with an inquiry about any insights the client may have since they last talked about an issue.

CHALLENGE

For the majority of the interview practitioners listen, focus, and structure the discussion on the client's most pressing and relevant issues, provide support and encouragement, and help clients explore feelings and thoughts and their reactions in significant relationships and to external events. When these processes take place within the context of a connected working relationship, the client is assisted in developing greater clarity and understanding, arriving at new positions or enabled to take new actions. This description of the process of helping sounds more fluid and straightforward than the process is in everyday practice. It is not unusual for the client and worker to experience moments and even periods where the client feels "stuck."

Many reasons may account for a lack of progress and the sense of repetitive discussions of reoccurring themes and patterns with little forward movement.

The interviewing skill of challenge, also referred to as confrontation or point-ing out discrepancies, has been identified as an additional helping tool (Egan, 2002; Hill and O'Brien, 1999; Ivey and Ivey, 2003; Murphy and Dillon, 2003). Challenge refers to making a comment that aims to help the client develop greater awareness of their thoughts, feelings, or behaviors through address-ing contradictions, discrepancies, fixed beliefs, or defenses (Hill and O'Brien, 1999). They are used when it seems to the worker that the client is unaware of aspects of her internal or external experience that are perpetuating the prob-lem situation and maintaining the status quo. For example, an elderly spouse tells her family that she is getting more and more exhausted caring for her hus-band who has Alzheimer's disease. However, after many home visits from the Seniors' Agency social worker, she rejects all offers of in-home care, day pro-grams he could attend, and respite care, saying that she would feel too guilty if someone else took care of him. The worker gently and supportively challenges her, saying, "I wonder how we can help you; you clearly need some help to care for your husband and yet feeling guilty about receiving it seems to leave you without help and becoming more and more exhausted."

When offering challenging comments, workers must be aware of their tone and give thought to how best to phrase their statements or questions. Fol-lowing a review of studies of confrontation, Hill and O'Brien (1999) conclude that they are powerful interventions that frequently, however, had a negative impact on the client. In the studies workers pointed out discrepancies to cli-ents; for example, although a client tells the worker in the interview that he plans to address his procrastination about studying, he is not doing anything to demonstrate that he is taking responsibility for his behavior and chang-ing his study habits. Clients tended to respond defensively, which in turn led to the practitioner responding with more confrontation, producing a down-ward cycle in their interaction and a rupture in the alliance. Hill and O'Brien (1999) recommend that when using the interviewing skill of challenge work-ers must offer their comments with empathy and in the context of a solid re-lationship. It is obvious that when we hear information that may sound like criticism our anxiety level may increase, and a reasonable response is to reject it. Hence thought needs to be given to how to offer a challenging comment in a way that keeps anxiety at an optimum level, enables the client to hear and think about the comment, but is not so bland that it has no impact on the cli-ent. Too much support, an apology before offering a challenge, or couching the comment in mild and general terms can result in the client's dismissal, canceling out its potential usefulness. For example, a middle-aged man lost his clerical job because of cutbacks in the public works department. He has undergone retraining and is now working in a manual job he feels is beneath him. In his meetings with the Employee Assistance social worker he has been critical about the other workers on his team and also has complained that they ignore him in their informal conversations. When it has become apparent to the worker that he is unaware of how often he has told her anecdotes about his critical comments to his fellow workers, she feels that a gentle challenge is in order. Her comment begins by acknowledging his disappointment with his current position. "We've talked about how hard it has been for you at this stage of your life to move from an inside to an outside job, and that's made you angry. You've also acknowledged that you prefer to have a job rather than be unemployed. Do you think there is some connection between the other men being unfriendly and the fact that you've been fairly critical of them?" In this example the worker summarizes a theme they have covered and makes reference to their joint discussions. She then poses her challenge as a question and offers it in a gentle and understanding tone. Since the client experiences her interest and concern for him, the challenge does not lead to a comment about their relationship, although the client responds that these men don't work as hard as his other coworkers. The worker returns to her challenge, "That may be so, but how do you think they might see you when you make these critical comments?" The client hears this comment and together they begin to discuss how he can refrain from making them.

In general, a stance that encourages reflective discussion between client and worker can to some extent neutralize the inherent tension that is part of hearing a potentially critical comment from a person one values or respects. There are a number of phrases that might serve as useful prefaces to challenging comments. "Have you noticed that..." "It is interesting that..." "I'm curious/puzzled by the fact that on one hand you say... and on the other hand..." "Can we take a moment to consider this..." "I'm trying to understand this..." When offering challenges, they should draw from examples that are currently under discussion. The worker might also draw in anecdotes the client has offered earlier in the session or in previous interviews. Their potency however is derived from their proximity to issues that are currently under discussion where the client is emotionally involved and engaged in trying to sort through a situation.

Ambivalent or mixed feelings may account for some discrepancies, and it is useful to highlight that two different feelings can exist at the same time and may result in confusion for the client. Often individuals talk about two contradictory feelings or thoughts, using the term *but*. For example, "I know this relationship is not good for me, but I love her." Such use of language implies that nothing can be done about resolving the situation, that the client's love holds him in a particular position. It can be helpful for clients when the worker rephrases the presence of two discrepant positions by using the term *and* as a way of recognizing that two states are possible, that their presence makes a resolution more difficult, and that each needs to be explored and considered in relation to each other. For example, the worker might comment, "You experience great pain in this relationship, you are uncertain about your partner's continuing interest and reliability, and you still feel connected and attracted. Can we further examine both sides of this dilemma for you and see how you can deal with these two opposing feelings?"

As with all the processes of the middle phase such as resolving ambivalence, dealing with being "stuck," searching for alternatives, issues are not simply clarified or addressed after one discussion. Challenges may need to be repeated several times and in different ways (Hill and O'Brien, 1999). As noted earlier, challenges, interpretations, and reframes are all interviewing strategies or skills that may stimulate the client to look at a situation differently. There is an intricate relationship between thoughts, feelings, behaviors, and our sense of self. Hence it is understandable that information that seemingly threatens an integrated and cohesive view of self is likely to take time to examine, process, understand, and perhaps, gain acceptance. When studying interviews where these strategies are used one is struck by the observation that clients frequently react to these worker interventions by initially refuting them, denying the substance in them, or debating with the worker. In some instances it is appropriate that the worker leave the theme. Professional helping is not about being "right," and the worker does not want to assume a position where he is debating with the client the superiority of his insights over the client's. A client's strong rejecting reaction to a worker's challenge, interpretation, or reframe can be considered useful information or data; it may indicate that the substance of the comment is not meaningful to the client or it may indicate that the client is not able at that moment to examine a view that is contradictory to the one he currently holds. In contrast are those instances when the worker persists in a gentle fashion, or returns to the substance of the comment in another way, and the client recognizes the issue and includes the new perspective in his thinking, feeling, and discussion. These later interactions can be thought of as the process of working through an issue. The difficulty for the worker is in deciding when to leave a challenging comment and when to persist in offering it in a different manner. Client reaction is the primary source of data to guide the practitioner, although clinical supervision and peer consultation can also provide assistance. Through analyzing these crucial moments in interviews with others, practitioners can gain insight into their own personal reactions in professional situations, separate out issues of professional skill and personal use of self, and obtain other perspectives on the client situation and ways of effectively intervening.

PUTTING IT TOGETHER

Interviewing skills have been discussed thus far in discrete terms. In our analysis of first sessions in positive outcome cases we found that the social workers used four sets of skills in a conversational manner to achieve the tasks of the first stage—gaining sufficient understanding of the clients' situation to proceed and build a helping relationship through providing empathy and support (Tsang, Bogo, and George, 2004). The first set of skills consisted of a considerable number of open-ended questions, requests for concreteness, and clarifications to encourage each client to elaborate on what the client initially offered. They also used these skills to obtain information from the client that described the client's ecological map. It was apparent that all of these social workers used the ecosystemic perspective while working in different fields of service, from an agency serving adolescents, to a community health center, to a mental health facility. The second set of skills involved the workers in offering periodic brief summary statements throughout the interview that pulled together information the client had shared up to that point. These summaries were offered in a way that invited the client to confirm that the worker had understood the client's message or to correct the worker's impression. Third, in these summaries the practitioners usually included some comments about the client's feelings and thoughts. These comments were drawn directly from what the client had shared or from what the client had subtly alluded to. The practitioners seemed to also use these summary statements as empathetic responses that provided support and led to further elaboration by the clients. In addition, these summaries and the clients' responses can be seen as sequences of interaction that led toward affirming a joint understanding of the client's experience of the presenting problem and related issues. In the words of one client, she feels that the worker "gets it." Frequently it took the better part of a one-hour interview for these experienced social workers to offer an elaborated summary that was inclusive enough to lead naturally into the client and worker setting up some very preliminary goals or plans. The fourth set of skills includes those that offer support, encouragement, or hope to clients. Practitioners used a range of techniques to respond on an emotional level to the client's confusion, pain, and distress. In some instances they validated painful emotions, in others they pointed out the client's strengths and courage in dealing with past difficult situations or feelings, and in others they identified any areas of positive and effective functioning on the part of the client.

This review of first sessions in the study reveals that the interviewing skills discussed in this chapter cannot be used in a mechanistic or formulaic manner. They are integrated in the personal styles of each of these experienced workers' and are used in a purposeful or intentional manner to achieve the tasks of the beginning stage in a way that is sensitive to the client's presentation of self and situation and comfort with the pace and timing in the interview. While empirical data from the middle and ending stage is not yet available for analysis, from clinical observations it is apparent that an even wider range of skills are used to achieve the many processes of these phases. Hence social workers are constantly traversing the arc of theories and concepts that help them explain and understand the client, processes, and principles that guide their intentions and skills that actually ground their interventions.

DEVELOPING INTERVIEWING SKILLS

Videotaping and analyzing tapes of interviews is one of the most effective ways for students to develop their interviewing skills and their ability to become self reflective practitioners, able to identify their own learning needs. Two processes can guide the review of tapes. First, the student can look at segments of the interview to consider the essence of what the client was trying to convey, the themes the segment reflected, and the student's intentions that led them to make the comments they did. Second, at the level of discrete interviewing skills, the videotape captures what was actually said and provides concrete data for students to use in assessing whether their statements were clear, how

BEHAVIORS THAT CAN BLOCK INFORMATION GATHERING AND CLIENTS' SHARING OF PERSONAL THOUGHTS, FEELINGS, OR BEHAVIORS

- Offering strong judgmental comments or ignoring the client's cultural and value system.
- Making inappropriate humorous comments or minimizing the situation.
- Not tracking the client by not responding to the client's messages, abruptly changing the topic, and responding with superficial or irrelevant comments to the client's messages that are emotionally laden.
- Interrupting the client.
- Providing too much structure and talking too much.
- Giving long explanations or "mini-lectures" about human behavior and social conditions.
- Providing too little structure and only minimal responses.
- Displaying discomfort that conveys that the topic under discussion is threatening or uncomfortable in some way.
- Being overprotective of the client in a way that implies he is too fragile to discuss difficult matters beyond a surface level.
- Offering premature problem solving by giving advice and suggestions.
- Overly focusing on problems and weaknesses without attention to strengths.
- Overly focusing on facts and external circumstances without enough attention to the client's subjective experiences.
- Overly focusing on irrelevant information and topics, persons other than the client, or sidetracks in general.
- Providing reassurance that is not based on solid data is defined as false reassurance. For example, reassurance that the situation will work out or that the worker believes the client has the ability to handle the situation successfully.
- Power struggles over what information is needed and to what extent.
- Arguing with the client, taking an authoritarian and dogmatic stance.
- Criticizing, belittling, or demonstrating a condescending attitude toward the client.

they were received by the client, what impact they had on the client, and how they served to further the interview or to interfere with its progress. When observing the skills, the tape can be stopped and alternate ways of phrasing a particular comment can be formed; a role-play can be conducted to reenact a particular segment while practicing different ways of putting the skill into action.

Many students identify the skills of reflecting feelings and in-depth exploration of feelings as most challenging. The feelings connected to the issues that generally bring individuals to a social worker are about anger, sadness or depression, fear and anxiety, shame, vulnerability, confusion, inadequacy, and discouragement. Social workers are also attuned to the positive emotions of happiness or joy, peace, love and caring, energy, and strength and mastery. First, it is useful to develop a language rich in expressive terms. For example, the feeling of anger can be described in many different ways, as annoyed, cranky, enraged, exasperated, frustrated, furious, hostile, mad, outraged, upset, and so on. A diverse repertoire of terms to help clients describe the particular aspect of these general emotions can be developed by each practitioner. Students can draw on their own vocabularies, terms used by colleagues and supervisors, and terms used by clients when describing their emotions. The second issue many students identify is the need to develop a balance between sensing when one is overly intrusive when reflecting feelings and when one is too distant and superficial in the interview. Timing and the stage of relationship development will have an impact on learning this skill. Specifically, as the relationship between the student and client develops and the client recognizes that disclosure and elaboration will be met with interest and response on the part of the student, rather than a shaming, critical, or negative comment, it becomes easier for both the student and client to discuss emotional issues. However, if the dialogue is conducted on a superficial level, the client will not have the opportunity to experience what it is like to reveal emotions. There is a circular or interrelated nature to the client's ability to disclose and the student's ability to reflect feelings. With opportunities to practice these skills, especially with feedback from field instructors, students are able to improve their level of competence and their comfort level (Bogo et al., in press).

From analyses and comparisons of student interviewing behaviors in class and in field practicum, a number of behaviors have been identified that interfere with effective interviewing (Bogo, 1989; Collins, 1990; Collins and Coleman, 2000; Hepworth, Rooney, and Larsen, 2002; Matarazzo et al., 1965). When learning the interviewing skills presented in this chapter, it may also be useful to attend to diminishing the frequency of behaviors that undermine the student's efforts to develop a productive partnership and to assist clients in presenting and elaborating on relevant aspects of their situations.

The final section of this text reviewed a number of generic interviewing skills that can be used in social work practice. As noted throughout, these skills constitute the fundamental building blocks that practitioners use to ground concepts and processes in their actual work with clients. As such they remain core to professional activity.

Social workers are faced with an ever expanding knowledge base that they access through formal continuous learning activities. Of equal importance is the rich learning that derives from reflection on their own practices, especially in relation to new findings and trends in the professional literature. One of the rewards of professional practice is the opportunity for continuous renewal and growth provided in this type of human service work.

REFERENCES

Ahn, H., and Wampold, B. E. (2001). Where oh where are the specific ingredients? A meta-analysis of component studies in counseling and psychotherapy. *Journal of Counseling Psychology*, 48(3), 251–257.

Ainsworth, M. D. S., Blchar, M. C., Waters, E., and Wall, S. (1978). *Patterns of attachment: A psychological study of the Strange Situation*. Mahwah, NJ: Erlbaum.

Anderson, H., and Goolishian, H. (1992). The client is the expert: A not-knowing approach to therapy. In S. McNamee and K. J. Gergen (Eds.), *Therapy as social construction* (pp. 25–39). Newbury Park, CA: Sage.

Applegate, J., and Bonovitz, J. (1995). *The facilitating partnership: A Winnicottian approach for social workers and other helping professionals*. Northvale, NJ: Aronson.

Atwood, G. E., and Stolorow, R. D. (1984). *Structures of subjectivity: Explorations in psychoanalytic phenomenology*. Hillsdale, NJ: Analytic.

Bachelor, A. (1988). How clients perceive therapist empathy: A content analysis of "received" empathy. *Psychotherapy: Theory, research, and practice*, 25, 227–240.

Bachelor, A. (1995). Clients' perception of the therapeutic alliance: A qualitative analysis. *Jounral of Counseling Psychology*, 42, 323–337.

Bachelor, A., and Horvath, A. (1999). The therapeutic relationship. In M. A. Hubble and B. L. Duncan and S. D. Miller (Eds.), *The heart and soul of change: What works in therapy* (pp. 133–178). Washington, DC: American Psychological Association.

Baldwin, M. W. (1992). Relational schemas and the processing of social information. *Psychological Bulletin*, 112, 461–484.

Bandura, A. (1986). *Social foundations of thought and action*. Englewood Cliffs, NJ: Prentice Hall.

Barrett, S. E. (1990). Paths toward diversity: An intrapsychic perspective. *Women and Therapy*, 9(1–2), 41–52.

Beck, A. (1976). *Cognitive therapy and emotional disorder*. New York: International Universities Press.

Beck, A., Rush, J., Shaw, B., and Emery, G. (Eds.). (1979). *Cognitive therapy of depression*. New York: Guilford.

Beck, J. S. (1995). *Cognitive therapy: Basics and beyond*. New York: Guilford.

Behroozi, C. S. (1992). A model for social work with involuntary applicants in groups. *Social Work with Groups*, 15, 223–238.

Berg, I. K. (1994). *Family-based services: A solution focused approach*. New York: Norton.

Bergin, A. E., and Garfield, S. L. (Eds.). (1994). *Handbook of psychotherapy and behavior change* (Vol. 4). New York: Wiley.

Berkman, B. (1996). The emerging health care world: Implications for social work practice and education. *Social Work, 41*(5), 541–552.

Beutler, L. E., Machado, P. P., and Neufelt, S. A. (1994). Therapist variables. In A. E. Bergin and S. L. Garfield (Eds.), *Handbook of psychotherapy and behavior change* (pp. 229–269). New York: Wiley.

Biestek, F. (1957). *The casework relationship*. Chicago: Loyola University Press.

Bisno, H., and Cox, F. (1997). Social work education: Catching up with the present and the future. *Journal of Social Work Education, 33*(2), 373–387.

Bocage, M., Homonoff, E., and Riley, P. (1995). Measuring the impact of the current state and national fiscal crises on human service agencies and social work training. *Social Work, 40*(5), 701–705.

Bogo, M. (Ed.). (1989). *Training program: Practice skills for social work students* (3rd ed.). Toronto, ON: Faculty of Social Work, University of Toronto.

Bogo, M. (1993). The student/field instructor relationship: The critical factor in field education. *Clinical Supervisor, 11*(2), 23–36.

Bogo, M., Globerman, J., and Sussman, T. (2004a). The field instructor as group worker: Managing trust and competition in group supervision. *Journal of Social Work Education, 40*(1), 13–26.

Bogo, M., Globerman, J., and Sussman, T. (2004b). Field instructor competence in group supervision: Students' views. *Journal of Teaching in Social Work, 24*(1/2), 199–216.

Bogo, M., and Power, R. (1992). New field instructors' perceptions of institutional supports for their roles. *Journal of Social Work Education, 28*(2), 178–189.

Bogo, M., Regehr, C., Hughes, J., Power, R., and Globerman, J. (2002). Evaluating a measure of student field performance. *Journal of Social Work Education, 38*(3), 385–401.

Bogo, M., Regehr, C., Power, R., Hughes, J., Woodford, M., and Regehr, G. (2004). Towards new approaches for evaluating student field performance: Taping the implicit criteria used by experienced field instructors. *Journal of Social Work Education, 40*(3).

Bogo, M., Regehr, C., Woodford, M., Hughes, J., Power, R., and Regehr, G. (in press). Beyond competencies: Field instructors' descriptions of student performance. *Journal of Social Work Education*.

Bogo, M., and Vayda, E. (1998). *The practice of field instruction in social work: Theory and process* (2nd ed.). New York: Columbia University Press.

Bolland, K. A., and Atherton, C. R. (1999). Chaos theory: An alternative approach to social work practice and research. *Families in Society: The Journal of Contemporary Human Services, 80*(4), 367–373.

Borash, M. (2002). Treating the involuntary client: Storming their defenses will get you nowhere. *Psychotherapy Networker, 26*,(March/April) 21–22.

Bordin, E. (1979). The generalizability of the psychoanalytic concept of the working alliance. *Psychotherapy: Theory, research, and practice, 16*, 252–260.

Bordin, E. (1994). Theory and research in the therapeutic working alliance. In A. O. Horvath and L. S. Greenberg (Eds.), *The working alliance: Theory, research, and practice* (pp. 13–37). New York: Wiley.

Bowlby, J. (1969). *Attachment and loss: Volume 1.* New York: Basic.

Bowlby, J. (1988). *A secure base: Parent-child attachment and healthy human development.* New York: Basic.

Brammer, L. M., and MacDonald, G. (1999). *The helping relationship: Process and skills.* Boston: Allyn and Bacon.

Brandell, J. (Ed.). (1997). *Theory and practice in clinical social work.* New York: Free.

Brandell, J. (2004). *Psychodynamic social work.* New York: Columbia University Press.

Brems, C. (2001). *Basic skills in psychotherapy and counseling.* Belmont, CA: Brooks/ Cole.

Bretherton, I. (1993). From dialogue to internal working models: The co-construction of self in relationships. In C. A. Nelson (Ed.), *The Minnesota Symposia on child psychology: Vol. 26, Memory and affect in development* (pp. 237–263). Hillsdale, NJ: Erlbaum.

Brown, L. S. (1994a). Boundaries in feminist therapy: A conceptual formulation. *Women and Therapy, 15*(1), 29–38.

Brown, L. S. (1994b). *Subversive dialogues: Theory in feminist therapy.* New York: Basic.

Bushman, B. J., Baumeister, R. F., and Stack, A.D. (1999). Catharsis, agression, and persuasive influence: Self-fulfilling or self-defeating prophecies? *Journal of Personality and Social Psychology, 76*, 367–376.

Carkhuff, R. (1993). *The art of helping.* Amherst: Human Resources Development.

Christensen, L. L., Russell, C. S., Miller, R. B., and Peterson, C. M. (1998). The process of change in couples therapy: A qualitative investigation. *Journal of Marital and Family Therapy, 24*(2), 177–188.

Cingolani, J. (1984). Social conflict perspective on work with involuntary clients. *Social Work, 29*, 442–446.

Clark, J. L. (2003). *Practitioners' experienced knowledge: Creating space for understanding in cross-cultural clinical practice.* Ph.D. dissertation, University of Toronto, Toronto.

Coady, N. (1991). The association between complex types of therapist interventions and outcomes in psychodynamic psychotherapy. *Research on Social Work Practice, 1*, 257–277.

Coady, N. (1993). The worker-client relationship revisited. *Families in Society, 74*(5), 291–299.

Coady, N. (1999). The helping relationship. In F. J. Turner (Ed.), *Social work practice: A Canadian perspective* (pp. 58–72). Scarborough, ON: Prentice Hall Allyn and Bacon Canada.

Collins, D. (1990). Identifying dysfunctional counseling skill behaviors. *Clinical Supervisor*, 8(1), 67–79.

Collins, D., and Bogo, M. (1986). Competency based field instruction: Bridging the gap between laboratory and field learning. *Clinical Supervisor*, 4(3), 39–52.

Collins, D., and Coleman, H. (2000). Eliminating bad habits in the social work interview. In L. Grobman (Ed.). *The field placement survival guide* (pp. 195–199). Harrisburg, PA: White Hat.

Compton, B. R., and Galaway, B. (1999). *Social work processes* (6th ed.). Pacific Grove, CA: Brooks/Cole.

Cormier, S., and Hackney, H. (1999). *Counseling strategies and interventions* (5th ed.). Needham Heights, MA: Allyn and Bacon.

Cowger, C. (1994). Assessing client strengths: Clinical assessment for client empowerment. *Social Work*, 39, 262–269.

Crits-Christoph, P., and Gibbons, M. B. C. (2002). Relational interpretations. In J. C. Norcross (Ed.), *Psychotherapy relationships that work* (pp. 285–300). New York: Oxford University Press.

De Shazer, S. (1985). *Keys to solution in brief therapy*. New York: Norton.

De Shazer, S. (1988). *Clues: Investigating solutions in brief therapy*. New York: Norton.

Dean, R. (2001). The myth of cross-cultural competence. *Families in Society: The Journal of Contemporary Human Services*, 82(6), 623–630.

DeJong, P., and Berg, I. K. (1998). *Interviewing for solutions*. Pacific Grove, CA: Brooks/Cole.

Devore, W., and Schlesinger, E. G. (1996). *Ethnic sensitive social work practice*. Needham Heights, Mass.: Allyn and Bacon.

Donner, S. (1988). Self psychology: Implications for social work. *Social Casework*, 69(1), 17–22.

Donner, S. (1996). Field work crisis: Dilemmas, dangers, and opportunities. *Smith College Studies in Social Work*, 66, 317–331.

Dore, M. (1993). The practice-teaching parallel in educating the micropractitioner. *Journal of Social Work Education*, 29(2), 181–190.

Drake, B. (1994). Relationship competencies in child welfare services. *Social Work*, 39(5), 595–602.

Dyche, L., and Zayas, L. H. (1995). The value of curiosity and naïveté for the cross-cultural psychotherapist. *Family Process*, 34(4), 389–399.

Dyche, L., and Zayas, L. H. (2001). Cross-cultural empathy and training the contemporary psychotherapist. *Clinical Social Work Journal*, 29(3), 245–258.

Edwards, J. B., and Richards, A. (2002). Relational teaching: A view of relational teaching in social work education. *Journal of Teaching in Social Work*, 22(1/2), 33–48.

Edwards, J. K., and Bess, J. M. (1998). Developing effectiveness in the therapeutic use of self. *Clinical Social Work Journal*, 26(1), 89–105.

Egan, G. (2002). *The skilled helper* (7th ed.). Pacific Grove, CA: Brooks/Cole.

Elson, M. (1986). *Self psychology in clincial social work*. New York: Norton.

England, H. (1986). *Social work as art*. London: Allen and Unwin.

Fairbairn, W. (1952). *An object relations theory of personality*. New York: Basic.

Falicov, C. J. (1995). Training to think culturally: A multidimensional framework. *Family Process*, 34(4), 373–388.

Fortune, A. E. (2002). Terminating with clients. In A. R. Roberts and G. J. Greene (Eds.), *Social workers' desk reference* (pp. 458–463.). New York: Oxford University Press.

Fortune, A. E., McCarthy, M., and Abramson, J. S. (2001). Student learning processes in field education: Relationship of learning activities to quality of field instruction, satisfaction, and performance among MSW students. *Journal of Social Work Education*, 37(1), 111–124.

Fosha, D. (2000). *The transforming power of affect*. New York: Basic.

Foster, R. P. (1998). The clinician's cultural countertransference: The psychodynamics of culturally competent practice. *Clinical Social Work Journal*, 26(3), 253–270.

Frank, J. D., and Frank, J. B. (1991). *Persuasion and healing: A comparative study of psychotherapy* (3rd ed.). Baltimore: Johns Hopkins University Press.

Franklin, C. (2001). Coming to terms with the business of direct practice social work. *Research on Social Work Practice*, 11(2), 235–244.

Freeman, M. L., and Valentine, D. (1998). The connected classroom: Modeling the evaluation of practice by evaluating the classroom group. *Journal of Teaching in Social Work*, 17(1/2), 15–29.

Fusko, L. (1999). The techniques of intervention. In F. J. Turner (Ed.), *Social work practice: A Canadian perspective* (pp. 48–57). Scarborough, ON: Prentice Hall Allyn and Bacon.

Gambrill, E. (1990). *Critical thinking in clinical practice*. San Francisco: Jossey Bass.

Gambrill, E. (1999). Evidence-based practice: An alternative to authority-based practice. *Families in Society: The Journal of Contemporary Human Services*, 80, 341–350.

Gambrill, E. (2001a). Educational policy and accreditation standards: Do they work for clients? *Journal of Social Work Education*, 37(2), 226–239.

Gambrill, E. (2001b). Evaluating the quality of social work education: Options galore. *Journal of Social Work Education*, 37(3), 418–429.

Garcia, B., and Soest, D. V. (2000). Facilitating learning on diversity: Challenges to the professor. *Journal of Ethnic and Cultural Diversity in Social Work*, 9(1/2), 21–39.

Garfield, S. L. (1994). Research on client variables in psychotherapy. In S. L. Garfield and A. E. Bergin (Eds.), *Handbook of psychotherapy and behavior change* (4th ed., pp. 190–228). New York: Wiley.

Gehart-Brooks, D. R., and Lyle, R. R. (1998). Client and therapist perspectives of change in collaborative language systems: An interpretive ethnography. Paper presented at the American Association of Marital and Family Therapists, Dallas, Texas.

Gergen, K. J., and Davis, K. E. (1985). *The social construction of the person*. New York: Springer-Verlag.

Germain, C. B. (1991). *Human behavior in the social environment: An ecological view*. New York: Columbia University Press.

Germain, C. B., and Bloom, M. (1999). *Human behavior in the social environment: An ecological view* (2nd ed.). New York: Columbia University Press.

Germain, C. B., and Gitterman, A. (1996). *The life model of social work practice: Advances in theory and practice* (2nd ed.). New York: Columbia University Press.

Gibbs, L. (2002). *Evidence-based practice for social workers*. Pacific Grove, CA: Brooks/Cole.

Gibbs, L., and Gambrill, E. (1999). *Critical thinking for social workers: A workbook*. Thousand Oaks, CA: Pine Forge.

Gilligan, C. (1982). *In a different voice*. Cambridge: Harvard University Press.

Glass, S. P., and Wright, T. L. (1997). Reconstructing marriages after the trauma of infidelity. In W. K. Halford and H. J. Markman (Eds.), *Clinical Handbook of Marriage and Couples Interventions*. New York: Wiley.

Globerman, J., and Bogo, M. (2002). The impact of hospital restructuring on social work field education. *Health and Social Work, 27*(1), 7–16.

Globerman, J., and Bogo, M. (2003). Changing times: Understanding social workers motivation to be field instructors. *Social Work, 48*(1), 65–73.

Gold, N. (1990). Motivation: The crucial but unexplored component of social work practice. *Social Work, 35,* 49–56.

Goldstein, E. G. (1995). *Ego psychology and social work practice* (2nd ed.). New York: Free.

Goldstein, E. G. (1997). To tell or not to tell: The disclosure of events in the therapists' life to the patient. *Clinical social work journal, 25,* 41–58.

Goldstein, E. G. (2001). *Object relations theory and self psychology in social work practice*. New York: Free.

Goldstein, H. (1990). The knowledge base of social work practice: Theory, wisdom, analogue, or art? *Families in Society, 71,* 32–42.

Goldstein, H. (1999). The limits and art of understanding in social work practice. *Familes in Society: The Journal of Contemporary Human Services, 80*(4), 385–395.

Goldstein, H. (2000). Social work at the millenium. *Families in society: The journal of contemportaty human services, 81*(1), 3–10.

Gottman, J. M., and Levenson, R. W. (1999). How stable is marital interaction over time? *Family Process, 38*(2), 159–165.

Green, J. W. (1995). *Cultural awareness in the human sevices* (2nd ed.). Boston: Allyn and Bacon.

Green, R. J. (1998). Race and the field of family therapy. In M. McGoldrick (Ed.), *Re-visioning family therapy* (pp. 93–110). New York: Guilford.

Greenberg, J., and Mitchell, S. (1983). *Object relations in psychoanalytic theory.* Cambridge: Harvard University Press.

Greenberg, L. (1999). Ideal psychotherapy research: A study of significant change processes. *Journal of Clinical Psychology, 55*(12), 1467–1480.

Greenberg, L. (2002a). *Emotion-focused therapy: Coaching clients to work through feelings.* Washington, DC: American Psychological Association.

Greenberg, L. (2002b). Integrating an emotion-focused approach to treatment into psychotherapy integration. *Journal of Psychotherapy Integration, 12*(2), 154–189.

Greenberg, L., and Pavio, S. C. (1997). *Working with emotions in psychotherapy.* New York: Guilford.

Greenberg, L., Rice, L. N., and Elliott, R. (1993). *Facilitating emotional change: The moment-by-moment process.* New York: Guilford.

Greenberg, L., and Bolger, L. (2001). An emotion-focused approach to the over-regulation of emotion and emotional pain. *Journal of Clinical Psychology, 57*(197–211).

Greene, R. W. (1994). *Human behavior theory: A diversity framework.* Hawthorne, NY: de Gruyter.

Grencavage, L. M., and Norcross, J. C. (1990). Where are the commonalities among the therapeutic common factors? *Professional Psychology: Research and Practice, 21,* 372–378.

Gutierrez, L. (1990). Working with women of color: An empowerment perspective. *Social Work, 35,* 149–153.

Gutierrez, L., Parsons, R. J., and Cox, E. O. (1998). *Empowerment in social work practice.* Pacific Grove, CA: Brooks/Cole.

Hanna, S. M., and Brown, J. H. (1999). *The practice of family therapy: Key elements across models.* Belmont, CA: Wadsworth.

Hardy, K. V. (1997). Steps toward becoming culturally competent. *Family Therapy News,* 13–19.

Hardy, K. V., and Laszloffy, T. A. (2002). Couple therapy using a multicultural perspective. In A. S. Gurman and N. S. Jacobson (Eds.), *Clinical handbook of couple therapy* (3rd ed., pp. 569–593). New York: Guildford.

Hartman, A. (1978). Diagrammatic assessment of family relationships. *Social Casework, 59,* 465–476.

Hartman, A. (1994). Social work practice. In F. J. Reamer (Ed.), *The foundations of social work knowledge* (pp. 13–50). New York: Columbia University Press.

Hartman, A. (1995). Diagrammatic assessment of family relationships. *Familes in Society: The Journal of Contemporary Human Services, 76*, 111–122.

Hazan, C., and Shaver, P. (1987). Romantic love conceptualized as an attachment process. *Journal of Personality and Social Psychology, 52*, 511–524.

Hazan, C., and Shaver, P. (1994). Attachment as an organizational framework for research on close relationships. *Journal of Personality and Social Psychology, 52*(511–524).

Heinonen, T., and Spearman, L. (2001). *Social work practice: Problem solving and beyond.* Toronto: Irwin.

Henggeler, S. W., Schoenwald, S. K., Borduin, C. M., Rowland, M. D., and Cunningham, P. B. (1998). *Multisystemic treatment of antisocial behavior in children and adolescents.* New York: Guilford.

Hepworth, D. H., Rooney, R. H., and Larsen, J. A. (2002). *Direct social work practice: Theory and skills* (6th ed.). Pacific Grove, CA: Brooks/Cole.

Hill, C. E., and Knox, S. (2002). Self-disclosure. In J. C. Norcross (Ed.), *Psychotherapy relationships that work: Therapist contributions and responsiveness to patients* (pp. 255–265). New York: Oxford University Press.

Hill, C. E., and O'Brien, K. M. (1999). *Helping skills: Facilitating exploration, insight, and action.* Washington, DC: American Psychological Association.

Hill, C. E., Thompson, B. J., Cogar, M. C., and Denman, D. W. (1993). Beneath the surface of long-term therapy: Therapist and client report of their own and each other's covert processes. *Journal of Counseling Psychology, 40*(3), 278–287.

Ho, D. (1995). Internalized culture, culturocentrism, and transcendence. *Counseling Psychologist, 23*(1), 4–24.

Holley, L. C., and Steiner, S. (2005). Safe space: Student perspectives on classroom environment. *Journal of Social Work Education, 41*(1), 49–64.

Hollis, F. (1964). *Casework: A psycho-social therapy.* New York: Random House.

Horvath, A. O. (2000). The therapeutic relationship: From transference to alliance. *JCLP/In session: Psychotherapy in practice, 56*(2), 163–173.

Horvath, A. O., and Bedi, R. P. (2002). The alliance. In J. C. Norcross (Ed.), *Psychotherapy relationships that work: Therapist contributions and responsiveness to patients* (pp. 37–69). New York: Oxford University Press.

Horvath, A. O., and Greenberg, L. (1986). The development of the Working Alliance Inventory. In L. Greenberg and W. Pinsof (Eds.), *The psychotherapeutic process: A research handbook* (pp. 529–556). New York: Guilford.

Horvath, A. O., and Symonds, B. D. (1991). Relation between working alliance and outcome in psychotherapy: A meta-analysis. *Journal of Counseling Psychology, 38*, 139–149.

Howe, D. (1995). *Attachment theory for social work practice*. London: MacMillan.

Hubble, M. A., Duncan, B. L., and Miller, S. D. (1999a). Directing attention to what works. In M. A. Hubble and B. L. Duncan and S. D. Miller (Eds.), *The heart and soul of change: What works in therapy* (pp. 407–447). Washington, DC: American Psychological Association.

Hubble, M. A., Duncan, B. L., and Miller, S. D. (Eds.). (1999b). *The heart and soul of change: What works in therapy*. Washington, DC: American Psychological Association.

Hunt, D. E. (1987). *Beginning with ourselves in practice, theory, and human affairs*. Cambridge: Brookline.

Hunter, S., and Hickerson, J. (2003). *Affirmative practice: Understanding and working with lesbian, gay, bisexual, and transgender persons*. Washington, DC: NASW.

Hyde, C. A., and Ruth, B. J. (2002). Multicultural content and class participation: Do students self-censor? *Journal of Social Work Education, 38*(2):241–256.

Ivanoff, A., Blythe, B. J., and Tripodi, T. (1994). *Involuntary clients in social work practice*. New York: de Gruyter.

Ivey, A. E., and Ivey, M. B. (2003). *Intentional interviewing and counseling*. Pacific Grove, CA: Brooks/Cole.

Johnson, S. M. (1996). *The practice of emotionally focused marital therapy*. New York: Brunner/Mazel.

Johnson, S. M. (2002). *Emotionally focused couple therapy with trauma survivors*. New York: Guilford.

Johnson, S. M., Makinen, J. A., and Millikin, J. W. (2001). Attachment injuries in couple relationships: A new perspective on impasses in couples therapy. *Journal of Marital and Family Therapy, 27*(2), 145–155.

Johnson, S. M., and Whiffen, V. E. (1999). Made to measure: Adapting emotionally focused couple therapy to partners' attachment styles. *Clinical Psychology: Science and Practice, 6*(4), 366–381.

Johnson, S. M., and Whiffen, V. E. (Eds.) (2003). *Attachment processes in couple and family therapy*. New York: Guilford.

Jordan, C., and Franklin, C. (2003). *Clinical assessment for social workers: Quantitative and qualitative methods* (2nd ed.). Chicago: Lyceum.

Jordan, J. V. (Ed.). (1997). *Women's growth in diversity*. New York: Guilford.

Jordan, J. V., Kaplan, A. G., Miller, J. B., Stiver, I. P., and Surrey, J. L. (1991). *Women's growth in connection: Writings from the Stone Center*. New York: Guilford.

Kadushin, A., and Kadushin, G. (1997). *The social work interview: A guide for human service professionals*. New York: Columbia University Press.

Kagle, J. D., and Giebelhausen, P. N. (1994). Dual relationships and profssional boundaries. *Social Work, 39*, 213–220.

Keefe, T. (1980). Empathy skill and critical consciousness. *Social Casework, 61*, 387–393.

Keenan, E. K. (2004). From sociocultural categories to social located relations: Using critical theory in social work practice. *Families in Society, 85*(4), 539–548.

Kennedy-Moore, E., and Watson, J. C. (1999). *Expressing emotion: Myths, realities, and therapeutic strategies.* New York: Guilford.

Kenyon, G. L. (2000). No magic: The role of theory in field education. In G. L. Kenyon and R. Power (Eds.), *No magic: Readings in social work field education* (pp. 3–23). Toronto: Canadian Scholars.

Kirkpatrick, L. A., and Hazan, C. (1994). Attachment styles and close relationships: A four-year prospective study. *Personal Relationships, 1*, 123–142.

Klein, M. (1964). *Contributions to psychoanalysis 1921–1945.* New York: McGraw Hill.

Knight, C. (2001). The skills of teaching social work practice in the generalist/ foundation curriculum: BSW and MSW student voices. *Journal of Social Work Education, 37*(3), 507–521.

Kohut, H. (1957). Introspection, empathy, and psychoanalysis: An examination of the relationship between mode of observation and theory. In P. H. Ornstein (Ed.), *The search for the self: Selected writings of Heinz Kohut: 1950–1978.* New York: International Universities Press.

Kohut, H. (1971). *The analysis of the self.* New York: International Universities Press.

Kohut, H. (1977). *The restoration of the self.* New York: International Universities Press.

Kohut, H. (1984). *How does analysis cure?* Chicago: Univeristy of Chichago Press.

Kolb, D. A. (1985). *The learning style inventory.* Boston: McBer.

Kondrat, M. E. (1999). Who is the "self" in self-aware: Professional self-awareness from a critical theory perspective. *Social Service Review, 73*, 451–477.

Laird, J. (1998). Theorizing culture: Narrative ideas and practice principles. In M. McGoldrick (Ed.), *Re-visioning family therapy* (pp. 20–36). New York: Guilford.

Laird, J. (1999). *Lesbians and lesbian families: Reflections on theory and practice.* New York: Columbia University Press.

Lambert, M. J. (1992). Implications of outcome research for psychotherapy integration. In J. C. Norcross and M. R. Goldfried (Eds.), *Handbook of psychotherapy integration* (pp. 94–129). New York: Basic.

Lambert, M. J., and Barley, D. E. (2002). Research summary on the therapeutic relationship and psychotherapy outcome. In J. Norcross (Ed.), *Psychotherapy relationships that work: Therapist contributions and responsiveness to patients* (pp. 17–32). New York: Oxford University Press.

Lambert, M. J., and Bergin, A. E. (1994). The effectiveness of psychotherapy. In A. E. Bergin and S. L. Garfield (Eds.), *Handbook of psychotherapy and behavior change* (pp. 143–189). New York: Wiley.

Landy, S. (2002). *Pathways to competence*. Baltimore, Maryland: Paul H. Brookes Publishing Co.

Lebow, J. (2002, January/February). Transformation now! (Or maybe later). *Psychotherapy networker, 26*, 31–32.

Lewis, H. (1991). Teacher's style and use of professional self in social work education. *Journal of Teaching in Social Work, 5*(2), 17–29.

Longres, J. F. (1996). *Human behavior in the social environment*. Itasca, IL: Peacock.

Lum, D. (1992). *Social work practice and people of color* (2nd ed.). Monterey California: Brooks/Cole.

Lum, D. (1999). *Culturally competent practice*. Pacific Grove, CA: Brooks/Cole.

Lum, D. (2000). *Social work practice and people of color: A process-stage approach* (4th ed.). Belmont, CA: Wadsworth.

McCullough, V. L. (1997). *Changing character*. New York: Basic.

McGoldrick, M., Giordano, J., and Pearce, J. K. (Eds.). (1996). *Ethnicity and family therapy* (2nd ed.). New York: Guilford.

McGoldrick, M., Pearce, J. K., and Giordano, J. (Eds.). (1982). *Ethnicity and family therapy*. New York: Guilford.

McIntosh, P. (1989). White privilege: Unpacking the invisible knapsack. *Peace and freedom*, 10–12.

Mackelprang, R., Ray, J., and Hernandez-Peck, M. (1996). Social work education and sexual orientation: Faculty, student and curriculum issues. *Journal of Gay and Lesbian Studies, 5*(4), 17–31.

Mackelprang, R., and Salsgiver, R. (1999). *Disability: A diversity model approach in human service practice*. Pacific Grove, CA: Brooks/Cole.

McMahon, M. O. N. (1996). *Social work practice*. New York: Allyn and Bacon.

McNamee, S., and Gergen, K. J. (Eds.). (1992). *Therapy as social construction*. Newbury Park, CA: Sage.

Mahalik, J. R., VanOrmer, E. A., and Simi, N. L. (2000). Ethical issues in using self-disclosure in feminist therapy. In M. M. Brabeck (Ed.), *Practicing feminist ethics in psychology*. Washington, DC: American Psychological Association.

Main, M., and Solomon, J. (1986). Discovery of an insecure-disorganized/disoriented attachment pattern. In T. B. Brazelton and M. Y. Yogman (Eds.), *Affective development in infancy* (pp. 95–124). Norwood, NJ: Ablex.

Martin, D. J., Garske, J. P., and Davis, M. K. (2000). Relation of the therapeutic alliance with outcome and other variables: A meta-analytic review. *Journal of Consulting and Clinical Psychology, 68*, 438–450.

Matarazzo, R., Phillips, J., Weins, A., and Saslow, G. (1965). Learning the art of interviewing: A study of what beginning students do and their patterns of change. *Psychotherapy: Theory, Research, and Practice, 2*, 49–60.

Meichenbaum, D. (1977). *Cognitive-behavior modification: An integrative approach.* New York: Plenum.

Memmott, J., and Brennan, E. M. (1998). Learner-learning environment fit: An adult learning model for social work education. *Journal of Teaching in Social Work, 16*(1/2), 75–98.

Meyer, C. H. (Ed.). (1983). *Clinical social work in the eco-systems perspective.* New York: Columbia University Press.

Miehls, D., and Moffat, K. (2000). Constructing social work identity based on the reflexive self. *British Journal of Social Work, 30*(339–348).

Miller, J. B. (1987). *Toward a new psychology of women* (2nd ed.). Boston: Beacon.

Mishna, F. (2003a). Issues in forming alliances. Toronto: Faculty of Social Work.

Mishna, F. (2003b). Psycho-social assessment. Toronto: Faculty of Social Work.

Mishna, F., and Rasmussen, B. (2001). The learning relationship: Working through disjunctions in the classroom. *Clinical Social Work Journal, 29*(4), 386–399.

Mitchell, S. A. (1988). *Relational concepts in psychoanalysis: An integration.* Cambridge: Harvard University Press.

Mohl, D.C. (1995). Negative outcome in psychotherapy: A critical review. *Clinical psychology: Science and practice, 2,* 1–27.

Murphy, B.C., and Dillon, C. (2003). *Interviewing in action: Relationship, process, and change.* Pacific Grove, CA: Brooks/Cole.

Nakanishi, M., and Ritter, B. (1992). The inclusionary cultural model. *Journal of Social Work Education, 28*(1), 27–35.

Nes, J. A., and Iadicola, P. (1989). Toward a definition of feminist social work: A comparison of liberal, radical, and socialist models. *Social Work, 34*(1), 12–21.

Nichols, M. P., and Schwartz, R. C. (2001). *Family therapy: Concepts and methods* (5th ed.). Boston: Allyn and Bacon.

Norcross, J.C. (1993). Tailoring relationship stances to client needs: An introduction. *Psychotherapy, 30,* 402–403.

Norcross, J.C. (Ed.). (2002). *Psychotherapy relationships that work: Therapist contributions and responsiveness to patients.* Washington, DC: American Psychological Association.

Northen, H. (1995). *Clinical Social work: Knowledge and Skills* (2nd ed.). New York: Columbia University Press.

Ogles, B. M., Anderson, T., and Lunnen, K. M. (1999). The contribution of models and teachniques to therapuetic efficacy. In M. A. Hubble and B. L. Duncan and S. D. Miller (Eds.), *The heart and soul of change: What work in therapy* (pp. 201–225). Washington, DC: American Psychological Association.

Okun, B. (2002). *Effective helping: Interviewing and counseling techniques.* Pacific Grove, CA: Brooks/Cole.

Orange, D. M. (1995). *Emotional understanding.* New York: Guilford.

Orange, D. M., Atwood, G. E., and Stolorow, R. D. (1997). *Working intersubjectively: Contextualism in psychoanalytic practice*. Hillsdale, NJ: Analytic.

Orlinsky, D. E., Grawe, K., and Parks, B. K. (1994). Process and outcome in psychotherapy—Noch einmal. In A. E. Bergin and S. L. Garfield (Eds.), *Handbook of psychotherapy and behavior change* (4th ed., pp. 270–378). New York: Wiley.

Palombo, J. (1985). Depletion states and selfobject disorders. *Clinical Social Work Journal*, 14, 32–49.

Palombo, J. (1987). Spontaneous self-disclosures in psychotherapy. *Clinical Social Work Journal*, 15, 107–120.

Parad, H. (1965). *Crisis intervention: Selected readings*. New York: Family Service Association of America.

Pearlman, L. A., and Saakvitne, K. W. (1995). *Trauma and the therapist*. New York: Norton.

Perlman, H. H. (1957). *Social casework: A problem-solving process*. Chicago: University of Chicago Press.

Perlman, H. H. (1979). *Relationship: The heart of helping people*. Chicago: University of Chicago Press.

Pinderhughes, E. (1989). *Understanding race, ethnicity, and power*. New York: Free.

Poorman, P. B. (2003). *Microskills and theoretical foundations for professional helpers*. Boston: Allyn and Bacon.

Poulin, J., and Young, T. (1997). Development of a helping relationship inventory for social work practice. *Research on Social Work Practice*, 7(4), 463–489.

Prochaska, J. M., and Prochaska, J. O. (2002). Transtheoretical model guidelines for families with child abuse and neglect. In A. R. Roberts and G. J. Greene (Eds.), *Social workers' desk reference*. New York: Oxford University Press.

Prochaska, J. O. (1995). Common problems: Common solutions. *Clinical Psychology: Science and Practice*, 2, 101–105.

Prochaska, J. O. (1999). How do people change? In M. A. Hubble and B. L. Duncan and S. D. Miller (Eds.), *The heart and soul of change: What works in therapy* (pp. 227–255). Washington, DC: American Psychological Association.

Prochaska, J. O., DiClemente, C. C., and Norcross, J. C. (1992). In search of how people change. *American Psychologist*, 47, 1102–1114.

Prochaska, J. O., and Norcross, J. C. (2002). Stages of change. In J. C. Norcross (Ed.), *Psychotherapy relationships that work: Therapist contributions and responsiveness to patients* (pp. 303–313). New York: Oxford University Press.

Proctor, E. K., and Davis, L. E. (1994). The challenge of racial difference: Skills for clinical practice. *Social Work*, 39(3), 314–323.

Racker, H. (1968). *Transference and countertransference*. New York: International Universities Press.

Rasmussen, B. M., and Mishna, F. (2003). The relevance of contemporary psychodynamic theories to teaching social work. *Smith College Studies in Social Work*, 74(1), 31–47.

Raw, S. D. (1998). Who is to define effective treatment for social work clients? *Social Work*, 43(1), 81–86.

Reamer, F. G. (Ed.). (1994). *The foundations of social work knowledge*. New York: Columbia University Press.

Reamer, F. G. (1999). *Social work values and ethics* (2nd ed.). New York: Columbia University Press.

Reamer, F. G. (2001). *Tangled relationships: Managing boundary issues in the human services*. New York: Columbia University Press.

Reamer, F. G. (2003). Boundary issues in social work: Managing dual relationships. *Social Work*, 48(1), 121–133.

Regehr, C., and Antle, B. (1997). Coercive influences: Informed consent in court-mandated social work practice. *Social Work*, 42, 300–306.

Reid, W. J. (1992). *Task strategies: An empirical approach to social work practice*. New York: Columbia University Press.

Reid, W. J. (1994). The empirical practice movement. *Social Service Review*, 68, 165–184.

Reid, W. J., and Epstein, L. (1972). *Task-centered casework*. New York: Columbia University Press.

Reid, W. J., and Fortune, A. E. (2003). Empirical foundations for practice guidelines in current social work knowledge. In A. Rosen and E. K. Proctor (Eds.), *Developing practice guidelines for social work intervention: Issues, methods, and research agenda* (pp. 59–79). New York: Columbia University Press.

Ribner, D. S., and Knei-Paz, C. (2002). Clients' view of a successful relationship. *Social Work*, 47(4), 379–387.

Ringel, S., and Mishna, F. (2005). Beyond avoidance and secrecy: Using students' practice to teach ethics. Paper presented at the APM, Council on Social Work Education, New York.

Roberts, A. R. (Ed.). (2000). *Crisis intervention handbook: Assessment, treatment, and research*. New York: Oxford University Press.

Rogers, C. (1951). *Client-centered therapy: Its current practice, implications, and theory*. Boston: Houghton-Mifflin.

Rogers, C. R. (1957). The necessary and sufficient conditions of therapeutic personality change. *Journal of Consulting Psychology*, 21, 95–103.

Rooney, R. H. (1992). *Strategies for work with involuntary clients*. New York: Columbia University Press.

Rooney, R. H. (2002). Working with involuntary clients. In A. R. Roberts and G. J. Greene (Eds.), *Social workers' desk reference* (pp. 709–713). New York: Oxford University Press.

Rosen, A., Proctor, E. K., and Staudt, M. M. (1999). Social work research and the quest for effective practice. *Social Work Research*, 23(1), 4–14.

Rosen, A., Proctor, E. K., and Staudt, M. (2003). Targets of change and interventions in social work: An empirically based prototype for developing practice guidelines. *Research on Social Work Practice*, 13(2), 208–233.

Rothman, J. (1992). *Guidelines for case management: Putting research to professional use.* Itasca, IL: Peacock.

Rothman, J. (2002). An overview of case management. In A. R. Roberts and G. J. Greene (Eds.), *Social workers' desk reference* (pp. 467–472). New York: Oxford University Press.

Rothman, J., and Sager, J. S. (1998). *Case management: Integrating individual and community practice.* Boston: Allyn and Bacon.

Sable, P. (1992). Attachment theory: Application to clinical practice with adults. *Clincial Social Work Journal*, 20(3), 271–283.

Safran, J. D., and Muran, J. C. (2000). *Negotiating the therpeutic alliance.* New York: Guilford.

Safran, J. D., Muran, J. C., Samstag, L. W., and Stevens, C. (2002). Repairing alliance ruptures. In J. C. Norcross (Ed.), *Psychotherapy relationships that work: Therapist contributions and responsiveness to patients* (pp. 235–254). New York: Oxford University Press.

Saleeby, D. (1992). *The strengths perspective in social work practice.* New York: Longman.

Saleeby, D. (2002a). The strengths approach to practice. In D. Saleeby (Ed.), *The strengths perspective in social work practice* (pp. 80–94). Boston: Allyn and Bacon.

Saleeby, D. (2002b). *The strengths perspective in social work practice* (3rd ed.). Boston: Allyn and Bacon.

Schamess, G. (1981). Boundary issues in countertransference: A developmental perspective. *Clinical Social Work Journal*, 9, 344–357.

Schon, D. (1983). *The reflective practitioner: How professionals think in action.* New York: Basic.

Schon, D. (1987). *Educating the reflective practitioner.* San Francisco: Jossey-Bass.

Schon, D. (1995). Reflective inquiry in social work practice. In P.M. Hess and E. J. Mullen (Eds.), *Practitioner-researcher partnerships: Building knowledge from, in, and for practice* (pp. 31–55). Washington, DC: NASW.

Schwartz, W. (1961). The social worker in the group. In *New perspectives on services to groups: Theory, organization, practice.* (pp.7–34). New York: National Association of Social Workers.

Seligman, M. E. (1990). *Learned optimism.* New York: Knopf.

Shapiro, J. R., and Applegate, J. S. (2000). Cognitive neuroscience, neurobiology, and affect regulation: Implications for clinical social work. *Clincial Social Work Journal*, 28(1), 9–21.

Sheafor, B., Horejsi, C., and Horejsi, G. (1997). *Techniques and guidelines for social work practice.* Boston: Allyn and Bacon.

Shulman, L. (1987). The hidden group in the classroom: The use of the group process in teaching group work practice. *Journal of Teaching in Social Work,* 1(2), 3–31.

Shulman, L. (1999). *The skills of helping individuals, families, groups, and communities.* Itasca, IL: Peacock.

Simpson, J. A. (1990). Influence of attachment styles on romantic relationships. *Journal of Personality and Social Psychology,* 59, 971–980.

Slonim-Nevo, V. (1996). Clinical practice: Treating the non-voluntary client. *International Social Work,* 39, 117–129.

Smith, M. K. (1995). Utilization-focused evaluation of a family preservation program. *Familes in Society: The Journal of Contemporary Human Services,* 76(1), 11–19.

Snyder, C. R., Michael, S. T., and Cheavens, J. S. (1999). Hope as a psychotherapeutic foundation of common factors, placebos, and expectancies. In M. A. Hubble and B. L. Duncan and S. D. Miller (Eds.), *The heart and soul of change: What works in therapy* (pp. 179–200). Washington, DC: American Psychological Association.

Solomon, S. E. (1993). Women and physical distinction: A review of the literature and suggestions for intervention. *Women and Therapy,* 14(3/4), 91–103.

Sprenkle, D. H. (Ed.). (2002). *Effectiveness research in marriage and family therapy.* Alexandria, VA: American Association for Marriage and Family Therapy.

Stolorow, R. D. (1994). The intersubjective context of intrapsychic experience. In R. D. Stolorow and G. E. Atwood and B. Brandchaft (Eds.), *The intersubjective perspective* (pp. 3–14). Northvale, NJ: Aronson.

Strean, H. (1979). *Psychoanalytic theory and social work practice.* New York: Free.

Strom-Gottfried, K. (2000). Ensuring ethical practice: An examination of NASW code violations. *Social Work,* 45(3), 251–262.

Sue, D. W., Ivey, A. E., and Pedersen, P. B. (1996). *A theory of multicultural counseling and therapy.* Pacific Grove, CA: Brooks/Cole.

Sullivan, H. S. (1953). *The interpersonal theory of psychiatry.* New York: Norton.

Tallman, K., and Bohart, A. C. (1999). The client as a common factor: Clients as self-healers. In M. A. Hubble and B. L. Duncan and S. D. Miller (Eds.), *The heart and soul of change: What works in therapy* (pp. 91–131). Washington, DC: American Psychological Association.

Task Force on Promotion and Dissemination of Psychological Procedures (1995). Training in and dissemination of empirically-validated psychological treatments: Report and recommendations. *Clinical Psychologist,* 48(1), 2–23.

Thyer, B. A. (2000). Editorial: A decade of research on social work practice. *Research on Social Work Practice,* 10(1), 5–8.

Thyer, B. A., and Myers, L. L. (1998). Supporting the client's right to effective treatment: Touching a raw nerve? *Social Work,* 43(1), 87–91.

Thyer, B. A., and Myers, L. L. (1999). On science, anti-science, and the client's right to effective treatment. *Social Work, 44*(5), 501–504.

Thyer, B. A., and Wodarski, J. S. (1998). First principles of empirical social work practice. In B. A. Thyer and J. S. Wodarski (Eds.), *Handbook of empirical social work practice* (pp. 1–21). New York: Wiley.

Timberlake, E. M., Sabatino, C. A., and Martin, J. A. (1997). Advanced practitioners in clincial social work: A profile. *Social Work, 42*(4), 374–386.

Tsang, A. K. T., and Bogo, M. (1997). Engaging with clients cross-culturally: Towards developing research-based practice. *Journal of Multicultural Social Work, 6*(3/4), 73–91.

Tsang, A. K. T., and George, U. (1998). Towards an integrated framework for cross-cultural social work practice. *Canadian Social Work Review, 15*(1), 73–93.

Tsang, A. K. T., Bogo, M., and George, U. (2003). Critical issues in cross-cultural counseling research: Case example of an ongoing project. *Journal of Multicultural Counseling and Development, 31*(1), 63–78.

Tsang, A. K. T., Bogo, M., and George, U. (2004). Engagement: Lessons from an outcome-process study on cross-cultural clinical practice. Toronto.

Turner, F. (Ed.). (1996). *Social work treatment: Interlocking theoretical approaches* (4th ed.). New York: Free.

Turner, F. (2002). Psychosocial therapy. In A. R. Roberts and G. J. Greene (Eds.), *Social workers' desk reference* (pp. 109–112). New York: Oxford University Press.

Waldman, F. (1999). Violence or discipline? Working with multicultural court-ordered clients. *Journal of Marital and Family Therapy, 25*(4), 503–515.

Walsh, J. (2000). *Clinical case management with persons having mental illness: A relationship-based perspective.* Pacific Grove, CA: Wadsworth-Brooks/Cole.

Walsh, J. (2002). Clinical case management. In A. R. Roberts and G. J. Greene (Eds.), *Social workers' desk reference* (pp. 472–476). New York: Oxford University Press.

Wampold, B. E. (2001). *The great psychotherapy debate:Models, methods, and findings.* Mahwah, NJ: Erlbaum.

Wampold, B. E., Mondin, G. W., Moody, M., Stich, F., Benson, K., and Ahn, H. (1997). A meta-analysis of outcome studies comparing bona fide psychotherapies: Empirically, "All must have prizes." *Psychological Bulletin, 122,* 203–215.

Watson, J. C., and Rennie, D. L. (1994). Qualitative analysis of clients' subjective experience of significant moments during the exploration of problematic reactions. *Journal of Counseling Psychology, 41*(4), 500–509.

Watzlawick, P., Beavin, J., and Jackson, D. (1974). *Change: Principles of problem formation and problem resolution.* New York: Norton.

Weerasekera, P. (1993). Formulation: A multiperspective model. *Canadian Journal of Psychiatry, 38*(5), 351–358.

Weick, A. (1999). Guilty knowledge. *Families in Society: The Journal of Contemporary Human Services, 80*(4), 327–332.

Weick, A., Rapp, C., Sullivan, W. P., and Kisthardt, W. (1989). A strengths perspective for social work practice. *Social Work, 34*, 350–354.

Wells, T. L. (1994). Therapist self-disclosure: Its effects on clients and the treatment relationship. *Smith College Studies in Social Work, 65*, 23–41.

White, M. (1991). Deconstruction and therapy. *Dulwich Center Newsletter, 3*, 21–40.

White, M., and Epston, D. (1990). *Narrative means to therapeutic ends.* New York: Norton.

Williams, C. C. (2002). Evaluation of an educational intervention to increase cultural competence in social workers. Doctor of Philosophy thesis, University of Toronto, Toronto.

Winnicott, D. W. (1956). On transference. *International Journal of Psycho-Analysis, 37*, 386–388.

Winnicott, D. W. (1958). *Through pediatrics to psychoanalysis.* London: Hogarth.

Winnicott, D. W. (1965). *The maturational process and the facilitating environment.* New York: International Universities Press.

Witkin, S. (1998). The right to effective treatment and the effective treatment of rights: Rhetorical empiricism and the politics of research. *Social Work, 43*(1), 75–80.

Wolf, E. S. (1988). *Treating the self: Elements of clinical self psychology.* New York: Guilford.

Woods, M. E., and Hollis, F. (2000). *Casework: A psychosocial therapy* (5th ed.). Boston: McGraw-Hill.

Woolley, S. R., Butler, M. H., and Wampler, K. S. (2000). Unraveling change in therapy: Three different process research methodologies. *American Journal of Family Therapy, 28*(4), 311–327.

Young, T. M., and Poulin, J. E. (1998). The helping relationship inventory: A clinical appraisal. *Families in Society: The Journal of Contemporary Human Services, 79*(2), 123–129.

INDEX

Abstract conceptualization stage of learning, 17–18

Acceptance in relationship building, 70–75, 111, 265

Action stage of change, 199–202

Active experimentation stage of learning, 18

Active listening techniques, 145, 241–46, 249

Advice and suggestions in interviewing, 263–64

Affective empathy, 88

Agency thinking, 200

Ahn, H., 96

Ainsworth, M. D. S., 91

Alliance, therapeutic, *see* Therapeutic alliance

Ambivalence in clients, 42, 126–27, 208–9

Arbitrary inference, 186–87

Artistic aspects of social practice, 11, 55, 68

Assessment phase: cognitive factors in, 53, 164; collaborative atmosphere development, 158–59, 239; cultural diversity issues, 165; data analysis, 165, 168–71; data gathering, 160–65, 166–68; goal setting in, 159

Attachment theory, 26, 90–94, 271

Attending techniques, 145, 241–46, 249

Audio/video taping of interviews, 230–31, 242, 245–46, 279, 281

Awareness-in-action, 22–23; *see also* Self-awareness in practitioner

Bachelor, A., 88

Beck, A., 186

Beginning stages of helping process: data analysis, 165, 168–71; data gathering, 160–65; initial stage, 151–59, 171–75; preparatory stage, 143–50

Behaviors: in assessment phase, 53, 164; blocking, 280, 281–82; nonverbal, 244–46, 264; overview of relationship building, 67–69, 75–77; and subjective experience, 25, 81–82, 88, 160–61, 256

Belief in helping process, 132–33

Belief systems/schemas, 85, 187–88, 268–69

Berg, I. K., 196–97

Bess, J. M., 27

Biological factors in assessment phase, 164

Blocking behaviors, 280, 281–82

Body language, 242, 244–46, 264

Bogo, M., 14, 20, 21, 38, 58, 80, 85, 157, 163, 230, 278, 281

Bohart, A. C., 197

Bonding, emotional: through acceptance, 73; in attachment theory, 91; in case management, 210; through empathy, 82–83; with involuntary clients, 97–98, 111–12; and long-term maintenance, 107–9, 110, 203–6; overview, 97–99; processing at ending phase, 221–25; through self-disclosure, 102–5; *see also* Therapeutic alliance

Borash, M., 112

Bordin, E., 97
Boundary issues, ethical, 106, 114–15, 117
Bowlby, J., 25–26, 90–91
Brainstorming, 200
Brown, L. S., 106

Capacity building: in change process, 128; through feedback, 220, 274; overview, 52–53; in strengths perspective, 137; by theme identification, 189
Carkhuff, R., 79
Case management model, 209–12
Challenge as intervention tool, 76, 198, 274–78
Change process: action stage, 199–202; case management model, 209–12; dynamics/focus of, 118–20, 127; expanded understanding, 183–84; in-depth exploration, 184–92; maintenance of working relationship, 203–6; models for, 120–22, 180–83; monitoring goal achievement, 206–9; new perspective development, 197–99; research in, 122–23, 124; social worker as process expert, 176–77; stages of change, 124–30; strengths perspective, 51–52, 130–31, 134–37, 192–97, 271; support, providing and fostering, 177–80, 255–57; see also Helping process
Clarification skills in interviewing, 238–41
Clark, J. L., 83, 156
Client-centered approach, 47–48, 55–56, 65–66
Clients: expectations of, 40, 93–94, 174–75, 259–60; willingness of, 194, 208–9; see also Relationship building
Close-ended questions, 235–37

Cognitive factors: in assessment, 53, 164; and empathy, 88; in in-depth exploration, 268–69; in intervention phase, 186–89
Collaboration, commitment to, 99–101
Common factors approach, 96–97, 130–34
Competence, professional, 10, 18, 45, 251, 281
Concrete experience stage of learning, 17
Concreteness, seeking through questioning, 238–41, 267
Confrontation as intervention tool, 76, 198, 274–78
Congruence in relationship building, 79–81
Consciousness-raising, 52, 192
Contemplation stage of change, 126–27
Context of practice: core concepts/practices, 50–54; introduction, 3–4, 5; knowledge base, 4–6, 10–15; learning processes, 15–19; linkage phase, 48–50; organizational, 8–9; professional response phase, 54–60; self-awareness/reflection, 20–33; and social worker, 6–8
Coping styles, 53–54, 130, 160–61, 193; see also Strengths perspective
Cotransference, 25
Countertransference, 24–26, 40–41, 103, 245
Critical theory vs. reflective process, 48
Crits-Christopher, P., 273
Cross-cultural counseling, 38, 47, 86–87; see also Cultural diversity issues
Crossing of boundaries, ethical, 106, 115
Cultural diversity issues: in assessment phase, 165; awareness of in practice, 146, 156–58; and emotional display,

251–52, 266; and empathy, 84–87; and ending phase of helping process, 216–17; and immigration, 38–40, 64–65, 87, 157–58; internalized culture, 37, 41–44; and interviewing, 243–46, 269; overview and contemporary practice profile, 35–41, 64–65; and self-disclosure, 104–5; *see also* Diversity; Ethnicity; Power/privilege/oppression dynamic

Cultural learner approach, 38–40, 85–87, 156

Cultural literacy approach, 36–37, 85–86

Culture, definition, 35

Data gathering and analysis for assessment, 160–65, 166–71

Davis, L. E., 70

DeJong, P., 196–97

"Demand for work" approach, 209

Developmental issues, themes for, 190–91

Dillon, C., 80, 82, 106, 114, 176, 225, 272

Direct questioning, 233

Disorganized/disoriented attachment style, 91–92

Distractions, minimizing, 145–46

Diversity: and common factors approach, 134; and empathy, 84–87; individual, 13, 37, 51; integrating perspective in practice, 156–58; and internalized culture, 37, 41–44; and self-disclosure, 104; *see also* Cultural diversity issues; Power/privilege/oppression dynamic

Duncan, B. L., 96, 126, 133, 174

Dyche, L., 38, 85, 156

Early relational experiences, 26, 190–91

Echoing questions, 234

Ecological-systemic perspective, 20, 119, 160–63, 210, 219

Ecomaps, 162, 242

Economic issues, 9, 52–53, 129

Edwards, J. K., 27

Elliott, R., 82

Emotions/feelings: in assessment phase, 53; and cultural diversity issues, 251–52, 266; interview stage access to, 233, 265–68; primary/secondary emotions, 185–86, 250–51, 270; and reflection techniques in interviewing, 249–52; and self-care of practitioner, 30; *see also* Bonding, emotional

Empathy: in challenges, 275; and diversity, 84–87; importance in therapeutic process, 25; interactivity of, 87–90; with involuntary clients, 112; overview, 81–84; preparatory, 149–50; and self-disclosure, 103

Empirical support of principles, 10–12, 56–58, 68, 122–23, 169–70, 180–82

Empowerment, *see* Capacity building

Ending phase of helping process, 213–25

England, H., 13

Environmental factors, *see* Societal environment

Environmental reevaluation, 192

Ethical considerations: boundaries, 106, 114–15, 117; ending phase relationships, 222–24; in ongoing client/practitioner relationship, 113–15, 117; practice principles, 3–4, 66; in self-disclosure, 102, 106–7

Ethnicity, 35, 41–44, 70; *see also* Diversity; Power/privilege/oppression dynamic; Societal environment

Evaluation of progress, 56–58, 206–9, 217–19; *see also* Feedback, client

Evidence-based practice approach, 10–12

Evocative responding, 267

Okun, B., 242

Open-ended questions, 232–35, 266–67

Oppression, *see* Power/privilege/oppression dynamic

Orange, D. M., 25

Organizational structure/mandates: and assessment formats, 165; client turnover pressure, 80; influence on ending phase, 213–14, 215; and limitations to practice, 52–53, 98, 129, 181; and practitioner well-bexg, 30; in social practice context, 8–9, 155; as threatening to clients, 132; validation of service scope, 260–61

Overgeneralization cognitive style, 187

Pacing, *see* Timing

Paraphrasing as response technique, 247–49

Parroting vs. paraphrasing, 248

Partnership, commitment to, 99–101

Pathways thinking, 200

Patterns, identifying, 189–92

Personalization, 187

Personal self, 3, 6–7, 73

Person-in-context, 20, 29–32; *see also* Self-awareness in practitioner

Perspective development, 197–99

Physical/psychological setting for practice, 144–48, 244–46

Physical well-being of practitioner, 32

Pinderhughes, E., 73

Planning: in action stage, 202; and goal setting, 127, 171–75; post-termination phase, 220–21; *see also* Assessment phase

Polarizing cognitive style, 187

Positive regard, 70–75, 111, 265

Positivist paradigm, 10, 12

Poulin, J., 100–1

Power, definition, 45

Power/privilege/oppression dynamic: and acceptance, 72; and client expectations, 175; in client/practitioner relationship, 52, 158, 222; in close-ended questioning, 235–36; and cultural diversity issues, 39–42; and involuntary clients, 111–13; overview, 23–24, 44–48; and self-disclosure, 104–5

Practice environment, preparing, 144–48

Practice principles: blocking behaviors, 280, 281–82; case management, 210–12; for change guidance, 120, 129; definition, 6; and ethics, 3–4, 66; internal working model development, 93–94; for relationship building, 116; "space and place" concept, 63–64, 126–27, 176, 203; "start where the client is" approach, 98, 154, 193

Precontemplation stage of change, 125–26

Preparation stage of change, 127

Preparatory empathy, 149–50

Preparatory stage of helping process, 143–51

Primary emotions, 185–86, 250, 270

Primary relationships of practitioner, 31–32

Principles of practice, *see* Practice principles

Privacy in practice environment, 144–45

Procedures and common practice approach, 133–34

Process, 22, 63–64, 138; *see also* Interventions

Processing styles, 186–87

Process-outcome research, 182, 192

Prochaska, J. M., 127, 129

Prochaska, J. O., 124, 125, 126, 127, 128–29
Proctor, E. K., 11, 70
Professional deportment, importance of, 4; *see also* Ethical considerations
Professional development, continuing, 46–48, 279, 281
Professional response phase (in ITP loop model), 49, 55–60
Professional self, 6, 22
Professional vs. non-professional helpers, 65–66
Progress, evaluation of, 56–58, 206–9, 217–19; *see also* Feedback, client
Prompting through questions, 232
Psychoanalytic/psychotherapeutic methods, 24–25, 50, 82, 95–97, 103, 120–21, 191
Psychodynamic factors in assessment, 164
Psychodynamic theory, 23, 24, 50
Psychoeducation, 261
Psychosocial theory, 10–12

Questioning techniques in interviewing, 232–41

Race, *see* Ethnicity; Power/privilege/oppression dynamic
Racker, H., 24
Reamer, F. G., 107, 114–15
Recording interviews, 230–31, 242, 245–46, 281
Referral, establishing nature of, 153
Reflection-in-action, 13–14
Reflection phase (in ITP loop model), 21–22, 58–59; *see also* Reflective process
Reflection techniques in interviewing, 249–52, 260, 265, 281

Reflective observation stage of learning, 17
Reflective process: and critical theory, 48; and evaluation, 56–58; and genuineness, 79; and internalized culture, 41–44; and learning, 16–17; *see also* Self-awareness in practitioner
Reframing techniques in interviewing, 269–71
Reid, W. J., 123, 210
Relabeling techniques, 269–71
Relational change, 119
Relational theory, 25–26
Relationship building: acceptance, 70–75, 111, 265; attachment theory, 26, 90–94, 271; behaviors overview, 67–69, 75–77; collaborative models for, 54; context overview, 62–65; empirical support for importance of, 95–101, 131; forming helping relationships, 24–25, 33; genuineness, 78–81; in initial stage of helping process, 153–54; with involuntary clients, 97–98, 109–12, 194; and long-term maintenance, 107–9, 110, 203–6; professionals' key components, 65–67; warmth and caring concern, 69, 75–77; *see also* Empathy; Therapeutic alliance
Research on social work practice: on change process, 122–23, 124; dearth of, 8; ethnographic study of therapy, 64; limitations of, 10–11; as practice tool, 57; process-outcome, 182–83, 192; *see also* Models/theories
Resources for help: access to, 45, 171, 211, 255–56; planning for post-termination phase, 220–21; psychoeducation, 261–62
Respect, 70